Teaching English Language Learners

Teaching English Language Learners

Michaela Colombo

University of Massachusetts Lowell

Los Angeles | London | New Delhi
Singapore | Washington DC

Los Angeles | London | New Delhi
Singapore | Washington DC

FOR INFORMATION:

SAGE Publications, Inc.
2455 Teller Road
Thousand Oaks, California 91320
E-mail: order@sagepub.com

SAGE Publications Ltd.
1 Oliver's Yard
55 City Road
London EC1Y 1SP
United Kingdom

SAGE Publications India Pvt. Ltd.
B 1/I 1 Mohan Cooperative Industrial Area
Mathura Road, New Delhi 110 044
India

SAGE Publications Asia-Pacific Pte. Ltd.
33 Pekin Street #02-01
Far East Square
Singapore 048763

Executive Editor: Diane McDaniel
Editorial Assistant: Theresa Accomazzo
Production Editor: Brittany Bauhaus
Copy Editor: Jenifer Dill
Typesetter: C&M Digitals (P) Ltd.
Proofreader: Jenifer Kooiman
Indexer: Molly Hall
Cover Designer: Janet Kiesel
Marketing Manager: Erica DeLuca
Permissions Editor: Adele Hutchinson

Copyright © 2012 by SAGE Publications, Inc.

Printed in the United States of America

Library of Congress Cataloging-in-Publication Data

Colombo, Michaela.

Teaching English language learners : 43 strategies for successful K-8 classrooms/Michaela Colombo.

p. cm.
Includes bibliographical references and index.

ISBN 978-1-4129-8029-6 (pbk. : alk. paper)

1. English language—Study and teaching—Foreign speakers. 2. Language and languages—Study and teaching. 3. Second language acquisition. I. Title.

PE1128.A2C673 2012 428.2′4—dc22 2010040647

This book is printed on acid-free paper.

11 12 13 14 15 10 9 8 7 6 5 4 3 2 1

Contents

Preface

As a teacher or as someone who is preparing to become a teacher, you have probably noticed that the population of students in U.S. schools is changing. Our students are becoming increasingly diverse in race, ethnicity, and language.

The purpose of this book of strategies is to help regular—that is, non-ESL—classroom teachers and preservice teachers better meet the needs of English language learners in the regular classroom setting. Increasingly, English language learners are being placed in regular classrooms and taught by teachers with varying degrees of preparation to meet their needs. I have worked with many of these teachers, and while some may have felt overwhelmed and pressured to accomplish more within the academic day, each of them strove to provide instruction that enabled every child in the classroom to be successful. Teachers who have found a way to meet the needs of English language learners in their classrooms are the inspiration for this strategy book.

This book is meant to be a useable resource for preservice teachers and regular classroom teachers who teach English language learners along with fully English-proficient students. It is appropriate for teachers of all content areas and as a professional development tool. While it is not a book for ESL specialists, whose knowledge base should exceed what is presented, it does provide regular classroom teachers with strategies for collaborating with ESL specialists and paraprofessionals for the benefit of English language learners in their classrooms.

The standards developed by Teachers of English to Speakers of Other Languages (TESOL), an international organization to improve the education of English language learners, provide a unifying framework for the strategies presented in this book. Using TESOL standards provides a common language, and although standards in states may differ slightly, state standards are easily aligned with the TESOL standards. TESOL standards include teacher knowledge, skills, and practice as well as performance indicators for student learning; both standards and performance indicators are included in this book.

Ten key features make this book accessible to readers who are using this book as part of course work assignments, as professional development, or as an independent guide.

1. Each unit is aligned with the TESOL teacher and student standards. In addition, student performance indicators are provided for Units III through VIII.

2. Each unit includes a listing of what readers will know, understand, or be able to do as a result of that unit.

3. The Introduction provides a brief history of educating English language learners in the United States, an overview of current programs, and student demographics. An overview of theories is presented in an easy-to-read table format.

4. The strategies included are doable within the context of the regular classroom and are accompanied by underlying theories and research, which allows teachers to understand why the strategies are likely to be effective with English language learners in the regular classroom and encourages the extension of strategies.

5. The implementation for each strategy is presented in an easy to follow, step-by-step format.

6. Each strategy is followed by a Strategy in Action section, which illustrates the strategy in a variety of regular classroom situations.

7. A Reflections section after the Strategy in Action section provides questions that can be used by a course instructor or independently by the reader.

8. A Strategy Resources section is included at the end of each unit opener and, when relevant, at the end of each strategy. The resources include further research that underlies the strategies, additional examples of strategies in use or ways to extend strategies, and videos that illustrate strategies in action. The Resources section provides the course instructor with additional reading and assignments for participants and provides the individual reader with materials for self study. Icons identify the type of resource:

   ▤ Research

   ▰ Video links

   ▤ Additional strategies

9. New terms are **glossed** within the text.

10. Charts and rubrics are included to help readers plan instruction and to measure progress of the English language learners in their classrooms.

> **Glossing** refers to bolding the word as it appears in the text and then providing a brief definition in the margins. Glossing new words in text has been shown to be more effective for English language learners than providing definitions in a glossary at the end of the text.

Acknowledgments

Many people have contributed to the quality of this strategies book. I would like to first acknowledge the many teachers in Massachusetts public schools with whom I have worked, as well as pre- and inservice teachers who were students in the Methods of Sheltered Instruction course I teach at the University of Massachusetts Lowell. Over the years, my students have held me accountable by demanding that I provide them with the strategies they needed. I thank them for this.

I would like to acknowledge Diane McDaniel, Executive Editor, and Ashley Conlon, Editorial Assistant, for their ongoing guidance and many helpful suggestions. I also would like to acknowledge the helpful suggestions of the reviewers listed here:

Susan J. Britsch, *Purdue University*

Anita Flemington, *University of La Verne*

Demetria Harvell, *Florida State University*

Joy Henderson, *California State University, Bakersfield*

Kathleen McInerney, *Chicago State University*

J. Sabrina Mims, *California State University, Los Angeles*

Eileen Ordu, *Plymouth State College*

Nancy Pappamihiel, *University of North Carolina–Wilmington*

Carine Strebel, *University of Central Florida*

Glen E. Tracy, *University of Nebraska–Kearney*

Introduction

As a teacher or as someone who will soon become a teacher, you have probably noticed the growing number of English language learners (ELLs) in your school system. ELLs are the fastest growing group of students in U.S. schools. It is estimated that approximately 5.1 million ELLs currently attend U.S. schools (U.S. Census, 2008), and this number is expected to continue to grow steadily (Goldenberg, 2008). Every day, more and more ELLs are being placed in regular education classrooms.

I wrote this strategy book to address the needs of the regular classroom teacher who is teaching one or more ELLs along with fully English proficient (FEP) learners. My intention is to provide you, the classroom teacher or preservice teacher, with strategies that are grounded in research and theory to enable you to provide appropriate instruction to this growing population of students. While it is not possible in a book of this nature to provide a comprehensive discussion of theories and research, the Resource section at the end of each unit provides additional readings. I recommend that you familiarize yourself with the theories and research presented within the units and within the Resource section and that you reflect on what is effective or likely to be effective with the ELLs you teach. As Carrier (2005) reminded us, to simply extract "strategies from books without an understanding of ELLs' unique language and learning needs is like building a house without understanding the basic principles of construction. Our house may begin to fall apart before we even move in" (p. 4).

HOW BEST TO USE THIS BOOK

This book is divided into nine units: the introduction, which you are now reading, and eight additional units. Each unit focuses on strategies in one area: managing the learning environment, working with other school professionals, assessment, comprehensibility, vocabulary, oral language development, reading and writing, and building home–school connections.

This Introduction provides an overview of the needs of regular classroom teachers, a brief history of the education of ELLs in U.S. schools, an explanation of the types of programs that currently exist for ELLs, and a brief description of several accepted theories for teaching ELLs. The Resource section at the end of this unit provides suggestions for further reading as well as links to videos that illustrate the theories and strategies.

After reading the Introduction, you may skip from unit to unit. Each unit begins with an overview of the broad underlying research and the TESOL student performance indicators for the strategies presented. The overview is useful for understanding the strategies presented within the unit. I encourage you to read this overview prior to reading the strategies and then to revisit it as you plan to implement the strategies with your students.

KNOWLEDGE AND SKILLS FOR REGULAR CLASSROOM TEACHERS OF ENGLISH LANGUAGE LEARNERS

As the strengths and needs of students in U.S. classrooms change, so too must the knowledge, skills, and practice of classroom teachers. In order for ELLs to become successful academically, they will need to receive ongoing, appropriate instruction from well-prepared and caring teachers. As a regular classroom teacher, or as a preservice teacher, you bring great strengths to the role of teaching ELLs: You have the necessary content-area knowledge and expertise to determine which concepts are necessary for all students to learn. This knowledge will guide your instruction of ELLs who are placed in your classroom and will ensure that they learn content-area concepts that lead to academic success.

While, as a regular classroom teacher, you cannot be expected to have the same level of expertise as a specialist in English as a Second Language (ESL), you will need to be sufficiently prepared to help the ELLs in your classroom to develop content-area knowledge and academic English language proficiency as they learn complex content in English.

STANDARDS FOR CLASSROOM INSTRUCTION FOR ENGLISH LANGUAGE LEARNERS

TESOL developed five broad classroom standards to guide instructional practices for ELLs in pre-kindergarten through Grade 12. The strategies in this book are aligned with TESOL standards, which are shown in Table 1.

Table 1	TESOL Standards for Instruction of ELLs
Standard 1	ELLs communicate for social, intercultural, and instructional purposes within the school setting
Standard 2	ELLs communicate information, ideas, and concepts necessary for academic success in the area of language arts
Standard 3	ELLs communicate information, ideas, and concepts necessary for academic success in the area of mathematics
Standard 4	ELLs communicate information, ideas, and concepts necessary for academic success in the area of science
Standard 5	ELLs communicate information, ideas, and concepts necessary for academic success in the area of social studies

Source: From *PreK–12 English Language Proficiency Standards* (p. 28), by Teachers of English to Speakers of Other Languages [TESOL], 2006, Alexandria, VA: Author. Reprinted with permission.

TESOL also provided performance indicators for these standards for ELLs with different levels of English proficiency. Performance indicators for instructional strategies are included in the units of this book to help you understand the specific supports that ELLs with different English-proficiency levels will need for each strategy. The performance indicators are approximations, and they are indicative of performance that is likely to occur when instruction is optimal.

In addition, TESOL and the National Council for The Accreditation of Teacher Education (NCATE) developed standards to guide the preparation of ESL specialists, whose role is to provide explicit language instruction in a variety of academic and social contexts and to ensure that ELLs have the oral and written English language they need across content areas (TESOL, 2010). The TESOL/NCATE standards are organized into five domains: Language, Culture, Instruction, Assessment, and Professionalism. Although regular classroom teachers may not receive the same depth of preparation in the area of language as ESL teachers, the TESOL/NCATE standards provide a framework to guide effective instruction for ELLs in all classrooms. Table 2 shows how units in this book are aligned with TESOL/NCATE standards. A link to the complete TESOL standards is included in the Resource section at the end of this unit.

Table 2 Alignment of TESOL Standards for Teachers and Units in this Book

Domain(s)	Standards	Unit Connections
Language	Know, understand, and use the major theories and research related to the structure and acquisition of language to help . . . ELLs develop language and literacy and achieve in the content areas. (TESOL, 2010, p. 27)	Introduction
Language, instruction	Know, understand, and use evidence-based practices and strategies to plan and implement standards-based, ESL and content instruction (TESOL, 2010, p. 44) in a supportive and collaborative classroom environment that provides multiple ways of presenting content.	Units I, V, VI, VII
Language	Know and understand English phonology, morphology, pragmatics, and syntax (a definition of each of these terms is included in Unit VII), and apply these to help ELLs develop listening, speaking, reading, and writing abilities in English.	Introduction, Units VI, VII
Language	Know and understand theories of second language acquisition and apply these to instruction.	Introduction, Units III through VII
Culture	Know, understand, and use major concepts, principles, theories, and research related to the nature and role of culture and cultural groups to construct supportive learning environments for ELLs. (TESOL, 2010, p. 39)	Introduction, Units I, VI, VII

(Continued)

(Continued)

Domain(s)	Standards	Unit Connections
Instruction	Plan and implement standards-based instruction in language and content areas.	Unit III
Assessment	Appropriately assess ELLs' language and content-area knowledge and understanding.	Unit III
Assessment, instruction	Effectively differentiate instruction according to ELLs' language and content-area assessments and grade-level standards.	Units III through VII
Instruction	Understand and apply theories and research in language acquisition and development to support ELL's English language and literacy learning and content-area achievement. (TESOL, 2010, p. 33)	Unit VI
Professionalism, culture	Acknowledge and understand the importance of school and family relationships for ELLs, establish and maintain positive school–family relationships, and collaborate with other professionals to provide appropriate instruction for ELLs.	Units II and VIII

Source: Adapted from *TESOL/NCATE Standards for the Recognition of Initial ESOL Programs in P-12 ESL Teacher Education,* by TESOL, 2010, Alexandria, VA: TESOL.

Although a complete discussion of the knowledge and abilities put forth by TESOL/ NCATE and referenced in Table 2 is well beyond the scope of this strategy book, the Resource section at the end of each unit provides sources for further reading. It is useful for teachers and prospective teachers of ELLs to be aware of the history of language education in the United States, the current programs that exist for ELLs, and the demographics of ELLs in U.S. schools.

LANGUAGE EDUCATION IN U.S. SCHOOLS: A HISTORICAL PERSPECTIVE

The presence of ELLs in U.S. schools is not a new phenomenon. Bilingual education programs were once quite common in the United States. A textile strike by immigrants in the Northeast in 1912 and World Wars I and II changed that dramatically. These historical events resulted in a distrust of immigrants, and speaking English became synonymous with loyalty to the United States. Consequently, bilingual programs were dismantled and ELLs were placed in U.S. schools with no support—an instructional situation that became widely known as *sink or swim*. Unfortunately, many ELLs were failed miserably by school systems during this sink or swim period.

To address educational inequities created by sink or swim, in 1970, a memorandum extended the Civil Rights Act of 1964 to explicitly protect language, and districts were required to take "affirmative steps" to provide English language development that would allow ELLs access to the curriculum. In 1974, in response to a class action suit by approximately 1,800 students of Chinese ancestry, the Supreme Court ruled that it was not sufficient to provide ELLs with the same facilities, textbooks, and teachers as

English proficient students; districts were required to provide ELLs with instruction that they could access. (Crawford, 2004)

LANGUAGE PROGRAMS FOR ENGLISH LANGUAGE LEARNERS IN U.S. SCHOOLS

The Office for Civil Rights (1985/1990) allows districts to implement any program that has "proven successful" based on a "sound educational program" (para. 26). Districts must include an explanation of how the program meets the needs of ELLs and whether the "district is operating under an approved state plan or other accepted plans" (para. 26). As illustrated in Table 3, several types of programs exist in U.S. schools today (Office for Civil Rights, 2005).

Table 3   Basic Language Development Programs in U.S. Schools Today

Program	Goal	Language of Instruction	Approximate Time in Program
Two-Way Immersion	Bilingualism and biliteracy for ELLs and native-English speakers	English and native language	Generally at least six years and may continue throughout student's education
Maintenance Bilingual	Bilingualism and biliteracy for ELLs	English and native language	Generally at least six years and may continue throughout student's education
Transitional Bilingual Education (TBE), late exit	English proficiency	English and native language	Generally five years
TBE, early exit	English proficiency	English and native language	Generally not to exceed three years
Sheltered English Immersion (SEI) and/or Specially Designed Academic Instruction in English (SDAIE)	English proficiency	English	Varies—one to three years is often the norm, but this can be extended
English to Speakers of Other Languages (ESOL) alone	English proficiency	English	Varies depending on proficiency levels of ELLs on entry into the program

Source: From *Teaching English Language Learners: Content and Language in Middle and Secondary Mainstream Classrooms,* by M. Colombo and D. Furbush, 2009, Thousand Oaks, CA: Sage.

An English to Speakers of Other Languages (ESOL) program may consist of two types of instruction: The ESOL teacher may work in the classroom with the classroom teacher or he or she may pull students from the classroom for individual or small group instruction.

Research is clear that ELLs who receive literacy instruction in their first languages make better progress in English literacy than those who are instructed in English only. As Goldenberg (2008) explained, this might seem counterintuitive based on common sense, but if we made all our decisions based on common sense "we would still believe that the sun revolves around a flat Earth" (p. 15). Research suggests that the programs with the most promise for ELLs are two-way bilingual programs in which ELLs continue to develop their first language while at the same time mastering challenging content and academic English (Goldenberg, 2008). Research also suggests that ELLs benefit from at least one period per day of instruction that is solely dedicated to the development of English language proficiency.

High-quality sheltered English immersion programs may be implemented when there is not a sufficient number of ELLs from any one language group to implement a two-way program. Sheltered English immersion programs are most effective for ELLs who have English proficiency levels from *Developing* to *Bridging* and who are on grade level in their first language. (Please see Table 4 for a description of English language proficiency levels.) In reality, ELLs who have *Starting* and *Emerging* levels of English language proficiency are often placed in regular education classrooms where all instruction is provided in English. Unfortunately, this is a less effective method for teaching ELLs who have lower proficiency levels and for ELLs who have major gaps in their schooling.

WHO ARE THE ENGLISH LANGUAGE LEARNERS IN U.S. SCHOOLS?

ELLs are a very diverse population of students. Some ELLs arrive in the United States as young children or adolescents from over 200 countries (Goldenberg, 2008). Other ELLs represent the first generation born in the United States, and still others are the third generation in their families born in the United States. According to the American Community Survey, over 19% of the U.S. population over the age of five speaks a language other than English at home (U.S. Census Bureau, 2008).

The languages other than English spoken most often in the United States are Spanish (62%); followed by Chinese (2.9%); Tagalog (Filipino) (2.6%); French, including Patois and Cajun (2.5%); Vietnamese (2.2%); German (2.1%); Korean (1.95%); Italian and Russian (1.5% each); Arabic (1.3%); and Portuguese (1.2%). The remaining 18.3% of people in the United States who speak a language other than English at home speak a variety of other languages (U.S. Census Bureau, 2008).

Like the general student population, ELLs differ from one another in terms of socioeconomic status, although ELLs are disproportionately represented in poverty statistics (Goldenberg, 2008). ELLs also differ from one another in their prior schooling, background knowledge, and proficiency levels in English and their first languages. Like all students, they differ cognitively, developmentally, and in their preferred styles of learning. What ELLs have in common is that they must construct all the knowledge that FEP learners construct, and they must do this in a language that they do not fully understand. At the same time ELLs are learning content, they must acquire the English language necessary to make sense of instruction and to express their knowledge and understanding.

ELLs have to develop proficiency in listening, speaking, reading, and writing in English. While social language, such as the language used on the playground, at lunch, and in the hallways to discuss day to day events, is acquired quite quickly—normally within a year or two—academic language, or the language of classroom instruction, develops much more gradually. Even with appropriate instruction, academic language proficiency may not fully develop for at least six years.

ELLs in early grades and ELLs who have significant gaps in their schooling must also learn to read in English as they learn the language itself. They will have to learn to read different genres (various types of fiction, nonfiction, and expository text) and to apply the writing conventions of standard English across genres and content areas.

Even after ELLs have developed the ability to read and write in English, frequent errors with grammar, syntax, and idioms are a normal part of language development. The research of Thomas and Collier (1997) suggested that to simply catch up to native English speakers, ELLs must make a 1.5-year gain for every year of growth that native English speakers make. Achieving academic success is extremely challenging, yet we know that with appropriate instruction, many ELLs do become successful.

For instructional purposes, the development of English proficiency can be categorized by five broad performance levels that detail what English language learners can understand and use (TESOL, 2006), shown in Table 4.

Table 4 TESOL Performance Levels for Five Levels of Language Proficiency

Level 1 Starting	*Level 2* Emerging	*Level 3* Developing	*Level 4* Expanding	*Level 5* Bridging
Language to communicate basic and concrete needs	Language based on simple and routine experiences	Language about familiar matters regularly encountered	Language at concrete and abstract levels, application of language to new experiences	Language within a range of longer oral and written texts, recognition of implicit meaning
High-frequency words and memorized chunks of language	High-frequency words and generalized vocabulary and expressions	General and specific academic vocabulary and expressions	Specialized and some technical academic vocabulary and expressions	Technical and academic vocabulary and expressions
Words, phrases, or chunks of language	Phrases or short sentences	Expanded sentences	Variety of sentence lengths and linguistic complexity	Varity of sentence lengths and linguistic complexity in extended discourse
Pictorial, graphic, or nonverbal representation of language	Oral or written language, making errors that often impede meaning	Oral or written language, making errors that impede communication but retain much of the meaning	Oral or written language, making minimal errors that do not impede overall meaning	Oral or written language approaching that of English-proficient learners

Source: Adapted from *PreK–12 English Language Proficiency Standards* (p. 39), by TESOL, 2006, Alexandria, VA: Author. Used with Permission.

CURRENT THEORIES IMPORTANT FOR LEARNING AND FOR TEACHING ELLS

Large numbers of books are written about theories of second language acquisition that help to inform teaching and learning. Obviously, a complete description of these theories is well beyond the scope of this strategy book. Thus, the purpose of the next few pages is simply to familiarize you with some commonly accepted theories and hypotheses that undergird the instructional strategies presented in this text. Table 5 shows the theory (hypothesis or model), the theorist, a description of the theory, and the broad instructional strategies or methodologies that have sprung forth from the theory. These theories, hypotheses, and models will be revisited in later units as strategies are introduced and illustrated.

Table 5 Common Theories (Hypotheses and Models), Theorists, and Instructional Implications

Theory Name	Theorist	Description and Implications for Instruction
Universal Grammar	Chomsky	*Description.* Chomsky's work revolutionized the way we understand language development. Universal Grammar refers to the system of rules that is common to all languages that exist in the world. Languages share both commonalities and differences (principles and parameters). With regard to principle, all languages express meaning by combining sounds to develop words, and combining words to make phrases, which are then used in a variety of contexts. With regard to parameters, languages differ in the ways meaning is expressed (sounds, words, phrasing, etc.). According to Chomsky, and many more recent linguists, the human brain contains a neurological structure that is referred to as the language acquisition device (LAD). The LAD enables children to naturally acquire the language(s) to which he or she is regularly exposed. *Implications for instruction.* ELLs have a sophisticated and developed primary language system. They know the rules of their own language—what sounds right. They will need ongoing opportunities to hear and to use language in meaningful circumstances in order to develop English sounds, syntax, grammar, and vocabulary. Chomsky (1965)
Common Underlying Proficiency	Cummins	*Description.* Cummins theorized that humans have one central and integrated system or processing center that can be accessed by multiple languages. Thus, the concepts that ELLs have learned in one language are available to the ELLs in additional languages.

		Implications for instruction. The Common Underlying Proficiency theory helps to explain the differences between teaching ELLs who are educated in their primary languages and teaching ELLs with interrupted schooling. An ELL who has learned a concept in his or her first language does not need to relearn the concept when it is encountered in English; rather, he or she must learn the English words for the concept. ELLs who are able to read in their first languages will transfer these abilities (with varying levels of support) to reading in English as they develop proficiency in academic English. ELLs with interrupted schooling will need to learn new concepts in a language they do not understand as they learn the language itself. It is beneficial to use one's primary language in the acquisition of another language. Cummins (1981) (see also Baker 2006; Colombo & Furbush, 2009)
Comprehensible Input Hypothesis (i +1)	Krashen	*Description.* Krashen hypothesized that acquiring a language occurs through ongoing exposure to input that is comprehensible to the listener and is just beyond the listener's current linguistic ability. Thus, the ELL must understand the language input, but the input must consistently require her to develop more sophisticated language. The input hypothesis is frequently referred to as *input + 1* or simply *i+1*. *Implications for instruction.* Instructional language must be made understandable to the language learner. In providing instruction, teachers must ensure that presentations and materials are always understandable to the ELL, but at the same time just a little beyond the ELL's current ability. (Strategies for making content comprehensible are discussed in Unit IV of this book.) Krashen (1985)
Acquisition vs. Learning Hypothesis	Krashen	*Description.* Language learners acquire language by using it in real communication. They learn about language through instruction and studying. According to Krashen, ELLs acquire the rules of grammar in the same way that children acquire the grammatical rules of their first language. Thus, while acquiring English, ELLs first produce words and then put words together to create meaningful utterances, rather than grammatically correct ones. *Implications for instruction.* Teachers should provide language-rich settings and ample opportunities for ELLs to hear and use English in meaningful ways. Unit I helps create a classroom setting for this to occur, and Unit VI provides strategies for engaging ELLs in meaningful academic conversations. Krashen (1981, 1985)

(Continued)

(Continued)

Theory Name	Theorist	Description and Implications for Instruction
Monitor Hypothesis	Krashen	*Description.* As language learners learn the rules of grammar, they begin to monitor their output for grammatical correctness. The monitor acts as an editor. According to Krashen, there is substantial variation in individuals with regard to their use of the monitor. Overactive use of the monitor may interfere with using English for communication. *Implications for instruction.* Once ELLs acquire basic grammatical rules, they are able to begin to monitor their output for correctness. To do this, ELLs need time to use language with peers and in think-pair-share situations before speaking to the larger group. While the focus is communication rather than correctness, practicing with a group of peers is likely to promote both. Krashen (1981)
Affective Filter Hypothesis	Krashen	*Description.* The affective filter refers to the emotional factors that allow or block language—the anxiety that a learner experiences. When the affective filter is high, language is blocked and learners have limited access to input and may be unable to produce output. Conversely, when the affective filter is low, learners can access input and produce output. *Implications for instruction.* Language learning environments should limit anxiety and fear so that ELLs' affective filters remain low. Well-planned, comprehensible activities in small groups are useful, as are providing ELLs with sufficient comprehensible input and time to practice language with a partner or within small groups before speaking in front of the larger group. Krashen & Terrell (1983)
Silent Period	Krashen	*Description.* The silent period is a normal stage of second language acquisition. When first exposed to a new language, the language learner takes in the language and begins to make sense of it, but often does not try to use the language. This silent period can be brief or prolonged. *Implications for instruction.* ELLs should not be pressured to speak. Teachers should make other students in the classroom aware of the possibility of a silent period so that students will understand if ELLs do not attempt to speak and will not pressure them to do so. Krashen (1985)

Theory Name	Theorist	Description and Implications for Instruction
Sociocultural Learning, Constructivism, and the Zone of Proximal Development	Vygotsky	*Description.* Individuals construct knowledge and understanding when working in collaboration with others. The Zone of Proximal Development (ZPD) refers to the difference between what a learner can do independently and what he or she is able to do with scaffolding or when collaborating with a more capable peer. *Implications for instruction.* The ZPD is relevant to all kinds of learning, including language learning. Within the classroom, ELLs need ample opportunities to use language with teachers and with students who have higher levels of English language proficiency. Several strategies for academic oral language proficiency in Unit VI and strategies for reading and writing in Unit VII are based, at least in part, on the ZPD. Vygotsky (1978)
Comprehensible Output (o + 1)	Swain	*Description.* Comprehensible output refers to the language that ELLs use when speaking with others. According to Swain, it is the use of language that enables ELLs to understand what they can and cannot do, what they have learned, and what they still need to learn. Through output, the ELL notices that her language is incorrect or that she is unable to say something. Thus, output provides for ongoing formative self-assessment, enabling the ELL to measure progress and note gaps. Output also promotes deep language processing and elaboration, which promotes language acquisition. *Implications for Instruction.* Teacher questions that require ELLs to elaborate on their responses encourage the development of language proficiency. Purposeful academic conversations in small groups also promote increased and improved output (Units V and VI include strategies that promote increased comprehensible output). Swain (1985, 2000, 2005)
Communicative Competence	Hymes, Canale, Swain	*Description.* Hymes introduced the theory of communicative competence, which recognizes the important of output as well as input. The theory of communicative competence was further developed by Canale and Swain and Canale. According to the theory, receptive and productive language proficiency develops as a result of meaningful communication in the target language. Canale identified four major types of communicative competence: grammatical, sociolinguistic, discourse, and strategic competence. *Implications for instruction.* ELLs benefit from ongoing opportunities within the classroom to use language for purposeful communication (Units I and IV through VII). Teachers should assess communicative competence to provide ELLs with meaningful feedback (Unit III). Canale (1983); Canale & Swain (1980); Hymes (1972)

(Continued)

(Continued)

Theory Name	Theorist	Description and Implications for Instruction
Four Quadrant Context-Embedded, Context-Reduced Model	Cummins	*Description*. The context-embedded versus context-reduced model provides a framework for understanding that language forms differ in their cognitive complexity, and context makes language less cognitively demanding. For example, speaking face to face provides context because the speaker and listener receive visual cues from one another, whereas speaking by telephone removes the visual cues (the context) and makes communication more difficult. A lecture accompanied by rich visuals has more context than one without. A complete discussion of the model is provided in Unit IV. *Implications for instruction*. ELLs benefit from instruction that is situated in context. The more context (visuals, graphics, realia, etc.) that the teacher can provide, the more comprehensible the content. Cummins (2000)
Social or Conversational Language vs. Academic Language	Cummins	*Description*. Social language is normally acquired within a year or two, whereas academic language (the language of the classroom) typically takes six or more years to acquire. The distinction between social and academic language was once referred to as Basic Interpersonal Communication Skills (BICS) versus Cognitive Academic Language Proficiency (and still is by many ESL teachers). *Implications for instruction*. Teachers should not confuse an ELL's ability to speak socially with her ability to perform course work. An ELL might appear to speak fluently and without an accent and still not have sufficient academic language to succeed in school. Teachers must provide structured time within their classes for academic conversations. Unit VI has strategies that help to build academic language. Cummins (1979, 2000)

Strategy Resources

Research

1. TESOL/NCATE Standards for ESOL Teachers. TESOL provides the entire TESOL/NCATE Standards for the Recognition of Initial TESOL Programs in P-12 ESL Teacher Education.

   http://www.tesol.org/s_tesol/seccss.asp?CID=219&DID=1689

2. *Teaching English Language Learners: What the Research Says and Does Not Say* is an important overview of current research and suggestions for practice provided by Claude Goldenberg (2008).

   http://www.edweek.org/media/ell_final.pdf

3. The executive summary of the National Literacy Panel, which focused on teaching language-minority students to read and write in English, provides an overview of the NLP's findings that providing instruction in the key components of literacy is necessary, but insufficient for ELLs who require instruction that develops oral proficiency.

   http://www.cal.org/projects/archive/nlpreports/Executive_Summary.pdf

4. Interview with Noam Chomsky on first language development

   http://www.chomsky.info/interviews/1987----.htm

5. Relationship between first and second language development

   http://www.cal.org/resources/digest/ncrcds04.html

6. Second language research and history of education for ELLs, by Dr. Jim Cummins

   http://www.iteachilearn.com/cummins/

7. *Second Language Acquisition and Second Language Learning*, by Dr. Stephen Krashen (1981), is available online at no cost. Chapter 5 discusses the role of first language in second language acquisition.

   http://www.sdkrashen.com/SL_Acquisition_and_Learning/index.html

▤ VIDEO LINKS

1. The E-library at Stanford University offers over 10 hours of video for teachers of ELLs, including second language acquisition, English language development, sheltering content-area instruction, and the impact of culture on ELLs. There is no fee for registration.

   http://ellib.stanford.edu/?q=public-video-library

2. Colorin Colorado and the American Federation of Teachers present a comprehensive online professional development series for middle and high school educators of ELLs.

   http://www.colorincolorado.org/multimedia/learn

3. Total Physical Response (TPR) demonstration on YouTube, with James Asher; provides theory and illustrates practice with adults, younger children, and youth.

   http://www.youtube.com/watch?v=ikZY6XpB214&feature=related

4. Language Development in infants—a study of innate language abilities—word segmentation in support of Universal Grammar—infants identify sounds not in their language

   http://www.youtube.com/watch?v=mZAuZ--Yeqo&feature=related

5. A four-minute introduction to Vygotsky

   http://www.youtube.com/watch?v=hx84h-i3w8U&feature=related

UNIT 1

Managing the Learning Environment

I have a classroom filled with students with different needs. How do I also prepare and deliver instruction to students who do not speak English?

—Middle School Teacher

Upon entering any classroom, one of the first things a visitor may notice is that students within the classroom look different from one another. They differ in gender, general body size and build, hair color, eye color, and skin tone. A review of the class roster would likely reveal that students differ in chronological age, and a review of the class grade book would suggest that students differ in their levels of achievement as measured by classroom assessments.

Less noticeable differences between students also exist; students differ from one another in stages of cognitive development, learning styles, current level of skill attainment in different content areas, and English language proficiency. Preservice and inservice teachers, both novice and veteran often express concern about how they will meet the needs of all the students in their classrooms, and especially the needs of English language learners (ELLs). They wonder how they can create a classroom culture that builds community while providing instruction that meets each student's needs.

This unit provides strategies for structuring and managing an inclusive classroom that values the strengths and meets the needs of all students—a classroom that builds community and celebrates difference. This section begins by providing a research-based foundation for the benefits of quality classroom management along with a vignette showing how one fourth grade teacher, Mrs. Allen, implements management strategies to help create an inclusive classroom. This vignette illustrates the ways in which Mrs. Allen has established and maintained clear classroom routines that foster an inclusive learning environment for ELLs and other students—the focus of Strategies 1 through 3. The unit continues by providing an overview of types of differentiation, accompanied by a second vignette that shows how Mrs. Allen manages differentiated materials for her classroom. Strategies 5 through 7 provide strategies for classroom management of differentiated assessment (Strategy 5) and instructional materials (Strategy 6) as well as for how to manage multiple groups during instructional time (Strategy 7). Although strategies for practice are illustrated in the fourth grade classroom, they are easily adaptable for lower or higher grades.

What You Will Learn

Unit I provides research, vignettes, and strategies to help you do the following:

1. Understand how clear routines contribute to the education of ELLs and all other students in the classroom.

2. Develop strategies to establish culturally responsive routines for classroom behavior.

3. Develop strategies for implementing appropriate instructional routines.

4. Develop strategies for welcoming ELLs into the classroom, including preparing other students as buddies.

5. Develop strategies for managing and organizing differentiated assessments.

6. Develop strategies for managing differentiated materials.

7. Develop strategies for managing groups within the classroom.

Unit I is aligned with TESOL standards for teachers (Table I.1) and standards for ELLs at all proficiency levels (Table I.2).

Table I.1	TESOL Standards for Teachers

Domain 2: Culture

2.f.   *Use a range of resources, including the Internet, to learn about world cultures, and specifically the cultures of students in their classrooms, and apply that learning to instruction. (TESOL, 2010, p. 43)*

2.g.   *Understand and apply concepts of cultural competency, particularly knowledge about how an individual's cultural identity affects their learning and academic progress and how levels of cultural identity will vary widely among students. (TESOL, 2010, p. 43)*

Domain 3: Planning, Implementing, and Managing Instruction

3.a.2.   *Create supportive, accepting classroom environments. (TESOL, 2010, p. 45)*

Domain 5: Professional Development, Partnerships, and Advocacy

5.b.5.   *Advocate for ELLs' access to academic resources. (TESOL, 2010, p. 74)*

Source: TESOL Teacher Standards Tables: TESOL (2010). Adapted from TESOL/NCATE Program Standards: Standards for Accreditation of Initial Programs in P–12 ESL Teacher Education. Alexandria, VA: TESOL.

Table 1.2	TESOL Standards for Students

TESOL Standards for Students 1–5

TESOL Standard 1: ELLs communicate for social, intercultural, and instructional purposes within the school setting.

TESOL Standards 2–5: ELLs communicate information, ideas, and concepts necessary for academic success in the area of language arts, mathematics, science, and social studies.

The effective management of classroom space, materials, and grouping structures creates an inclusive classroom climate that promotes positive social, intercultural, and instructional communication between ELLs and other students and provides opportunities for individual, small group, and large group work—increasing ELLs' access to academic information, ideas, and concepts.

Specific performance indicators for academic conversations, vocabulary, reading, and writing for ELLs at each proficiency level are found in the units that are dedicated to these areas.

Source: TESOL (2006).

CLASSROOM MANAGEMENT

Quality classroom management sets the stage for effective instruction and learning for ELLs and other students in the classroom. In a systematic review of literature in the area of classroom management, Simonsen, Fairbanks, Briesch, Myers, and Sugai (2008) found evidence suggesting that effective classroom management results in positive student outcomes. Some features of classroom management are the effective use of space, clearly adhered to routines that are responsive to the needs of students, procedures that ensure all students know the routines and rules of the classroom and school, and an environment that is welcoming to all students.

In the following vignette, Mrs. Allen illustrates how she manages an inclusive classroom, including managing classroom space, setting culturally responsive rules and routines, establishing these routines within the classroom, and welcoming the newly arriving ELL.

Mrs. Allen's Fourth Grade Classroom

Mrs. Joanne Allen has been teaching the fourth grade for over 20 years. Her student population has consisted of predominantly fully English proficient (FEP) learners who are classified as regular education students (for the purpose of this text, *regular education students* refers to students who can access the regular curriculum without modification [non-special needs, non-ELL students]). Normally, Mrs. Allen's fourth grade class consists of between 20 and 25 students, and it has generally included at least a few students who speak English as a second language and a few students who also receive special education services.

In mid-October, six weeks after the start of the school year, Mrs. Allen was notified that a new student, Jorge Alvarado, had enrolled in school and would be joining her class the following day. The guidance counselor explained that Jorge's placement data, including a language proficiency assessment and the results of the home language survey, which are described in later in this unit, would be forwarded to Mrs. Allen prior to Jorge's arrival. Mrs. Allen understood that she would need to review Jorge's placement data to ensure appropriate instruction for him, yet based on feedback she had received from district and building ESOL professionals, Mrs. Allen was confident that she had already developed strategies for managing space, rules, and routines that created a supportive learning environment for ELLs and, therefore, a welcoming environment for Jorge.

MANAGING DIFFERENTIATION IN INCLUSIVE CLASSROOMS

Mrs. Allen knows that to meet Jorge's needs she will need to differentiate the instruction she provides for him. For several years, she has been working to differentiate instruction to meet the diverse needs of the students in her classroom. For example, Carlos grasps new mathematical concepts immediately, whereas Jane requires additional instruction and more guided practice. Elisa excels in science, whereas Juan shines in writing and English language arts. Julia reads through content-area texts without obvious effort, yet Carol requires additional instruction and support to effectively grasp meaning and glean conceptual knowledge from expository texts. Charles, who speaks English as a first language, can access instruction via lectures with few visuals, whereas Farrah, who has a *Developing* level of English proficiency, needs visuals and appropriate time to process language via wait time, think-pair-share, and other small group activities. Mrs. Allen knows that although every student in this class must master key concepts delineated in state and local curriculum frameworks, each student best learns these key concepts in a slightly different way and therefore requires learning experiences that differ in type, duration, and intensity. (Please see Table 4 for proficiency level descriptions.)

ELLs differ from their FEP peers and from one another in cognitive development and learning styles; they also differ in levels of proficiency in academic English, culture, background knowledge, and previous schooling. A differentiated classroom provides an environment that promotes learning for ELLs as well as other students in the classroom.

While it may be intuitive that differentiated instruction benefits all students, veteran and novice teachers often ask, "How do I manage a differentiated classroom? How do I organize and keep track of differentiated assignments, materials, and assessments?" and "Multiple groups make sense to me, but how do I juggle multiple groups in one class?" Teachers are right to ask these questions; without skillful management, differentiation can result in chaos. Therefore, while later units of this book provide strategies showing how to differentiate to account for English language proficiency and academic needs, this unit illustrates how to effectively manage a classroom where instruction and grouping are differentiated.

BEGINNING WITH IDENTIFYING STUDENT OUTCOMES

An effectively differentiated classroom begins by determining what every student must understand as a result of the instructional unit (Wiggins & McTighe, 1998, 2005). ELLs and all other students receive instruction that enables them to access and develop deep understanding of academic concepts and to demonstrate their mastery of concepts. (This is discussed further in Unit III: Strategies for Assessment). A differentiated classroom does not provide individualized instruction; rather, all students in the classroom learn the same concepts, yet assessments, instructional materials, and, at times, specific content vary in accordance with students' learning styles, strengths, needs, and English language proficiency. Teachers in effectively differentiated classrooms know their content, including national, state, and local curriculum frameworks, and they know their students. Thus, they are able to identify the core concepts that all students must master and plan instruction to teach these concepts in ways that meet the different needs of the students in their class. To do so, teachers differentiate instruction in three major ways: content, process, and product (Tomlinson, 2001; Tomlinson & Edison, 2003; Tomlinson & McTighe, 2006).

DIFFERENTIATING CONTENT

The goal of differentiated instruction is to ensure that each student, regardless of learning style, current ability level, or level of English language proficiency, is able to demonstrate mastery of key content-area concepts at varying levels of complexity. For example, Mrs. Allen knows that her state frameworks require every student to demonstrate an understanding of fractions as ratios of whole numbers, parts of units, and parts of collections. Based on assessment data (classroom and standardized), she also knows that her students differ in stages of cognitive development, readiness, and English language proficiency. Mrs. Allen plans her unit with the end in mind; all students will demonstrate mastery of the concept of fractions. In working with the diverse strengths and needs of students within her classroom, Mrs. Allen provides increasingly complex content and word problems for students who quickly grasp the concept and additional support with simpler problems to students who need more time to master the concept. She conducts mini-lessons in content-area vocabulary to ensure that lack of academic language proficiency does not interfere with learning mathematical concepts. She provides word problems at various levels of linguistic complexity to make content comprehensible and provide ongoing practice with the academic English language that frequently appears in word problems.

Easified refers to text that is rewritten in simpler, more comprehensible language (Bhatia, 1983).

Mrs. Allen knows that ELLs, and many other students in the classroom, learn best when content is made accessible through visuals, focused small group activities (to process content and language), and texts that have been made simpler by **easifying** and **glossing**. When easifying text, she often uses a parallel structure; the original text is displayed on the left side of the page and the easified version is on the right. This provides students access to both the original and the easified versions.

Glossing refers to highlighting vocabulary words and phrases in text and providing meanings on the page or in a glossary.

Unit IV of this book provides strategies for simplifying text through easification and glossing.

DIFFERENTIATING PROCESS

Mrs. Allen begins each school year by learning more about the ways her students learn. She observes their behaviors and output as they work in small groups and individually, complete pencil and paper tasks, use visuals, and use manipulatives to solve math problems. She tries to gauge students' academic English language proficiency levels and their content-area reading ability as they read directions and try to solve word problems. She also monitors the ways in which students solve mathematical problems. She has learned, for example, that students from many South American countries engage in a different process as they solve division problems.

Mrs. Allen begins each unit by administering a preinstructional assessment, which provides a snapshot of students' mathematical skills and academic language proficiency. After reviewing assessments, Mrs. Allen groups students. She frequently regroups students according to results of ongoing formative assessments of their written work, observations of discussions, and individual instructional meetings that she conducts with students. (Preinstructional, formative, and summative assessment strategies are provided in Unit III of this book.) Mrs. Allen varies her content-area instruction using manipulatives and visual representations of fractions as appropriate. To make the language used in mathematical problems more accessible, she provides problems in glossed English text, and when possible she provides some problems written in the language of her student.

DIFFERENTIATING PRODUCT

Product refers to what the students produce to enable teachers to measure their progress toward concept mastery: tests, performances and other presentations, artwork, completed graphic organizers, participation in group work, and so on. In a differentiated classroom, product is adjusted so that every student has the opportunity to demonstrate concept mastery irrespective of her or his English language proficiency level, reading level, or writing level. Products are designed to measure content-area understanding *and* growth in academic language; however, the two are not conflated. Strategies 5 through 7 in this section focus on the management of differentiated assessments and instructional materials and on the flexible grouping of students. (Unit III of this book provides step-by-step strategies for designing and implementing differentiated assessments.)

A Glimpse Into Mrs. Allen's Classroom

A glimpse into Mrs. Allen's fourth grade classroom reveals students who appear engaged and on task working in small groups in various areas of the classroom. Mrs. Allen is conferencing with a group of four students in the reading area, another group of students is at the far end of the classroom discussing various readings they have completed, a third group is at the computer station, and yet another group is collaborating on a poster assignment. There are four ELLs in this classroom; the remainder of the students are FEP learners. During this observation, two ELLs work together and the other two ELLs work in two separate groups. A chart at the front of the room lists the student groupings for today's science class.

Managing Classroom Space in an Inclusive Classroom

Strategy

1

THEORY AND/OR RESEARCH UNDERLYING THE STRATEGY

Clear classroom management makes effective use of space (Church, 2007), facilitates the ability of all learners to focus on instruction (Watson & Houtz, 2002), and includes expectations for academic and social behavior. These factors contribute to making the classroom an accepting and predictable place that provides context for instruction, which is consistent with theories of second language instruction (Cummins, 2000).

The physical organizational structure of classrooms is critical to management, effective teaching, and productive learning, and requires careful planning with consideration for the age and developmental levels of the students (Clayton & Forton, 2001). Although teachers may have no control over the size or location of their classrooms, they can be deliberate about the way they use the space they have (Saphier & Gower, 1997) and can organize the space to ensure opportunities for interactive communication. ELLs need to engage with other students in meaningful and purposeful "social, intercultural, and instructional" conversations and to "communicate information, ideas, and concepts" (TESOL, 2006, p. 28) across the content areas.

The spatial design of a classroom provides a framework for the classroom curricula, and thus is critical to effective differentiation of instruction. Clustering desks in groups will surely provide opportunities for interactive discussions. Yet not all students work well in group settings for all activities, and therefore spaces must also be provided for students to work quietly and independently.

Space must be deliberately planned to facilitate class meetings, large group and small group discussions, independent work, quiet space, a listening station for ELLs and other students who may benefit from listening to audio recordings, and other various learning activities dependent on the grade level of students. This space must include *hallways* through which students can pass without interrupting others and places for materials that are easily accessible to students and teachers; experienced teachers know that a traffic jam interferes with instructional time and learning. Waiting for materials, waiting to meet with the teacher, and waiting to begin activities create confusion and waste time (Clayton & Forton, 2001; Saphier & Gower, 1997).

IMPLEMENTING THE STRATEGY

The following organizational strategy, based on the work of Clayton and Forton (2001) and Saphier and Gower (1997), will facilitate the effective use of classroom space.

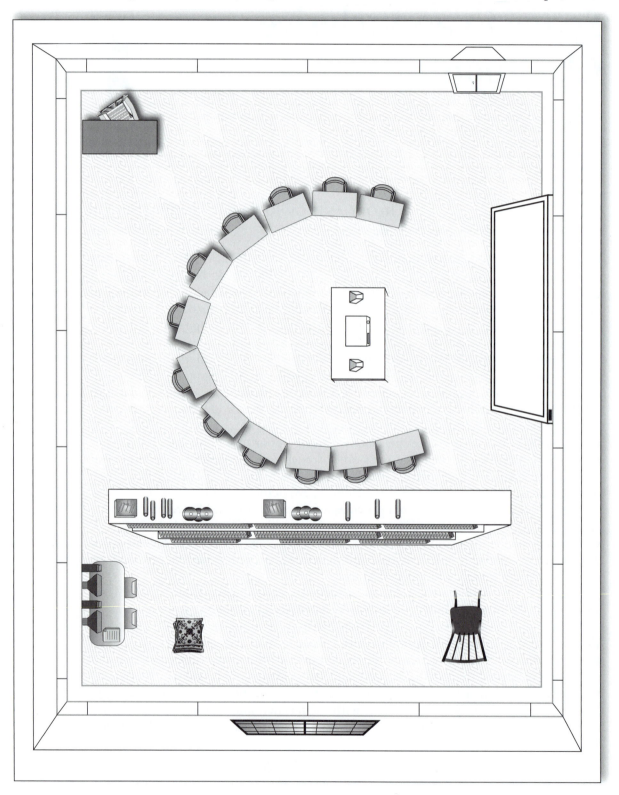

1. Think like a designer, and consider each type of activity that will enhance classroom curricula (content and language) and that the room configuration, therefore, must support.

2. Think about the physical size of students and the amount of space they will need to form lines, pass one another as they transition from activity to activity, come together as a group, engage in independent reading and writing, and engage in academic discussions across content areas.

3. Decide the best configuration to foster ongoing academic conversations between ELLs and FEP learners.

4. Consider the traffic flow as students transition from one activity to the next, and ensure that materials are readily accessible in different places to avoid waiting.

5. Develop a blueprint for the classroom space, working first on paper to ensure careful design.

6. If you are currently teaching, stage the classroom and try out the space with students during the first few weeks of the year. Observe student interactions and the flow of students during transitions and as they gather materials. Solicit the input of students to make adjustments to the space as appropriate.

7. If you are not currently teaching, visit schools and classrooms. If possible, observe the use of instructional space when the classroom is empty and then observe the space during instruction and transitions. What are the strengths and problems with the use of space? Create a sketch, rearranging the space to capitalize on the strengths and minimize identified problems.

STRATEGY IN ACTION

Mrs. Allen designed her classroom to maximize academic discussions in small and large groups and to provide quiet spaces for students to read, listen to audio recordings of texts, conference with her, and systematically use the two classroom computers.

Students' desks are arranged in a large horseshoe shape that faces the front whiteboard; each student can see all of the other students and Mrs. Allen when she is teaching a lesson. Mrs. Allen keeps her technology cart in the center of the horseshoe. With this seating arrangement, students can easily turn their desks to face one another or work in small groups depending on the purpose of the activity. A three-foot walk way on all sides of the horseshoe ensures that students are able to transition between activities without confusion.

Mrs. Allen used several long, three-foot-high bookcases placed end-to-end as a divider, which creates a reading area on the windowed side of the classroom. She placed the bookcases so that students are able to enter the area on the right and exit on the left, thus preventing traffic jams. On the floor is a comfortable and washable rug. A rocking chair, several large throw pillows, and cushions of various sizes enable students to be comfortable as they read. A small table that stands at one end of the area is equipped with audio players; here, students can listen to a variety of books available in audiotape or CD format. (Students also use this area to meet with Mrs. Allen for small group lessons and to plan projects across the content areas.) The bookcases allow Mrs. Allen to see students in the area at all times and to see students who are working in other areas of the classroom when she meets with groups. Mrs. Allen uses the tops of the bookcases to store supplies that students will need for reading, writing, and artwork. These are sorted and in plastic file boxes, easily accessible to students. (Math and science supplies are stored systematically on shelves on the other side of the room.) Mrs. Allen's reading area is replete with various types of fiction and expository texts, books on cassette and CD, and print-outs of electronic materials written in English, Spanish, and Portuguese. (This year Mrs. Allen has two ELLs who read on grade level in Spanish and one who reads near grade level in English.)

Mrs. Allen placed her desk in the back corner of the room as a conferencing center where students come to discuss their work and engage in academic conversation with her. In the opposite corner are two classroom computers. Mrs. Allen bookmarked a variety of content-related sites, including sites available in Spanish and Portuguese. On the wall next to the computers is a sign-up sheet for computer time.

REFLECTIONS

1. What classroom configurations have you tried to effectively utilize space? Which were successful and which were problematic? What factors may have contributed to success or the lack thereof?

2. On an 8 × 11 sheet of paper, map out your classroom so that it will facilitate the use of space for social and academic interaction between students, social and academic interaction between teacher and students, quiet time, and access to appropriate instructional materials, including audio players.

   a. What does (or would) this classroom look like? How is space used?

   b. What would it sound like as students transitioned from activity to activity?

   c. How would each space facilitate the instruction of your curriculum and the social and academic interaction of students at the grade level in which you teach?

   d. How does the space facilitate social and academic interaction between students and between teacher and students?

   e. How would children feel as they enter and work in this classroom?

   f. Would there be space for them to work in groups and to read and write quietly?

   g. When mapping out the classroom on paper, what are the challenges and what seems to work well?

Interactive tool for designing classroom space with related articles from *Instructor Magazine*

http://teacher.scholastic.com/tools/class_setup/

Strategy 2

Setting Culturally Responsive Rules and Routines for an Inclusive Classroom

THEORY AND/OR RESEARCH UNDERLYING THE STRATEGY

Effective management is culturally responsive and acknowledges that not all students share the cultural expectations of the teacher in terms of communication, learning styles, and body language (Cartledge & Lefki, 2008). Setting big-picture, open-ended classroom guiding principles helps to define the overarching philosophy of the classroom and set expectations for classroom climate without establishing rules that may not be culturally congruent for all students. Principles in expressions such as "Be safe, Be Responsible, Be Respectful" (Simonsen et al., 2008) can become classroom themes that convey expectations. Such expressions take into account individual differences and are thus likely to be effective for all learners, regardless of home culture and language. They can also be interpreted collectively by members of the classroom community, thus promoting social justice and engaging students in a democratic process. Another advantage of adopting the same open-ended expression (with its many interpretations) is that it can be easily translated into multiple languages, which can be posted throughout the classroom to demonstrate the value for language diversity.

IMPLEMENTING THE STRATEGY

1. Decide on an open-ended classroom slogan that frames the expectations for student behavior and performance, such as "Be Safe, Be Responsible, Be Respectful" or "Be responsible for your actions." Have the slogan translated into other languages that are spoken by students in the classroom. (Older students might be asked to develop the slogan or to help with translation.)

2. During the first day of school, write the slogan on large poster board and place it in a prominent place within the classroom.

3. Explain to students that safety, responsibility, and respect are non-negotiable aspects of the classroom community and are built on democracy and social justice, and include the voices of all students. (Christensen & Karp, 2003). A

slogan like this is likely to mean different things for different students, which is why open dialogue about the slogan is important.

4. Review rules of dialogue with students: Each student listens actively while his or her partner is speaking, does not interrupt, and shows respect in both spoken and body language. In addition, each student contributes her or his ideas.

5. Using a think-pair-share format, ask each student to describe what *safe, respectful,* and *responsible* (or other words you have chosen) mean to them. (Circulate and ensure that students observe the rules of dialogue.)

6. Have individual students report out as you affirm their responses, writing each new response on the whiteboard.

7. Ask students to discuss the generated responses in small groups and reach consensus about rules that operationalize the interpretations that group members view as most important.

8. Ensure that the slogan and its interpretations are socially just, promote respect for all cultures and language groups, and convey an overall sense of a community in which all voices are heard.

9. Create a poster with slogan and student interpretations.

10. Provide time for each student to sign the poster, indicating that they will support the agreed-upon rules.

11. Display the poster prominently in the classroom.

12. Revisit and adjust interpretations and rules as seems appropriate for students in the classroom.

STRATEGY IN ACTION

Mrs. Allen begins each school year by engaging students in the process of operational-izing the expression that provides the philosophy for her classroom: "Be Safe, Be Respectful, Be Responsible." She provides each student with a laminated copy of the rules of dialogue to tape to the upper left hand corner of his or her desk. Mrs. Allen also displays the rules of dialogue for the group using an overhead projector; she reads through them as students follow along. She asks students to interpret each rule.

Mrs. Allen finds it useful to model the rules of dialogue with a paraprofessional and one of the school's ESL teachers. They model the process of following and then breaking rules. She explains, "Students love catching us breaking a rule. They raise their hands when they see an infraction. Once they point out the infraction to us, we reenact the scene demonstrating adherence to the rule." Once students demonstrate understanding of each rule, Mrs. Allen assigns a think-pair-share activity in which students discuss behaviors that meet each rule that class members have generated. For example, Tania and Alicia began with the rule, "Pay attention when others are talking" and generated the following behaviors that meet this rule: Listen when Mrs. Allen is speaking, listen in groups and let each person have a turn, and listen with your body language—look at the person and do not make faces. Mrs. Allen has facilitated this activity alone, but having extra adults in the room for just an hour is very helpful. She has found that parents are also sometimes willing to serve as cofacilitators.

REFLECTIONS

1. How will you ensure that you provide an environment that is accessible and appropriate for the age and developmental level of your students and respectful of the cultural differences of all students in your classroom?

2. Develop a key slogan for use in your classroom. How will your slogan help to promote an inclusive and respectful environment? Review the slogan to ensure that it is user-friendly for the age and developmental level of the students you teach or will teach.

3. How might you ensure that all students, regardless of English language proficiency, have the opportunity to operationalize the slogan? Think about the potential glitches and problems you might encounter and how you might address each of these.

STRATEGY RESOURCE

Creating Culturally Responsive Classroom Environments

http://www.colorincolorado.org/article/c43/

Establishing Routines in an Inclusive Classroom

Strategy

3

Clear classroom routines provide context that facilitates the use of social and academic language across the content areas. The predictability of classroom routines results in greater comprehensibility of the language used within the classroom. Routines, for taking attendance, managing general supplies, transitioning between activities, moving into groups, taking turns, maintaining noise levels, and so on are fundamental to the effective ELL-supportive classroom.

A middle school mathematics teacher described in Colombo and Furbush (2008) provided a clear illustration of how routines facilitate the grouping and regrouping of students during classroom instruction. This teacher arranged students' desks in four desk clusters. Each desk in the cluster had a laminated number taped to the upper right-hand corner. In the center of each cluster was a label on which the name of a famous mathematician, such as Archimedes, Fibonacci, Germain, or Pythagoras, was written. She assigned each student to a group with careful consideration of English language proficiency and content knowledge. During the first week of school, she *explicitly brought the routine to students' attention:* "I have placed you in groups to begin instruction. During the year, we will form many different groups. You will notice that at the center of each cluster of desks is the name of a famous mathematician." She called for volunteers to read the name of the mathematician for their cluster. She *specifically* told students that at the beginning of each math class, she would call the name of their group and direct them to a meeting space, such as the math corner, the reading area, the computer area, or to her desk. She showed them the route they would take so there would be no traffic jams. She asked students to explain the routine to *ensure that they had internalized it,* and then called one group at a time *to model* the transitioning routine. She *consistently conveyed positive expectations* for students: "I know that you will be able to do this in less than two minutes so we can begin our lessons on time."

During the first weeks of school, the teacher models the routine and provides guided practice, ensuring that students transition efficiently and quietly so that time is not wasted. She is *persistent* in her expectations that students will adhere to the routine.

Once students have mastered this routine, she is able to vary the grouping structure she uses, each time providing students with clear expectations, modeling, and practice.

Routines can also provide a clear road map for "work habits and work procedures" (Saphier & Gower, 1997, p. 87), such as using the classroom word wall to access vocabulary words and checking to ensure the correct spelling of words (see Unit V of this book), accessing math assignments from the differentiated assignment box (see Unit III of this book), selecting appropriate reading materials (see Units IV and VI of this book), using the correct format for lab reports, self-checking reading comprehension, and so on.

IMPLEMENTING THE STRATEGY

1. Decide on a routine that you believe is important to the efficient flow of your classroom or the work habits of all students, such as a routine for moving into groups, forming a line, submitting completed work, effectively using time when assignments have been completed, using word walls to correctly spell words that have been learned, or any other routine that will facilitate a learning environment and good work habits.

2. Explicitly bring the routine to students' attention.

3. Provide clear and specific steps for the routine so that ELLs at all proficiency levels as well as other students understand what they will do.

4. Clearly explain and review the steps of the routine with students so that students will internalize them, and check student understanding.

5. Convey positive expectations that students will adhere to the routine.

6. Model each step of the routine.

7. Persistently adhere to and require students to adhere to the routine. (Saphier & Gower, 1997)

STRATEGY IN ACTION

Mrs. Allen established clear routines for grouping, classroom behavior, and academics that facilitated the instruction of ELLs and other FEP learners in her classroom. Students' use of the classroom word wall in editing is one academic routine that Mrs. Allen established early in the year. Table 3.1 provides a glimpse of each step of this strategy in action.

REFLECTIONS

1. Consider the types of student behavior (social and academic) that are most important to meeting TESOL Standards 1 through 5. What types of routines that

facilitate classroom flow will promote these standards in your specific classroom? What types of routines that facilitate academic work habits promote these standards in your specific classroom?

2. How will you ensure all students are clear about the routines they must follow, and how will you consistently enforce the routines that are most useful to you in a positive manner that conveys your high expectations?

Table 1.3   Routines—Strategy in Action

Teacher Guideline for Implementation	Mrs. Allen's Classroom
Teacher explicitly brings a routine to the attention of students.	Mrs. Allen explains to students that they are responsible for correctly using and spelling the words they have been taught.
Teacher is specific, explaining all the details of the routine.	She clearly explains to students that they must use the words on the word walls appropriately and spell them correctly. (Word walls are discussed in Unit V.)
Teacher repeats the routine to ensure that students have internalized it.	During the first month of the year, Mrs. Allen reviews the steps of the routine for using the word walls for choosing words and for correctly spelling words on assignments.
Teacher conveys positive expectations that students will follow the routine.	Mrs. Allen tells students, "I know that you will use the word wall to correctly use and spell the words that we have learned."
Teacher models the routine.	Mrs. Allen engages students in a think aloud. "I want to say that there was *too* much salt in the water," she tells them. She then models writing, pauses, and thinks aloud: "I know that *too* can be spelled in three different ways. Ahh . . . I see *too* on the word wall with the example *too much*. I know that I should write *too*."
Teacher consistently and persistently adheres to the routine.	When students submit written work with word wall and word bank words spelled incorrectly, Mrs. Allen circles the incorrect word, writes *ww* (word wall) or *wb* (word bank) over the word, and requires students to correct it (Cunningham & Hall, 1998)

STRATEGY RESOURCES

1. Classroom Rules and Procedures

   http://www.learnnc.org/lp/pages/735

2. Establishing Classroom Routines and Procedures

   http://www.brighthub.com/education/k-12/articles/3107.aspx

Strategy 4

Welcoming the ELL and Preparing and Assigning a Buddy

THEORY AND/OR RESEARCH UNDERLYING THE STRATEGY

When ELLs enter U.S. classrooms, they must learn the rules and routines of a new culture as they learn another language (Colorín Colorado, 2007). These dual tasks are difficult under any circumstance, and for ELLs in U.S. schools, these tasks must be accomplished in tandem with learning academic content. Balancing these tasks may cause trauma; it certainly requires cultural adjustment. Colorín Colorado (2007) summarized the stages of cultural adjustment that ELLs may experience:

- Euphoria: an initial period of excitement about their new surroundings.

- Culture shock: anger, hostility, frustration, homesickness, or resentment toward the new culture.

- Acceptance: gradual acceptance of different surroundings.

- Assimilation/adaptation: embrace and adapt to new surroundings and new culture. (para. 2)

Teachers can minimize trauma and maximize the possibility of adjustment by thoughtfully and carefully planning for the arrival of the ELL.

IMPLEMENTING THE STRATEGY

This strategy is presented in two parts: before the ELL arrives (Steps 1–6), which is focused on preparing other students in the classroom for the arrival of the ELL, and after the ELL arrives (Steps 7–11), which concentrates on classroom activity after the ELL is in the classroom.

Before the new ELL arrives

1. Review the ELL's records (assessments, home language survey, report cards from previous schools, and any other available information) to learn as much about her or him

as possible. Also, schedule time to talk to the guidance counselor or to the parents through an interpreter to determine if there is anything else in the ELL's background that you might need to know. For example, Farrah's Iraqi neighborhood experienced bombings and conflict with automatic weapons on a regular basis. For some time after she arrived in the United States, Farrah was easily startled and frightened by loud noises, such as the sound made by a dropped textbook and quick movement. Although Farrah's teacher could not eliminate all books from falling or a window from closing quickly, she could sensitize students to the fact that these sounds and movements might frighten Farrah.

2. Prepare the entire class by explaining something about the home language and culture of the ELL (Shore, 2005). With older students, allow time for students to conduct research about the country of origin of the ELL.

3. If the ELL speaks a language that uses the Latin alphabet, have students use the Internet or bilingual dictionaries to generate a short, age-appropriate list of words in the language of the ELL, which they later can ask the ELL to pronounce and teach to them. (For younger students, teach several key words.) Older children who speak the language of the newly arriving ELL may help with pronunciation. They may also help with different alphabet systems.

4. Explain and reinforce the importance of welcoming the new student to in- and out-of-class activities. Welcoming the ELL is an important part of the class routine and demonstrates the importance of including the newly arriving ELL.

5. With students, plan a tour of the school, which includes places (gym, cafeteria, bathrooms, principal's office, nurse's office, etc.), people (principal, nurse, and other teachers who will work with the ELL, such as the ESL teacher and the physical education, music, and art specialists). Review the routines that every student must know, such as which bus to take, where to line up for the bus, and how to proceed through the cafeteria line. Review specific procedures that every student must know: for example, having one's agenda signed before leaving the classroom for the bathroom, nurse's office, and so on.

6. Select and prepare a buddy for the ELL—if possible, ensuring that the buddy speaks the same first language (Freeman & Freeman, 1990), and make the job of buddy a prestigious and desirable one (Freeman & Freeman, 2007). The responsibility of a buddy is to make sure that the ELL can find her or his way around the school and is invited into out-of-class activities.

When the ELL arrives

7. Ask the ELL to say her or his name slowly and clearly and repeat it back, checking for correct pronunciation. Ensure that classmates learn the correct pronunciation of the ELL's name.

8. Demonstrate value for the ELL's first language by asking him or her to teach the class new words when he or she is ready. (Do not pressure the ELL to speak in any language. See the introduction of this book for information on the silent period.)

9. Have students show the research they found on the country of the ELL. Encourage the ELL to explain something about her or his country in English, her native language, or a combination of the two if he or she is willing to do so. If another student, teacher, or paraprofessional speaks the same language, solicit his or her support in interpreting.

10. Be careful not to assume that the ELL would like to discuss his or her experiences. If ELLs have come from situations of trauma caused by war, extreme poverty, or uprooting, they may not wish to discuss their situations.

11. Conduct read-alouds in the language of the ELL (Freeman & Freeman, 2007). Other teachers, paraprofessionals, and parents are excellent resources for this task.

STRATEGY IN ACTION

Mrs. Allen has only one day to prepare her class to welcome Jorge Alvarado into the classroom. As part of the morning meeting, Mrs. Allen shares the news that a new student will arrive, that his name is Jorge Alvarado, and that he is from the Dominican Republic. She asks if students know where the Dominican Republic is located and calls on two students to help her locate it on the class map. She points out its proximity to the equator and asks the class to hypothesize about the climate. Do they think it is warmer or colder there than it is in their New England classroom? She asks students if they know anyone else from the Dominican Republic. Nick volunteers the names of several major league baseball players. The mention of these players provides a segue for Mrs. Allen's next question, "Do you know what language is spoken in the Dominican Republic?" Several of the students volunteer that Spanish is spoken in the Dominican Republic. When she tells the students the new student's name is Jorge, two students make connections to Jorge Posada, a catcher for the New York Yankees.

Mrs. Allen asks the class to think of times when they have been placed in new situations in which they did not know other children or adults. She allows time for several students to share their experiences. Mrs. Allen then brainstorms with students about the things that everyone in the school building must know. The students and Mrs. Allen generate a list. Next, they discuss the people in the building that every student needs to know. (If Jorge's English proficiency had been at *Level 1, Starting* or *Level 2, Emerging,* Mrs. Allen would have also worked with students to find the Spanish definitions for the names of key places and people.) Mrs. Allen explains that all the students are responsible for helping Jorge feel at home and designates Andy, a student who would ride the same bus as Jorge, as his special buddy. (If any of the students spoke Spanish as a first language, Mrs. Allen would likely have designated one of these students as a buddy.)

After lunch, the students use the classroom computers and the bilingual dictionaries to generate a list of words in Spanish for items found in the classroom (blackboard, desk, chair, closet, books, door, window, etc.). Each student is responsible for one word, which she or he writes in English and in Spanish on a strip of oak tag that Mrs. Allen distributed. Two volunteers tape the words to the objects they represent.

When Jorge arrives the next day, Mrs. Allen and the class welcome him, and Mrs. Allen introduces him to Andy. She explains that Andy will be his buddy and will take the bus home with him in the afternoon. Andy tours the classroom with him to show him the words. Jorge smiles and reads each word aloud in Spanish. Members of the class repeat the words. Mrs. Allen calls on another student to show Jorge the map and indicate the Dominican Republic and New England. At the end of the school day, Mrs. Allen contacts one of the eighth grade teachers who she knows has at least one student from the Dominican Republic in her classroom. She arranges for the student to come to the class to read in Spanish the following week.

REFLECTIONS

1. Review the strategy and discuss the steps with a colleague, and determine which would be easy to implement and which might be more difficult.

2. Reflect on times that you have felt like a stranger or an outsider and on the actions of others that lessened or might have lessened your sense of aloneness.

STRATEGY RESOURCES

1. 🗎 Pair Your Newcomers With Buddies, by J. Haynes

   http://www.everythingesl.net/inservices/buddies.php

2. 🗎 Welcoming Second Language Learners

   http://teacher.scholastic.com/products/instructor/second.htm

3. Making Refugee Students Welcome

   http://www.ascd.org/publications/educational_leadership/apr09/num07/Making_Refugee_Students_Welcome.aspx

Strategy

5

Managing Differentiated Assessments

How do I keep track of all the different variations of assessments and make sure that each student is making progress?

—Grade 2 Teacher

THEORY AND/OR RESEARCH UNDERLYING THE STRATEGY

When teachers differentiate assessments, they must have a clear and useful data management system (Tomlinson, 2001) to ensure that they can access and use assessment data to inform instruction and ensure that each student is making progress (Gottlieb, 2006). In this strategy, three teachers provide glimpses of how to manage differentiated assessments.

IMPLEMENTING THE STRATEGY

Developing appropriate differentiated assessments requires a deep understanding of one's content area as well as an understanding of the developmental levels of one's students in terms of language and content. Effectively managing differentiated assessment data for each student in the classroom requires a clear and organized system for data storage and retrieval. Without this organized data system, differentiation is unlikely to be successful.

1. Decide on a system for organizing the papers and other assignments that students will submit as formative and summative assessments.

2. Evaluate the space within your classroom. Consider the arrangement of student desks and the available storage.

3. Think about the classroom traffic flow and the way to most effectively distribute and collect folders or papers to ensure that all assignments can be distributed and collected in the first and last two minutes of the class.

4. Establish a system for using folders and files or other organizational methods for placing and storing assessments.

5. During the first week of school, establish a clear routine for managing the file system.

6. Explain the routine to students and provide time for them to practice this routine.

7. Reinforce the routine so that it becomes automatic for students.

8. Develop a clear and manageable plan for reviewing assessments and providing student feedback once the system is in place.

STRATEGY IN ACTION

Ms. Cara Williams, a teacher in a self-contained fifth grade classroom, has found a data management system that has enabled her to measure the ongoing progress of each student. When she first began to differentiate content and assessments, Ms. Williams sorted through student work, trying to remember the modifications and adjustments she had made to the assignments for different students in her classroom. Although she could see student progress when she compared a student's work on large quarterly summative assessments, she often found it difficult to keep track of student growth and areas of need evidenced in formative and informal assessments. She had an overall sense of student growth, but this was far from exact. Knowing that assessment should inform instruction, Ms. Williams decided to implement an effective data management system that would enable her to measure the progress of any given student at any point in time. She decided that a portfolio system would be most useful for this purpose.

After deciding which assessments would best show student mastery of concepts, Ms. Williams purchased large accordion files (one to be used by each student in her classroom) to manage assignments submitted by each of her fifth grade students. Similar to file cabinets, the accordion files are part of Ms. Williams' permanent data management system and, thus, are recycled each year. Each file has been numbered and assigned to a student. At the beginning of the year, Ms. Williams makes it clear to students that they are responsible for maintaining the accordion files and that they should not mark or damage them in any way.

As part of her supply requisition each year, Ms. Williams orders multicolor folders, and she uses one color to correspond with each major content area she teaches: Math assignments are placed in the red folder, writing assignments in blue, science work in yellow, and social studies in green. Stapled to the inside of each folder is a work log with columns to record the name of the assignment and the date it is submitted. During the first few days of the school year, Ms. Williams works with students to establish an effective routine for folder use, which includes recording each assignment that is placed in the folder on a student log and returning each folder to the accordion file.

To facilitate student access to the folders and to ensure that instructional time is not wasted, Ms. Williams visualized her student desk area as four quadrants, with approximately equal numbers of students in each quadrant. She divided student portfolios accordingly and arranged groups of accordion files in each of the four corners of the classroom. Every week, she assigns one student from each quadrant to distribute the content-area color-coded folders to the students in his or her quadrant and to return student folders to the appropriate accordion file.

Each day, Ms. Williams reviews folders of students in one quadrant of the classroom. She makes notes regarding student progress, which enables her to conference with students in a systematic way.

Teachers Who Travel From Room to Room

Mrs. Sandy Jones uses a similar system, but she is without her own classroom and travels from classroom to classroom each day to meet her five classes of students. Mrs. Jones distributes students' folders at the beginning of each period and collects them at the end. Each day, she reviews the folders of students from one class, ensuring that at the end of the week, she has reviewed student progress for each student in each of the five classes she teaches.

Mr. Carlos Rivera adopted a similar system. He uses two sets of different colored plastic magazine files for each of his five science classes. Mr. Rivera places one set of files on each side of the room. A manila folder for each student in each class is housed within a color-coded magazine file, depending on the side of room on which the student sits. Having two files on opposite sides of the room reduces traffic flow and facilitates the efficient and time-effective distribution and collection of folders.

Ms. Clara Panak also uses magazine files for her third grade class. Students have five color-coded folders in which they store their assignments and assessments. Like Ms. Williams, Ms. Panak imagined her classroom divided into quadrants. She placed five student files in each quadrant. Each student retrieves her or his file at the beginning of the day, which provides them with access to the folders they need for different subjects. Students place their work in their folders, complete the student log, and then return the folders to their files, and the files to the designated location at the end of the school day.

Mr. Scott Brown teaches middle school math to five classes of students each day. He uses a similar system to Ms. Williams and Mrs. Jones, but rather than folders for each class, he uses a binder system to manage the assessment and assignment data for his students. Each student begins the year with a two-inch, three-ring binder. At the beginning of each instructional unit, Mr. Brown distributes a list of the goals and objectives for the unit and the key assignments. This list and all the materials that Mr. Brown distributes are three-hole punched so that students may easily store them in their binders. Students also place every assignment and journal entry into their binders. On Monday through Thursday, Mr. Brown collects binders from students according to their last names; students whose last names begin with A through D submit binders on Monday, students whose last names begin with E through L submit binders on Tuesday, and so on. Mr. Brown reviews one set of binders each evening and conferences with students during the instructional period the following day. By collecting binders across several days, Mr. Brown ensures that he has time within instructional periods to discuss progress and concerns with each student.

REFLECTIONS

1. In reading the Strategy in Action section, what ideas for managing assessments did you find that might be effective in your classroom?

2. Develop a system for implementing differentiated assessments within your classroom, including the physical system (the materials you will use, e.g., file cabinets

and files, accordion or magazine files, binders), the placement of the system for easy retrieval by you and students, a system for accessing assessments and measuring student progress, and a system for meeting with students to discuss progress. What challenges can you anticipate, and how might you resolve them?

STRATEGY RESOURCES

1. 📄 Educate Interactive—A description of differentiated assessment with several useful links

   http://www.educateinteractive.org/best_practices/differentiated_assessments.html

2. TeAchnology—The Online Teacher Resource provides a section on alternative assessment, alternative assessment, and rubrics.

   http://www.teach-nology.com/currenttrends/alternative_assessment

Strategy

6

Managing Differentiated Instructional Materials

How do I organize all these different materials, like visuals and text at different reading levels?

—Middle School Teacher

How do I make differentiated materials available to students?

—Pre-Service, Secondary Teacher

THEORY AND/OR RESEARCH UNDERLYING THE STRATEGY

Differences in learning styles, developmental levels, reading levels, and levels of proficiency in academic English require a variety of materials to make content accessible and to build academic language skills. Providing visuals, video, and graphic organizers builds comprehensibility of instruction for ELLs (Echevarria, Vogt, & Short, 2003; Krashen, 1981), which increases the likelihood that instruction will be meaningful to students with different learning styles. Providing text at different reading levels makes readings more accessible to ELLs and builds academic language (Nation, 2008; Schmitt, 2008).

Teachers who are new to the classroom and experienced classroom teachers who are new to differentiation can begin by collecting a few new items (visual or text) that increase the comprehensibility of content-area instruction for each unit they teach. Having an organizational system in place enables teachers to build a tool chest of differentiated materials to meet the needs of ELLs as well as FEP learners in their classrooms and to steadily add to this tool chest. Having a system for using differentiated materials within the classroom also ensures that students will have access to materials that are appropriate to their level of English proficiency.

IMPLEMENTING THE STRATEGY—PART I (ORGANIZING MATERIALS)

1. Determine content-area concepts and units that you teach or will teach.

2. Decide on the core materials you will use: texts, Internet sites, visuals, and so on.

3. Determine the English language proficiency levels of ELLs in your classroom. If you do not know the English proficiency levels of students who are or will be placed in your classroom, assume a classroom population that includes at least one ELL at each of the following TESOL levels: *Emerging, Developing, Expanding,* and *Bridging.* (Please see Table 4 for proficiency level descriptions.)

4. Determine reading levels of students in your classroom, including ELLs and FEP learners. If this is not known prior to the start of the year, it is useful to assume a range in reading ability from two years below to two years above grade level.

5. Decide on a system that will facilitate management and enable you to systematically and consistently add to your tool chest of differentiated materials. For example, Mr. James uses clear plastic file boxes for each quarter, with each unit in a different colored hanging file. Ms. Bell uses accordion boxes for each math unit she teaches. You might also organize a file cabinet or a large canvas bag filled with manila file folders for each instructional unit you teach. The secret to the system is that it needs to be one that is effective for you.

6. For each unit that you will teach, begin to collect additional published reading materials at various levels (old texts, magazine articles, student-generated writing), audios (commercially available and recorded by teachers or other students), commercially available videos, and Internet materials (YouTube and other videos).

7. Add each new item to the appropriate unit file. For readings, label the file according to subject and reading/English proficiency level.

STRATEGY IN ACTION

Mr. Patrick St. James, a middle school social studies teacher, uses his textbook as a reference book. He has used the Internet, *National Geographic,* and professional organizations to which he belongs to collect text at different reading levels and in Spanish and Portuguese, the two languages spoken by ELLs in his classroom. Mr. St. James also uses online resources such as the *National Archives, National Geographic,* and *Google Images* as sources for images. When Mr. St. James first started collecting materials, he found it was difficult to keep track of them from year to year. For example, one year he had dedicated many hours to collecting materials about world cultures and religions, a topic in his sixth grade curriculum. He worked both at home and at school and, thus, had bookmarked Internet sites in both locations. He also printed various materials and shared the originals with students. He placed some materials in his classroom file cabinet, others in his home office, and still others in different bags he carried from school to home. The following year, as he prepared to teach the topic, he was able to readily access only a small portion of the materials that he had collected. This is when Mr. St. James decided he needed a system for managing his materials.

Mr. St. James decided to file his materials in transparent plastic file boxes, each purchased for just a few dollars. The first year he bought four boxes, one to hold the materials for each semester of the school year. Mr. St. James purchased colored hanging folders, using a different color for each unit, and then carefully labeled manila folders for each document and photo within the unit. Once Mr. St. James established this system, he began to add videos and the student written work that he had vetted for quality of writing and content-area accuracy to his units. (The processes for using student writing as differentiated materials are included in Strategy 20 of this text.) Mr. St. James found that the written work of other students often provided entry for many ELLs and other students in his classroom. He also discovered that his students (ELLs and FEP learners alike) were more willing to revise and edit their work when they knew that it might be included in a resource packet for other students.

Ms. Mia Bell, a seventh and eighth grade mathematics teacher described in Colombo and Furbush (2009), stored the differentiated materials she collected in a number of accordion-style file boxes. Each file box housed a mathematics unit and was labeled for easy identification. She stored the boxes in a bookcase that was easily accessible to her. Whenever Ms. Bell located materials such as student work, Internet or journal writings, or ideas, she added them to the appropriate file, and thus continually built her instructional materials. Ms. Bell also worked at creating rubrics for each assignment at each English language proficiency level. She had a section in each box for these rubrics. Using teachers' journals, sample texts, and texts and workbooks no longer used in the system, Ms. Bell collected math word problems at various levels of difficulty. Ms. Bell also glossed and easified vocabulary on cards for two purposes: It makes academic content vocabulary more comprehensible and it calls students' attention to new words, which increases their opportunities to learn these words. (Strategy 20 provides a step-by-step guide for glossing and simplifying text.) Ms. Bell printed these word problems on 5 × 7 index cards, which she laminated for durability. She organized these cards by concepts and level of difficulty.

Implementing the Strategy—Part II (Making Differentiated Materials Available to Students)

1. Review the learning outcomes for an instructional unit.

2. Review materials you will use to teach the unit, including the course textbook and other materials that you have collected. Consider how each item (reading, graphic organizer, visual, recording, etc.) will enable students to meet specific learning outcomes.

3. Select materials that will make the established learning outcome accessible to all students. For example, materials that students will access to prepare for a discussion on the effects of population growth include six pages in the course textbook, a reading from a science journal for students that extends the textbook, a YouTube video with accompanying graphic organizer, a simplified version of the textbook, and an exemplary essay written by a student from the previous year.

4. Assign materials depending on the English proficiency level of students, ensuring that each student can access the content-area concepts and prepare to actively participate in the following day's discussion.

5. Explain to students what they should learn (or be able to do) as a result of the specific assignment. For example, "As a result of tonight's homework you will be prepared to actively contribute to tomorrow's small group discussions on the

effects of population growth" or "You will read the primary source documents on child labor laws to prepare for tomorrow's discussion on the Progressive Era."

STRATEGY IN ACTION

Mr. Todd Martin's fifth grade class has just begun a unit on immigration. One learning outcome for the unit is "Students will discuss the hardships and barriers encountered by various immigrant groups." The textbook provides a broad overview of immigration, but Mr. Martin finds that the textbook is too dense for many of his students and often fails to make history relevant to them. He continues to use the textbook to provide an overview and to help his students develop the ability to read expository text. He also supplements the textbook with materials that he and his team have collected over the past two years: primary source documents (visuals and written documents), online virtual museums, videos, and several children's books written at various reading levels, including some picture books. To help all students master the content-area learning outcome, Mr. Martin reviews the English proficiency levels of students in the classroom and the levels of the materials that he has collected. For the first reading assignment, he determines that everyone will read the four pages in the text that relate to immigration. Using a copy of the text, Mr. Martin glossed key words and made explanatory notes in the margins. He keeps a master copy on file and makes six copies of the easified text for the four ELLs in his classroom and for two FEP learners who, for various reasons, are experiencing difficulties with academic reading. He distributes these to the six students. For additional reading and materials, he guides students to choose materials (hard copy and electronic) that they will be able to access depending on their current English language proficiency and academic reading levels. Mr. Martin's differentiation of materials grants each student in his classroom access to the same content-area concepts and promotes their interactive participation in ongoing classroom discussion.

REFLECTIONS

1. Review a content-area unit that you teach. What are the learning outcomes for the unit? What materials have you collected to make these learning outcomes available to students of various English language proficiency levels and various reading levels? Are the materials accessible? Do they sufficiently challenge students to work at the upper level of their abilities?

2. Reflect on the advantages of providing to students materials that address the same learning outcomes, but are at various reading and language levels. How might using materials that are differentiated for academic English proficiency and reading levels meet the needs of all students in the classroom?

3. Think about systems you might implement for organizing differentiated materials. What potential benefits and challenges do you envision with each system?

Strategy Resources

1. 📄 Differentiated instruction and ability grouping (are not the same!)

   http://teachers.net/gazette/MAY08/sigmon/

2. 📄 Differentiated instruction (Reading Rockets)

   http://www.readingrockets.org/article/c64

Managing
Multiple Groups

Strategy
7

Engaging the class in whole group instruction is effective for presentations, introductions of materials, and for preparing all students to engage in the content-area unit. Working in small groups gives students more time to engage in academic discussions about the content. While lessons delivered to the entire class may be easier to manage, effectively working with students in smaller flexible groups for at least some of the instructional period increases the likelihood that the individual needs of students will be met (Tomlinson, 2001). Working purposefully in small content-area groups allows ELLs to engage in academic conversations with peers, thereby increasing academic language proficiency. Managing these small groups requires careful planning to avoid confusion and wasted instructional time.

THEORY AND/OR RESEARCH UNDERLYING THE STRATEGY

Comprehensible input (Krashen, 1982) and comprehensible output (Canale & Swain, 1980) are necessary for the development of a second or additional language. The opportunity for comprehensible input and output is likely to increase when ELLs and FEP learners collaborate in small groups. The small group setting is conducive to trying out new academic vocabulary and language structures.

Student grouping should be flexible and should depend on the purpose of the instruction and the needs of students. For example, heterogenous grouping works for activities such as jigsaws, where members of each group are responsible for becoming experts in one area of the content and then teaching this to members of other groups. Flexible homogeneous grouping can enable teachers to work with students based on specific identified needs and strengths. For example, students who grasp a science concept quickly and are motivated by the unit content are likely to benefit from focused work that extends their understanding (Tomlinson, 2001). Students who are having difficulty with the concept may need additional support and direct instruction from the teacher. ELLs may benefit from focused study of academic content-area language as they are learning new concepts. Both heterogeneous and homogeneous groupings require that teachers develop strategies for managing differentiated groups; students must be able to group and regroup efficiently and know explicitly what they are to do during group work, including what to do when they have questions or when they have completed their group assignment.

IMPLEMENTING THE STRATEGY

1. Review the learning outcomes you have established for the instructional unit and the initial assessment (pretesting, KWL (Know, Want to Know, Learned), or observation) of students' understanding of the content.

2. Determine how grouping will benefit students' acquisition of content-area concepts and academic language. For example, will students use terms and academic vocabulary to discuss an issue from the unit? Will groups of students become experts in one area and then present their findings to other groups in a jigsaw activity? Might a group of students who have demonstrated conceptual knowledge work together to complete more intensive enrichment activities, while another group of students receive additional support? (Grouping should be flexible and dependent on the specific purposes of the task and the identified needs and strengths of the students. Regrouping should be the norm rather than the exception.)

3. Design a system that will enable you to easily group students. (Calling out students' names is cumbersome and time consuming.) Try using colored index cards, regular playing cards (a number, symbol, or suit for each group), or picture cards from children's games. Display a chart showing the symbol that represents each group and where the group should meet. Distribute cards to students.

4. If group activities will vary, and generally they will, type instructions on sheets or on cards so that precious instructional time is not lost reviewing instructions several times. Use visuals or audios for students who have difficulty reading.

5. Set clear routines for moving into groups, moving furniture, and maintaining a low noise level (see Strategy 3).

6. Establish an anchor activity in which students will engage when they have completed their work (a box of brain teasers, "I'm done" activities on cards or sheets of paper, established journaling activities, puzzles, spelling or word building games or activities, etc.). Having an anchor activity ensures that every student knows what she or he should do when her or his assignment is completed.

7. Establish a routine for students to follow if they have questions while you are working with another group. (Ask two friends, try to figure out the answer, write down the question, or work on anchor activity until teacher is free.) Or assign a go-to person for each group who will adopt the role of question answering expert.

8. Assign an expert of the day in each group who will review student work before it is submitted. (Once students believe they have completed an assignment, they show it to the expert for approval before submitting. The expert must approve the work before it is submitted.)

9. Ensure that students know the routine for submitting work (folders, files, binders, etc.).

Source: Adapted from *How to Differentiate Instruction in Mixed-Ability Classrooms* (2nd ed., pp. 35–38), by C. Tomlinson, 2001, Alexandria, VA: Association for Supervision and Curriculum Development.

STRATEGY IN ACTION

As one component of an immigration unit, Mr. Martin assigned his students various populations who immigrated to the United States: populations from Ireland, China, Italy, Japan, and Mexico. In previous lessons, Mr. Martin prepared students to engage in jigsaw activities (Aronson, Blaney, Stephin, Sikes, & Snapp, 1978). (The jigsaw is a cooperative grouping activity in which each student is responsible for one component of the final product. Members of jigsaw groups should be diverse in terms of ability, ethnicity, and language proficiency. ELLs, however, who have *Starting* or *Emerging* levels of English language proficiency [See Table 4] should be paired with another student, preferably a student from the same language group.)

Mr. Martin has grouped students for the purposes of content and language. Content-wise, he wants students to gain a depth of understanding that goes beyond what is provided in the text. He wants students to be able to relate to the experiences of children who immigrated to the United States. He also wants to develop the academic language ability of all students in the classroom, and especially that of his ELLs. He collected reading materials (expository and narrative), photos, and Internet sites, which he bookmarked. He also created a graphic organizer as a tool to help students organize and share concepts and information. He organized the subtopics about immigration into five groups (Irish immigration, Chinese immigration, Italian immigration, Japanese immigration, and Mexican immigration) and prepared colored index cards for each group. He also organized students by group number (1–4) and printed numbers on the back of the index cards. As students enter the room, he distributes a colored, numbered index card to each student to indicate the group to which they belong.

There are 22 students with various English language proficiency levels in Mr. Martin's class. Twenty of these students have proficiency levels greater than *Expanding,* one student (Maya) has an *Emerging* level of proficiency, and another student (Ana) has a *Developing* level of proficiency. For this lesson, Mr. Martin divides the 20 students with English proficiency at levels greater than *Expanding* into four groups of five students each. Each member of each group will be responsible for learning more about one population that immigrated to the United States. To provide Maya and Ana with additional support, Mr. Martin pairs Maya (*Emerging Proficiency*) with Sandra, a student who is bilingual in English and Spanish. Maya joins Sandra's group as a sixth member. Ana (*Developing Proficiency*) is assigned to work with Blake, who is a monolingual English speaker, and joins Blake's team. Mr. Martin provides numerous materials about the immigration of Mexican Americans to the United States; many of these are written in Spanish. He assigns this subtopic to the group in which Maya is working. Mr. Martin has also easified materials about Irish immigration; he assigns Irish immigration to the group in which Ana and Blake are working.

Mr. Martin organized and placed reading and resource materials for each immigrating including materials that have been glossed and easified, in a folder marked with a corresponding color (yellow, Irish; orange, Chinese, etc.). Thus, each expert on each type of immigration knows exactly where to find her or his materials. Each colored folder holds sufficient graphic organizers for each student in the group. Internet sites have been bookmarked for quick and easy access and printing. Anchor or "I'm done" activities are always located in a box on the bookshelf. This ensures that students have ready access to anchor materials if they complete their assignment before the allotted time.

Charts posted on the board at the front of the room facilitate the grouping and regrouping of students. See Tables 7.1 and 7.2.

Table 7.1 Meeting Groups (Days 1 and 3)

Meeting Groups—Monday, 1:00–1:45 and Wednesday, 1:00–1:45

Student	Group 1	Group 2	Group 3	Group 4	Computer Time
Yellow	Irish immigration	Irish immigration	Irish immigration	Irish immigration	1:10–1:25
Orange	Chinese immigration	Chinese immigration	Chinese immigration	Chinese immigration	1:25–1:40
Pink	Italian immigration	Italian immigration	Italian immigration	Italian immigration	Tuesday
Green	Japanese immigration	Japanese immigration	Japanese immigration	Japanese immigration	Tuesday
White	Mexican immigration	Mexican immigration	Mexican immigration	Mexican immigration	Tuesday

Anchor activities: Vocabulary builders, making words

Table 7.2 Meeting Groups (Day 2)

Topic Expert Meeting Groups—Tuesday, 1:00–1:45

Student number	Yellow	Orange	Pink	Green	White
1	Irish immigration	Chinese immigration	Italian immigration	Japanese immigration	Mexican immigration
2	Irish immigration	Chinese immigration	Italian immigration	Japanese immigration	Mexican immigration
3	Irish immigration	Chinese immigration	Italian immigration	Japanese immigration	Mexican immigration
4	Irish immigration	Chinese immigration	Italian immigration	Japanese immigration	Mexican immigration
Computer Time	X	X	1:00–1:15	1:15–1:30	1:30–1:45

Anchor activities: Vocabulary builders, making words

On Monday, students meet in their numbered groups, and each student collects her or his materials. They read printed materials and view photos and videos individually, using the graphic organizer to record information, concepts, and ideas. The goal of each student is to become an expert in the immigration experiences of one immigrating population. On Tuesday, experts meet together in like groups (e.g., all students who studied Irish immigration collaborate and compare their work to ensure that they have been both thorough and accurate). On Wednesday, experts return to their original groups to teach their area of expertise to their original group members.

Mr. Martin's use of numbered, colored index cards enables him to group and regroup all students efficiently. Placing materials in folders with colored cards provides each group with ready access to the appropriate materials. The chart at the front of the room allows students to know what they will do and with which group they will work. Mr. Martin's designation of an expert student for each group increases the likelihood that he will be able to circulate and work with one group at a time without being interrupted.

REFLECTIONS

1. What lessons that you teach might be enhanced through heterogeneous group work?

2. After reading Strategy 7 and Mr. Martin's implementation of the strategy, what promises and potential areas of concern do you anticipate with implementing heterogeneous grouping with ELLs in the mainstream classroom?

3. What routines will you put in place in your classroom to facilitate the effective use of instructional time, and thus student learning?

STRATEGY RESOURCES

1. 📄 Instructional Grouping—Created for online learning, and applicable to any type of grouping and age group

   http://www.tltgroup.org/gilbert/millis.htm

2. 📄 Jigsaw Classroom—An overview, procedures, and tips for implementation

   http://www.jigsaw.org/overview.htm

3. 📄 Group Work in the Classroom

   http://www.brighthub.com/education/k-12/articles/19619.aspx

4. Managing a One Computer Classroom, by C. Hornik

   http://www.teachersnetwork.org/ntny/nychelp/manage/onecomputer.htm

UNIT II

Working With Other Professionals

The ESL teacher is very nice, but I don't even know what the ELLs in my classroom do when they go to ESL.

—Grade 5 Teacher

I observed a class today and the para[professional] just worked with one student. I am not even sure what he was doing. I was thinking that soon I would have my own classroom and I would have no idea how to work with a para.

—Preservice Teacher

As the population of students in regular education classrooms changes, the roles and responsibilities of the regular classroom teacher must also change. Teachers, who once may have closed their classroom doors and managed their classes in isolation, may well find that they now need to work collaboratively with other educators, specialists, and paraeducators in order to provide the most appropriate instruction for the students in their classrooms. Research suggests that collaboration is likely to have positive implications for teachers—lessening the sense of isolation that teachers report experiencing (Abdallah, 2009a). In fact, in a review of research on teacher attrition, Abdallah (2009b) found that isolation was a prominent reason teachers left the teaching profession.

The quality of relationships between teachers and other educators in their schools and school communities seems to promote teacher longevity (Alliance for Education, 2008), and the collegiality that can come from working together has been found to support teachers in challenging situations and to inspire teachers' confidence in their work (Abdallah, 2009a). Teacher collegiality and a sense of well-being between teachers are likely to have positive effects on student outcomes (Nias, 1998).

ELLs, in particular, are likely to benefit from collaborative relationships between their regular classroom teachers, ESL specialists, and paraeducators or tutors. As Brown (2005) explained, ESL specialists have a depth of knowledge in the area of second language acquisition that they can share with regular classroom teachers. Optimal collaboration between regular classroom teachers and ESL specialists should be planned, ongoing, and systematized. Although chatting in the hallways between classes and sharing advice in the teacher's lounge can be valuable, it leaves important conversations to chance. In contrast, scheduling ongoing collaborative team planning meetings increases the likelihood that both teachers will learn from one another and be able to plan more appropriate instruction for ELLs. In addition, planning together provides a sense of collegiality and can serve to reduce individual planning time (Abdallah, 2009b).

Collaboration with paraeducators also has the potential to improve instruction for both ELLs and FEPs. According to the National Resource Center for Paraprofessionals, ELLs are one of the populations of students who frequently receive support services from paraeducators. The services provided by paraeducators can be improved through thoughtful collaboration between teachers and paraeducators and creating well-defined roles and responsibilities (Pickett, Likins, & Wallace, 2003).

The focus of this unit is collaboration between regular classroom teachers and other educators (ESL specialists, paraeducators, and tutors) for the benefit of ELLs. Three strategies are presented in Unit II: Strategy 8, Collaborating With the ESL Specialist; Strategy 9, Communicating Effectively With the Paraeducator; and Strategy 10, Making the Specialist and Paraeducator Part of the Classroom.

WHAT YOU WILL LEARN

The strategies, vignettes, and research provided in Unit II will help you to do the following:

1. Work collaboratively and effectively with ESL teachers, paraeducators, and tutors.

2. Connect with the ESL specialist and use the specialist's expertise as a resource.

3. Communicate effectively with the tutor or paraeducator.

4. Include the ESL specialist, paraeducator, and tutor in the classroom.

The strategies presented in Unit II benefit ELLs at all proficiency levels and are aligned with TESOL Standards for Teachers, as illustrated in Table II.1.

Table II.1	TESOL Standards for Teachers

Professionalism

5.b.3. *Work with other teachers and staff to provide comprehensive, challenging educational opportunities for ELLs in the school. (TESOL, 2010, p. 73–74)*

5.b.4. *Engage in collaborative teaching in general education, content-area, special education, and gifted classrooms. (TESOL, 2010, p. 74)*

Source: TESOL Teacher Standards Tables: TESOL (2010). *TESOL/NCATE Standards for the Recognition of Initial ESOL Programs in P–12 ESL Teacher Education.* Alexandria, VA: TESOL.

The Nature of Professional Collaboration

ELLs clearly benefit from interactions with fully English proficient (FEP) peers and from full access to grade-level content that a regular classroom setting provides for several reasons: ELLs are integrated into the instructional setting, they have the opportunity to hear English in authentic settings, they have the opportunity to practice their English skills with FEP learners and find out whether they are being understood, and they have access to the regular curriculum. ELLs also have the right to have the regular classroom curriculum presented so that it is comprehensible and so it provides ongoing opportunities for them to participate in instruction in meaningful ways. Professional collaboration between the regular classroom teacher, the ESL specialist, and the paraeducator is likely to facilitate this accessibility. These collaborations can take many forms and will look different from classroom to classroom. For example, the instructional relationship between the regular classroom teacher and the ESL specialist is likely to be different from the relationship between the classroom teacher and the paraeducator. Several qualities, however, are common to any successful collaboration: mutual respect; ongoing, open communication; and clearly defined roles and responsibilities. The following vignette illustrates a collaboration that is building between Mrs. Marcia Bourque, the regular classroom teacher; Ms. Jan Ellis, the ESL specialist; and Mr. Ali, the English-Arabic classroom tutor.

Mrs. Marcia Bourque's Third Grade Classroom

Mrs. Marcia Bourque, a third grade classroom teacher, recently received notification that Adam, an English language learning student from Iraq, will be placed in her classroom. She immediately made a mental note to speak with Ms. Jan Willis, the elementary-level ESL specialist at her school. Ms. Willis has been a valuable resource in supporting instruction for the two other ELLs in Mrs. Bourque's classroom, and Mrs. Bourque is fully aware that a team approach will best meet Adam's needs.

To prepare for her meeting with Ms. Willis, Mrs. Bourque reviews the language proficiency intake assessment data (intake assessments are detailed in Unit III of this book). Reviewing the results of the intake assessment provides Mrs. Bourque with Adam's English proficiency level and suggests the amount of ESL support Adam is likely to need. It also helps Mrs. Bourque prepare detailed questions for Ms. Willis with regard to modifying Adam's instruction, providing effective instructional groupings, and developing appropriate content-area assessments. Mrs. Bourque also wants to set a schedule to ensure that she and Ms. Willis can work together most effectively to meet Adam's needs. Ideally, Mrs. Bourque would like to have Ms. Willis work in the classroom with her—supporting Adam and the two other ELLs. She is, however, mindful of Ms. Willis's schedule. The district has had an influx of ELLs and, because of budget constraints, has not yet employed additional ESL teachers.

When Mrs. Bourque reviews the intake assessment data she sees that Adam's proficiency level is *Emerging*. The tester has made a note on the assessment report indicating that Adam seemed distressed during the testing and did not appear comfortable speaking. Mrs. Bourque knows that in the past when Arabic-speaking ELLs were enrolled in the school, the district employed an Arabic-speaking tutor. Because there are no other Arabic speakers in the third grade, or in any of the elementary school for that matter, Mrs. Bourque thinks that a tutor who speaks Adam's language will be helpful in easing Adam's affective filter. (Affective filter is discussed in the introduction to this book.) Mrs. Bourque also makes a note to ask Ms. Willis about arranging for the tutor. She contacts Ms. Willis, and they agree to a mutually convenient time to meet.

During their meeting, Mrs. Bourque and Ms. Willis review Adam's records together. They look through the upcoming curricular units and discuss areas in which Adam is likely to encounter difficulties and where he might most benefit from ESL support. Because Ms. Willis currently provides support for two other students in Ms. Bourque's room, she has books and materials and is accustomed to building language that complements and supports Mrs. Bourque's curriculum. However, the two other ELLs to whom Ms. Willis provides services have greater English proficiency (*Developing* and *Expanding*), and because they both speak Spanish as a primary language, they are able to support one another. Adam, however, will need additional support. Based on Adam's needs, Mrs. Bourque and Ms. Willis collaboratively decide on a three-pronged approach for services: Ms. Willis will provide direct ESL instruction to Adam outside the regular classroom and some direct ESL support in the classroom, and she will act in a consultant role. As a consultant, she will advise Mrs. Bourque with regard to making the curriculum comprehensible and modifying assignments to meet Adam's needs.

A review of Ms. Willis's schedule indicates that she will be able to provide services in Mrs. Bourque's classroom for two hours each week. She will also provide ESL instruction to Adam in one 50–minute session outside the classroom each day. Ms. Willis agrees with Mrs. Bourque that a tutor who speaks Arabic will be very important in helping Adam access instruction and—perhaps more important, at least initially—in lowering Adam's affective filter and making him feel welcome in the classroom. Ms. Willis telephones Mr. Ali and they work out an arrangement for him to be in the classroom for one hour a day three days a week. This is an imperfect arrangement, but it appears to be the best they can arrange given scheduling conflicts. Mr. Ali, Mrs. Bourque, and Ms. Willis meet the day before Mr. Ali is to begin in the classroom. They spend a few minutes exchanging pleasantries and catching up, and once rapport is established, they turn their attention to the discussion of services for Adam. Each of them has different professional strengths, and each contributes to the discussion meaningfully. Prior to the end of the meeting, they agree on an initial plan with clearly defined roles and responsibilities. They also agree that they will revisit the plan in two weeks.

The first meeting has been productive. Working as a team, the classroom teacher, ESL specialist, and paraeducator have set an instructional plan in action, and they know that to best support Adam, they will need to communicate on an ongoing basis. They set a schedule to meet on Wednesday mornings for 20 minutes to discuss modifications, assessments, and best instructional groupings for Adam, knowing that these will change as he acquires greater English proficiency.

BROAD GUIDELINES FOR COLLABORATION

The American Federation of Teachers (n.d.) set forth guidelines for collaboration between teachers and paraeducators, and these guidelines are equally relevant for teachers and ESL specialists. Several of these were illustrated in the vignette:

1. Ensure that responsibilities are clear to all.

2. Set a clear schedule for instructional and any other responsibilities.

3. Set a clear schedule for meetings.

4. Describe what will happen in the classroom and who will do what.

5. Ensure that each party knows his or her schedule, what he or she will be responsible for preparing for meetings, and how he or she will work in the classroom.

6. Once this has been established, maintain an ongoing check-in procedure for the classroom teacher, ESL specialist, and paraeducator.

7. Determine if you are meeting often enough.

8. Check to make certain you are sharing important information about the ELL's performance and progress in both English and content-area concepts.

9. Discuss what has worked well.

10. Discuss any areas you would like to improve: redefining roles and responsibilities, setting learning goals for the ELL, and so on.

11. Honestly evaluate the relationships within the team and ensure that team members are working together as coworkers.

12. Ensure that each member has the opportunity to discuss challenges, concerns, and ideas for improving instruction for the ELL.

13. Ensure that each member of the team believes that the work is distributed fairly and that each plays an important role in the instructional process.

Source: Adapted from *Creating a Classroom Team: How Teachers and Para-Professionals Can Make Working Together Work.* (n.d.). American Federation of Teachers, Washington, DC: Author.

STRATEGY RESOURCES

1. ◼ Video: Ann Lou Pickett, the president of the National Resource Center for Paraprofessionals, speaks about working with paraprofessionals.

   (Running time: 2:24)

   http://www.youtube.com/watch?v=QFSbNhPg9jc&feature=related

2. ▤ Creating a Classroom Team: How Teachers and Paraprofessionals Can Make Working Together Work, from The American Federation of Teachers

   http://www.aft.org/pdfs/psrp/psrpclassroomteam0804.pdf

3. What Keeps Good Teachers in the Classroom? Understanding and Reducing Teacher Turnover

   http://www.all4ed.org/files/TeachTurn.pdf

4. ▤ The National Resource Center for Paraprofessionals

   http://www.nrcpara.org

Strategy

8

Connecting With the ESL Specialist

There are many ways that regular classroom teachers and ESL specialists can collaborate. In a review of team teaching for classrooms in which the focus was teaching another language, Wang (2010) identified the following co-teaching models that are likely to work well when co-teaching to provide instruction for ELLs:

1. Traditional team teaching: Both teachers simultaneously provide instruction to one group of students. For example, the regular classroom teacher may present a lecture while the ESL specialist demonstrates with visuals, graphic organizers, and so on. The ESL specialist might also model a lesson with the regular classroom teacher playing a more supportive role (Brown, 2005).

2. Collaborative: The teachers co-construct the course, actively discuss their ideas, and model their thinking in front of students. In a variation of this model, ESL specialists might also work as consultants (Brown, 2005) to collaboratively plan and debrief curriculum and individual lessons with the regular classroom teacher. The consultant model can be a particularly effective use of time when the ESL specialist's schedule requires him or her to provide services to many ELLs and therefore makes it impossible for the ESL specialist to be present in the regular classroom for sufficient periods of time.

3. Complimentary-Supportive: One teacher provides the instruction and the other teacher provides additional support. This model is frequently used when ESL specialists teach within the regular education classroom, and it can be effective as long as teaching roles are reversed periodically and the ESL specialist sometimes provides instruction.

4. Parallel Instruction: The class is divided into groups and each teacher provides instruction to her or his group. This teaching model is usually blended with others and can be effective if the ESL specialist and regular classroom teacher have sufficient time to plan and debrief.

5. Differentiated Split Groups: Students are divided into groups based on strengths and needs, and each teacher works with a group, differentiating instruction based on the needs of the students within the group. This model can work very well as long as the ESL specialist is not always teaching ELLs alone, thus forming two separate groups

and separating ELLs from the stream of the regular classroom. This creates an island that segregates ELLs from FEP learners rather than building a community of learners (Giangreco, Yuan, McKenzie, Cameron, & Fialka, 2005).

It is important that the regular classroom teacher and the ESL specialist collaboratively decide on an instructional model based on the needs of ELLs and other students within the classroom as well as on the strengths of each teacher. Regardless of the model, the ESL teacher must be an integral part of planning and delivering instruction.

THEORY AND/OR RESEARCH UNDERLYING THE STRATEGY

Appropriate instruction for ELLs effectively blends content and language. Collaboration between regular classroom teachers who are experts in content and ESL specialists who are experts in second language teaching and learning has the capacity to provide this appropriate instruction. Collaboration among teachers for instructional purposes has positive influences for the education of students (Lieberman, 1986, 1990; Little, 1992; McLaughlin & Talbert, 2010; Moore Johnson, 2010), and it is likely to improve educational opportunities for ELLs when it is implemented so that the regular classroom teacher and the ESL specialist share responsibility for planning and teaching lessons and when each teacher is valued for his or her expertise (Haynes, 2007).

IMPLEMENTING THE STRATEGY

1. Identify the ESL specialist for your building and grade level, and introduce yourself to him or her early in the academic year—relationship building lays the groundwork for future collaboration. View the ESL specialist as a valuable instructional resource who has the specialized knowledge necessary to help make your curriculum accessible to ELLs and to help you develop strategies to build the academic language of ELLs in your content area.

2. Understand that the schedule of the ESL specialist may be limited. He or she is often responsible for keeping records, consulting with regular classroom teachers, and providing direct instruction to ELLs. This schedule can become particularly hectic if the ESL specialist works in multiple school buildings.

3. Sometimes the ESL specialist is the person who will inform you that an ELL will be placed in your classroom. If this is the case, make time to review the incoming placement assessment data with the ESL specialist. If this is not the case, review the ELL's placement data first, and then make an appointment with the ESL specialist. Reviewing the intake assessment prior to the meeting and knowing the English language proficiency level and prior schooling experiences of ELLs will enable you to identify areas of concern and to prepare questions.

4. During the meeting, work collaboratively to establish an instructional plan that will meet the needs of the ELL.

5. Make collaborative decisions regarding roles and responsibilities. Decide what type of teaching each of you will do as well as the supporting role that each of you will play. (See models for co-teaching at the beginning of this strategy.) If you will share teaching responsibilities, decide who will give and grade assignments.

6. Maintain careful records of the ELL's progress to discuss with the ESL specialist—he or she should also maintain records to discuss with you. (Unit III provides strategies for assessment and record keeping.) Knowing the progress of the ELL, what he or she is able to do with modifications, and what remains difficult will enable the ESL specialist to provide you with guidance and recommendations for instruction.

7. Provide the ESL specialist with instructional materials—ensure that the ESL specialist has a textbook and supplemental materials so that he or she can plan instruction or be prepared to support instruction that you have planned.

STRATEGY IN ACTION

In the opening pages of this unit, you met Mrs. Bourque, a regular classroom teacher who received notification that Adam, a new student with *Emerging* English proficiency, will be placed in her classroom. You also met Ms. Willis, the building ESL specialist. Mrs. Bourque and Ms. Willis have established a collegial relationship prior to the meeting about Adam, which facilitates their planning of services. In addition, because two other ELLs are in Mrs. Bourque's classroom, Ms. Willis already has a copy of books and other instructional materials used by Mrs. Bourque's students. The two teachers decide on a three-pronged approach to instruction. In addition to providing Mrs. Bourque with recommendations for making content instruction and assignments comprehensible, Ms. Willis will include Adam in a small group ESL class outside the regular classroom for one period each day until he develops sufficient proficiency in English to participate meaningfully in instruction. Ms. Willis will also work in the classroom for two 50-minute periods each week. Mrs. Bourque and Ms. Willis decide that they will co-teach during social studies because it is such a language-heavy subject. They will use a complimentary-supportive model of co-teaching along with differentiated split groups (described near the beginning of this strategy), and Mrs. Bourque and Ms. Willis will alternate taking the role of lead teacher. During differentiated split groups, Adam will be placed in Ms. Willis's group. The other two ELLs, who have made steady progress in social studies with Mrs. Bourque, will likely stay with her group. Mrs. Bourque and Ms. Willis further decide that they will ask Mr. Ali to participate in an occasional social studies lesson—culture and geography play prominent roles in the third grade social studies curriculum. It would be exciting for all the students to learn more about Iraqi culture, language, and geography. They agree that having Mr. Ali present would help students to view him as an integral member of the instructional team. They also know that the attention to Iraqi language and culture will demonstrate that they value Adam's heritage.

With regard to grading, Ms. Willis will help Mrs. Bourque make modifications to assignments, and the two teachers will collaborate as necessary to discuss Adam's progress. Ultimately, Mrs. Bourque will be responsible for grading Adam's regular classroom work. Ms. Willis will grade his ESL work and will keep Mrs. Bourque closely informed. Both teachers will be prepared to discuss progress with a sample of Adam's work at the weekly meetings they have established.

REFLECTIONS

1. Does Mrs. Bourque and Ms. Willis's plan for collaboration have potential to be successful? Why, or why not?

2. How might all students benefit from a collaborative teaching situation such as the one that Mrs. Bourque and Ms. Willis have developed?

3. What are some of the potential issues of concern in their plan?

Strategy 9

Communicating Effectively With the Paraeducator

Increasingly, regular classroom teachers who serve the needs of students with diverse educational needs, including ELLs, are called on to be responsible for integrating paraeducators into the classroom, supervising their work, and monitoring their performance (Pickett et al., 2003). The paraeducator plays an important role in the instruction of ELLs. Frequently, he or she speaks the same language as the ELL and is a member of the community in which the ELL lives.

As a classroom teacher who works with a paraeducator, you will need to balance valuing the strengths and opinions of the paraeducator with the understanding that the paraeducator is not a formally prepared teacher and should not be responsible for planning, implementing, or assessing instruction. This is especially true for paraeducators who work with ELLs, whose needs are even more complex than those of FEP learners.

THEORY AND/OR RESEARCH UNDERLYING THE STRATEGY

In a discussion of the teacher-paraeducator relationship, Causton-Theoharis, Giangreco, Doyle, and Vadasy (2007) used the analogy of an executive chef and a sous-chef. The executive chef plans the menu, chooses the ingredients, and does most of the cooking. The sous-chef is invaluable to the process, yet is not "responsible for planning the meals, [is] not afforded the autonomy to adapt the recipes, and [does] not do the majority of the cooking" (p. 56). An effective chef is also one who treats the sous-chef with respect and as a valued coworker. The American Federation of Teachers (AFT) (n.d.) illustrates the importance of respect and value with the following quote from a paraeducator: "Something as simple as the way the teacher introduces me as her co-worker rather than as 'her aide' shows the level of respect she has for me" (p. 5).

IMPLEMENTING THE STRATEGY

1. Meet with the paraeducator outside of classroom time to get to know him or her and his or her experiences, strengths, and needs. During this time, discuss expectations—both the paraeducator's expectations and your own.

2. Set clear roles and responsibilities for ongoing communication and for classroom work. Paraeducators should provide supplemental instruction. Because ELLs are learning English at the same time they are learning content, teaching them is extremely complex—even more complex than teaching FEP learners. The classroom teacher and the ESL specialist will provide 80% of the classroom instruction (Giangreco, 2003).

3. Clearly explain your philosophy and expectations for classroom climate and rules, including the level of student talk, movement, and so on.

4. Clearly explain the routines you have established for your classroom.

5. Engage the paraeducator in the planning process when possible.

6. Discuss pedagogy and instructional methods and ensure that the paraeducator or tutor feels competent with the instructional methods.

7. Explain where classroom resources and materials are kept.

8. Provide clear and ongoing training to paraeducators that is based on their strengths and needs and on the lessons they will teach. For example, one strategy that is recommended in Unit VII is The Language Experience Approach. If the paraeducator is to use this approach with ELLs, he or she needs professional development to do so. Take the time to explain the purpose and value of the Language Experience Approach, provide a list of the steps and the purpose for each step, and allow the paraeducator to observe the approach as you implement it with an ELL. Debrief following the observation.

9. Provide ongoing and supportive feedback to paraeducators by taking the time to discuss with them what has gone well in the classroom and why, and provide open and constructive feedback for behaviors which the paraeducator needs to improve.

10. Check in with the paraeducator often to openly discuss roles and goals.

STRATEGY IN ACTION

Mrs. Bourque meets with Mr. Ali the day before he is scheduled to come into her classroom to work with Adam. Mrs. Bourque begins the conversation by getting to know Mr. Ali. She asks him about his prior experience and his work in the schools. She tells him that she is very pleased that he will work within her classroom and that she hopes that he will be able to help other students learn something about Iraq—its geography, culture, and language. She explains that this will benefit Adam by giving his primary language, culture, and country of origin value in the classroom, and it will greatly broaden the experiences of all the other students.

Mrs. Bourque explains the class rules and routines to Mr. Ali and provides him with the overview of classroom rules and expectations that she sent home to families the first week of school. She explains that she will prepare all classroom instruction and will provide Mr. Ali with her weekly plans during their Wednesday meetings; Mr. Ali's role is to make the instruction comprehensible to Adam. She also gives Mr. Ali copies of the books and instructional materials she is using in the classroom. Mr. Ali will work with Adam both in and out of the classroom. Out of the classroom, he will preview and review instruction with Adam in Arabic, and inside the classroom he will work with Adam and a small group of FEP learners to support instruction, providing clarification in Arabic as needed. Mrs. Bourque also asks Mr. Ali if he could make a brief weekly phone call home to keep Adam's family aware of his progress. At the end of the meeting, they exchange e-mail addresses so they can communicate quickly should the need arise.

REFLECTION

1. How did Mrs. Bourque help to prepare Mr. Ali for his role in the classroom? Is there anything else she might have done?

Making the Specialist and Paraeducator Part of the Classroom

Strategy
10

T he ESL specialist and the paraeducator play important roles with ELLs in the regular education classroom when they are integrated into the classroom and when their services are used appropriately. Strategy 10 provides a list of things to do and behaviors to avoid when involving other educators in the classroom. Many of the suggestions come from the field of special education where there is a greater body of research on the benefits and potential pitfalls of including additional instructional support staff in the classroom. While the student populations are different, many of the concerns regarding creating and maintaining an inclusive classroom for ELLs are the same.

THEORY AND/OR RESEARCH UNDERLYING THE STRATEGY

Although specialists and paraeducators can provide important instruction and instructional support for ELLs, without careful planning their presence in the classroom can also interfere with developing an inclusive classroom environment in which ELLs are fully and meaningfully integrated. Given the responsibilities and the work loads of teachers today, a teacher may understandably be concerned about meeting all the needs of the students in her classroom without additional support. One problem identified by researchers (Giangreco, 2010; Giangreco, Smith, & Pinckney, 2006; Giancreco et al., 2005) is that when students are assigned to work with paraeducators, they are isolated from the regular classroom teacher and from the rest of the classroom. A similar situation might exist when the ESL specialist works within the classroom with an ELL or a small group of ELLs. This is different from the co-teaching situation as described in Strategy 8, in which both teachers provide instruction to groups of students and the ESL specialist is viewed by all students as one of their teachers.

Another problem identified by Giangreco (2010), Giangreco et al. (2005), and Giangreco et al. (2006) is that too often instruction is provided by the paraeducator, which results in substandard instruction for the students whose needs are the most complex and who therefore need the most support. Based on my experience, a similar situation exists in regular education classrooms with ELLs. If paraeducators are present, they, rather than teachers, often provide the instruction to ELLs.

The existing research points to the need to fully integrate the ESL specialist and paraeducator into the classroom. This strategy provides some useful steps to help you do so.

Implementing the Strategy

1. Introduce the ESL specialist or paraeducator to the classroom as if he or she were an honored guest—a guest who will be adding to the quality of the classroom instruction for all students.

2. Clearly explain to students that the specialist or paraeducator will be working with groups of students or individual students.

3. Ensure that the paraeducator supports the instruction of groups of students—that he or she plays an integral role within the classroom and is not only there to support the ELL. While this is her or his primary responsibility, the ELL and others will be more comfortable if the paraeducator provides the ELL with physical space.

4. From time to time, ask the paraeducator to monitor the rest of the class while you dedicate instructional time to working directly with ELLs. Your expertise and one-on-one instructional support will benefit the ELL.

Strategy in Action

Mrs. Bourque introduces Ms. Willis and Mr. Ali to the students in the classroom and explains that they are fortunate to have a team of teachers who will be providing instruction. Mrs. Bourque and Ms. Willis team teach during social studies, and approximately once a week Mr. Ali teaches with them. After a large group presentation, the presence of three capable adults facilitates small group work and enables all students to benefit from the adults' perspectives.

Reflections

1. How is Mrs. Bourque's classroom inclusive?

2. What are the benefits to ELLs and to FEP learners?

3. Given your grade level and content area, what ideas do you have to include an ESL specialist? How would you include a paraeducator? What would this look like in a specific lesson? How would you prepare the lesson and prepare the specialist and paraeducator to participate in the instruction in a meaningful way?

UNIT III

Strategies for Assessment

How do I assess what English language learners know when they cannot adequately express their understanding of content?

—Marta, Inservice Teacher in a Graduate Methods Course

Well-planned assessment is integral to effective instructional practice; it guides instruction, and it helps teachers and students keep track of student learning and progress Well-planned assessment also helps teachers make ongoing decisions that ensure instruction is well matched to student needs.

Effective assessments for ELLs measure both content-area understanding and language development. Measuring English language development is critical for ELLs, and it also benefits many other students in the classroom. Indeed, it is difficult to imagine a classroom in which at least some students who speak English as a primary language would not benefit from assessment data that could be used to improve their ability to speak academically, to read across the content areas, and to write well in various subject areas.

This unit delves into the planning and implementation of effective assessment. It begins with a theoretical framework that supports the use of assessment to inform instruction and then provides an overview of three types of classroom assessment: preinstructional, formative, and summative. The unit continues with a vignette about Ms. Katie Parsen, a third grade teacher who uses assessment to guide the instruction of her students, both ELLs and FEP learners. This vignette illustrates how Ms. Parsen uses content and language assessment to plan instruction that meets the needs of the diverse groups of students in her classroom. The unit continues with six strategies for planning and implementing effective assessment for ELLs, starting with using initial

Table III.1	Types of Assessments	
Type of Assessment	*Purpose*	*Time of Implementation*
Preinstructional	To know students' preparedness prior to planning instruction; to set content-area benchmarks and English language benchmarks and outcomes	Prior to beginning an instructional unit
Formative	To measure ongoing progress toward benchmarks and outcomes; to adjust instruction	Ongoing—analogous to a streaming video
Summative	To determine whether students have met established learning outcomes	At the end of an instructional unit

assessment data to determine the strengths and needs of individual ELLs (Strategy 11), planning different forms of assessment (Strategy 12), designing content-area and language-based learning outcomes with lesson objectives (Strategy 13), planning differentiated assessments according to language proficiency (Strategy 14), planning and using formative assessments (Strategy 15), and planning and implementing summative assessments, including portfolio assessment (Strategy 16). The assessment strategies presented in this unit are effective for ELLs in regular education classrooms and also benefit FEP learners who have varying abilities and learning styles. Strategies are adaptable across grade levels.

WHAT YOU WILL LEARN

Unit III provides theory, research, vignettes, and strategies to help you do the following:

1. Know how to access and interpret incoming assessment data to understand the strengths and needs of ELLs.

2. Understand the relationship between assessment and instruction.

3. Understand the importance and the roles of preinstructional, formative, and summative assessments.

4. Plan various forms of assessments (written, oral, visual, performance).

5. Develop strategies for setting content-area and language learning outcomes and lesson objectives.

6. Differentiate content-area and language assessments according to English language proficiency.

7. Develop techniques for formatively assessing students and strategies to use the resulting data.

8. Develop strategies for designing and implementing summative assessment, including the use of portfolios.

CLASSROOM ASSESSMENT: AN OVERVIEW

The award-winning landscaper or gardener begins a new project with a clear picture of the end result—the purpose the area will serve and the aesthetic sense it will provide. Beginning with this clear picture in mind, she is then able to carefully plan both the project as a whole and each phase of the work to achieve the desired end result. Without this clear picture, it would be difficult, if not impossible, for her to reach her objectives.

Effective instruction also begins with a clear understanding of the desired end results—the overarching concepts students must master, the learning outcomes inherent in these concepts, and the student products that will demonstrate mastery of these learning outcomes, such as solving real-life mathematical problems, applying the steps of the scientific method to an authentic problem, demonstrating an understanding of social justice, or communicating by means of a well-written letter. Wiggins and McTighe (1998, 2005) referred to this type of planning as *backward design,* or planning the assessment and the products students will produce to demonstrate their conceptual understanding prior to planning lessons.

Students' ability to use academic language is critical to their success in school and ultimately in life. Effective instruction for ELLs, therefore, includes careful planning for academic language development, which begins with appropriate language assessment (Gottlieb, 2006). Teachers must have a clear picture of the language abilities and skills that ELLs will need to access instruction in the content area (listening and reading) and the skills and abilities ELLs will need to demonstrate their content-area mastery (speaking and writing). Clear and intentional attention to the development of academic language has potential to improve the academic language abilities of both FEP learners and ELLs.

Assessment of content and language takes multiple forms and can be either formal (papers, presentations, tests, quizzes, artwork, posters, etc.) or informal (observations, quick-checks, interviews with students, etc.). As illustrated in Table III.1, assessment can be preinstructional, formative, or summative, with each type of assessment playing an important role in measuring the progress of each student.

Preinstructional assessment enables teachers to set appropriate learning outcomes and benchmarks for language development based on a student's content-area understanding and English proficiency level. Formative assessment is ongoing—part of the flow of instruction. It provides a "video stream" of student progress (in content and language) across the instructional unit and is used to drive instructional decisions (Heritage, 2007). In addition, formative assessment helps students become more self-directed as they learn both to gauge where they are in the process of meeting learning outcomes and what their specific gaps may be. It provides measures of progress toward meeting the benchmarks that lead to mastery of established learning outcomes in both content and language. Formative assessment helps teachers understand when they need

Table III.2	Preinstructional, Formative, and Summative Assessment in Ms. Parsen's Classroom

Preinstructional Assessment: Enables teachers and students to measure what students understand and can do as well as what students need to learn. The results of preinstructional assessment enable teachers to set benchmarks for student progress. Preinstructional assessment can be formal or informal.

In Practice

Content	Language
The requisite mathematical knowledge in a math class in which students will solve authentic problems by adding two-digit numbers includes an understanding of place value and the ability to add single-digit numbers. If results of preinstructional assessment indicate that John and Sasha do not have this knowledge, Ms. Parsen will need to include instructional activities to build their knowledge and understanding. She sets immediate benchmarks for Sasha and John that will prepare them for adding two-digit numbers and will allow them to quickly catch-up with their peers. Pedro and Liz on the other hand, have already mastered the ability to solve word problems requiring the addition of two-digit numbers. Results from preinstructional assessment suggest that Ms. Parsen should provide Pedro and Liz with enrichment by increasing the difficulty and interest level of word problems. Ms. Parsen sets learning and instructional outcomes for Pedro and Liz to ensure they continue to make progress with more sophisticated word problems.	Students such as Thalia can successfully solve word problems that require the addition of two-digit numbers using the Spanish version of the math text. Thalia needs to develop English vocabulary for related math expressions such as *sum* and *all together.* She may also have difficulty with other words commonly associated with problem solving in mathematics, such as *examine, explore, compose,* and *estimate.* Preinstructional assessment informs Ms. Parsen that Thalia will benefit from content-area enrichment as well as instruction and practice that will build academic language. Based on appropriate assessment, Ms. Parsen sets language and content learning outcomes for Thalia. Other ELLs will need support with language and may also need reinforcement with concepts or focused content-area instruction. Pre-instructional assessment enables Ms. Parsen to set appropriate learning outcomes and develop instructional strategies for these students as well.

Formative Assessment: Provides ongoing evidence of student progress in meeting instructional benchmarks in content and language. Formative assessment can be formal or informal.

In Practice

Content	Language
Formatively, Ms. Parsen assesses students to measure their progress in meeting the benchmarks on the way to concept mastery. She assesses understanding during lessons (observations, conversations, quick checks, etc.) and continually makes instructional decisions based on the data she collects. For example, the learning goal for John and Sasha is adding two-digit numbers; benchmarks include an understanding of place value and the ability to add single-digit numbers. Ongoing formative assessment enables Ms. Parsen to ensure that John and Sasha continue to learn and to meet these benchmarks.	Formative assessment of language skills (productive and receptive) enables Ms. Parsen to ensure that ELLs are making continual progress in the acquisition of academic English. It also enables her to plan instruction that is comprehensible and appropriately challenging ($i + 1$), which is discussed in the introduction of this book.

Summative Assessment: Measures student achievement toward established end-result goal. Summative assessment is formal (recorded), but can vary widely in form.		
In Practice		
Content	*Language*	
The final unit assessment measures student mastery of the learning outcomes that were established at the beginning of the unit: for example, mastery of simple word problems that require two-digit addition.	ELLs at *Starting* and *Emerging* levels may solve math problems in their first language and may include the academic terms that have been taught and are on word walls,* such as *sum, all together,* and *estimate.* ELLs with *Developing* language proficiency solve problems in a glossed or easified English math book (Unit IV of this book). ELLs with *Expanding* English proficiency are able to explain the process by which they solve word problems in English.	
* Word walls are used for high-frequency, commonly misspelled words (e.g., *to, too, two*) and for words that are common across various content areas (e.g., *analyze, approach, concept, context, factor*). Strategies for word walls are provided in Strategy 27 in Unit V of this book. (See Table III.4 for proficiency level descriptions.)		

to reteach and reinforce, as well as when they need to extend instruction and provide enrichment. Summative assessment measures the degree to which ELLs and others have mastered content-area concepts and developed English language abilities at the end of a given instructional period.

Ms. Parsen's Second Grade Classroom

Ms. Katie Parsen, a second grade teacher, consistently uses assessment to plan and implement instruction for students in her mixed language proficiency second grade classroom. At the beginning of each school year, she reviews available state standardized testing (for language and content) for students, other standardized test scores, report cards, and sample work from the previous year. She reviews student portfolios if these are available and places high value on the rich data they provide about the student's strengths and needs. She also carefully reviews the intake assessments for each newcomer ELL in her class. Data from these multiple assessments provide Ms. Parsen with a broad idea of the instructional level of each student in her classroom—a place to begin planning instruction. Ms. Parsen then assesses her students at the beginning of every instructional unit, on an ongoing basis during the flow of daily instruction, and at the end of the unit. The daily use of assessment data to plan instruction and help students to self-assess their understanding enhances student learning (Stiggins, 2005).

Ms. Parsen begins with preinstructional assessment to inform her about the current content-area and language level of ELLs and FEP learners as they begin a unit of study. As Table III.2 illustrates, preinstructional assessment enables her to plan and deliver instruction that is congruent with students' needs, which may include reinforcing requisite skills, providing instruction in the target concept, or extending instruction with enrichment.

Ms. Parsen knows that her students differ widely in preparation, cognitive ability, preferred learning styles, and language development. She plans assessment that measures content knowledge

(Continued)

(Continued)

apart from language ability. In *the case of the mathematics example, Ms. Parsen encourages students to manipulate rods, create written representations of the digits and their sums, and solve the problem using the following algorithm: x + x = ___. Ms. Parsen's students then verbally explain their thought processes to her.*

Regardless of the content she is assessing, Ms. Parsen knows there are often multiple ways for students to show their mastery of concepts. She knows that ELLs in her classroom will have an easier time demonstrating mastery of science and social studies concepts through labeled drawings and models. She also knows that providing choice to all students (FEP learners as well as ELLs) improves student opportunities to demonstrate conceptual mastery. So while Ms. Parsen sometimes specifies the format of assignments (written paragraph, oral report, etc.), other times she allows students to decide the format. By providing all students with choice, Ms. Parsen does not single out ELLs or provide them with what fully English proficient students might otherwise consider an unfair advantage.

With regard to summative assessment, Ms. Parsen places more weight on assessments ELLs and other students complete toward the end of the instructional unit; in this way, she measures student mastery of concepts, rather than the speed at which students mastered concepts. The strategies in this unit demonstrate the types and forms of assessments that teachers like Ms. Parsen use to measure students' starting places and progress and are consistent with TESOL standards for teachers (Table III.3) and for ELLs at all proficiency levels (Table III.4).

Table III.3	TESOL Standards for Teachers

Domain 3: Planning, Implementing, and Managing Instruction

3.a.5. *Plan for instruction that embeds assessment, includes scaffolding, and provides reteaching when necessary for individuals and small groups to successfully meet learning objectives. (p. 46)*

Domain 4: Assessment

4.a.1. *Demonstrate an understanding of the purposes of assessment as they relate to ELLs, and use results appropriately. (p. 59)*

4.a.2. *Knowledgeable about and, able to use a variety of assessment procedures for ELLs. (p. 59)*

4.a.3. *Demonstrate an understanding of key indicators of good assessment instruments. (p. 60)*

4.c.1. *Use performance-based assessment tools and tasks that measure ELLs' progress. (p. 66)*

4.c.3. *Use various instruments and techniques to assess content-area learning (e.g., math, science, social studies) for ELLs at varying levels of language and literacy development. (p. 67)*

Source: TESOL Teacher Standards Tables: TESOL (2010). *TESOL/NCATE Standards for the Recognition of Initial TESOL Programs in P–12 ESL Teacher Education.* Alexandria, VA: TESOL.

Table III.4	TESOL Standards for Students, Performance Indicators, and Assessment Ideas

TESOL Standard 1: ELLs communicate for social, intercultural, and instructional purposes within the school setting.

TESOL Standards 2–5: ELLs communicate information, ideas, and concepts necessary for academic success in the area of language arts, mathematics, science, and social studies.

Proficiency Level	Descriptor	Assessment Ideas (Gottlieb, 2006, p. 30)*
1—Starting	An ELL with *Starting* proficiency has little to no English language skills with the exception of basic survival language. ELLs can communicate their concrete basic needs, use high-frequency words and memorized chunks of language, such as "I go . . . nurse, office, bathroom their (etc.)?" accompanied by gestures. With support in writing, ELLs will use high-frequency words, phrases, or chunks of language, such as "I like . . . ."	Identify objects, illustrations, symbols, or words by pointing or naming; match and label pictures and words; follow one-step directions; sort objects or illustrations with words into groups; illustrate and label words in graphic organizers; make collages or photo journals about stories or topics.
2— Emerging	An ELL with *Emerging* proficiency has acquired enough language to express simple and routine experiences, for example, "We go to the library. . . ." She or he continues to rely on high-frequency words and also is able to use generalized vocabulary and expressions and short sentences, such as "The water went from sand. . . ." in describing a science lab activity where vocabulary is provided.	Name and describe objects, people, or events with phrases; plot timelines, number lines, or schedules; follow multistep directions; define and categorize objects, people, or events with visual or graphic support; analyze and extract information in charts and graphs; sequence pictures with phrases.
3—Developing	An ELL with *Developing* proficiency is able to use language about familiar matters that are regularly encountered. For example, after engaging in ongoing comprehensible discussions about the responsibility of voting, having access to vocabulary cards or a vocabulary word wall, and time to compose his thoughts, an ELL at the developing level is able to express his point of view using academic language and expressions. At this level, an ELL is able to communicate meaning although he will make many errors that impede communication. When writing, the ELL at this level is able to use expanded sentences, although these will contain mechanical errors.	Compare and contrast objects, people, events with sentences; outline speech and text using graphic organizers; use information from charts, graphs, or tables; make predictions or hypotheses based on illustrated stories, events or inquiry; take notes; produce short stories, poetry, or structured reports with support.

(Continued)

(Continued)

Proficiency Level	Descriptor	Assessment Ideas (Gottlieb, 2006, p. 30)*
4—Expanding	At *Expanding* proficiency, an ELL is familiar and comfortable with concrete and abstract language. She is able to use some specialized and technical academic language in content-area classes and vary sentence length, structure, and level of complexity. Although at this proficiency level, the ELL makes errors in speaking and writing, these errors do not interfere with meaning or her overall ability to communicate within the classroom.	Explain processes or procedures with extended discourse/paragraphs; produce original modules, demonstrations, or exhibitions, summarize and draw conclusions from speech and text; construct charts, graphs, and tables; discuss pros and cons of issues; use multiple learning strategies.
5—Bridging	At this proficiency level, the ELL's use of academic English approximates that of a native speaker. Errors may be made, but these do not interfere with meaning or communication. An ELL at this level may need support with idioms and expressions that require context, such as "the Achilles heel of the Confederate army was . . . ."	Justify and defend positions through speeches, multimedia reports, or essays; research and investigate academic topics using multiple resources; explain relationships, consequences, or cause and effect; debate issues; react and reflect on articles, short stories, or essays of multiple genres from grade-level materials; author poetry, fiction, nonfiction for varied audiences.

Sources: Descriptors—Adapted from *PreK-12 English Language Proficiency Standards,* by TESOL, 2006, Alexandria, VA; Author. Assessments—*Assessing English Language Learners: Bridges from Language Proficiency to Academic Achievement* (p. 30), by M. Gottlieb, 2006, Thousand Oaks, CA: Corwin Press. Used with permission.

*The assessment ideas are broadly representative of what ELLs will be able to do when provided with appropriate and comprehensible instruction that enables them to access and understand the concepts being taught. As indicated in the introduction to this book, language acquisition is developmental. ELLs will progress from Starting to Emerging to Developing proficiency at a faster pace than they will progress from Developing to Expanding to Bridging proficiency levels.

Using Initial Assessment Data to Determine the Strengths and Needs of ELLs

Strategy 11

One source of assessment that is available to teachers when ELLs first arrive in their classrooms is the intake assessment. Reviewing this assessment enables teachers to understand the process by which ELLs are identified, how English language proficiency is assessed, and the English language proficiency level of a newly arriving ELL. Strategy 11 provides steps for reviewing and interpreting initial assessment data, and it addresses the often asked question, "How do I even know where to begin to provide instruction to the ELLs placed in my classroom?"

The best place for teachers to begin to learn about a newly arriving ELL may be the ELL's cumulative folder, which likely contains a home language survey, an English language assessment data, and report cards from previous schools, if available. (Unfortunately, it is often difficult to obtain complete records of previous schooling for ELLs who come from countries plagued by war, civil unrest, or abject poverty.) Naturally, it is important to request the folder from guidance department personnel so that information that is sensitive or protected can be removed.

THEORY AND/OR RESEARCH UNDERLYING THE STRATEGY

Districts must ensure that all ELLs, regardless of placement, receive services that promote English language development (Office for Civil Rights, 2000). Smaller school districts with few ELLs may implement an informal system for identifying students who need English language support, but larger systems or systems with greater numbers of ELLs must have a formal identification and assessment process in place to determine the need for specialized programs of instruction. While the assessment process may differ in form and format, from system to system the flow chart in Figure 11.1 provides an example of the identification, assessment, and placement processes for ELLs.

Figure 11.1   Student Placement

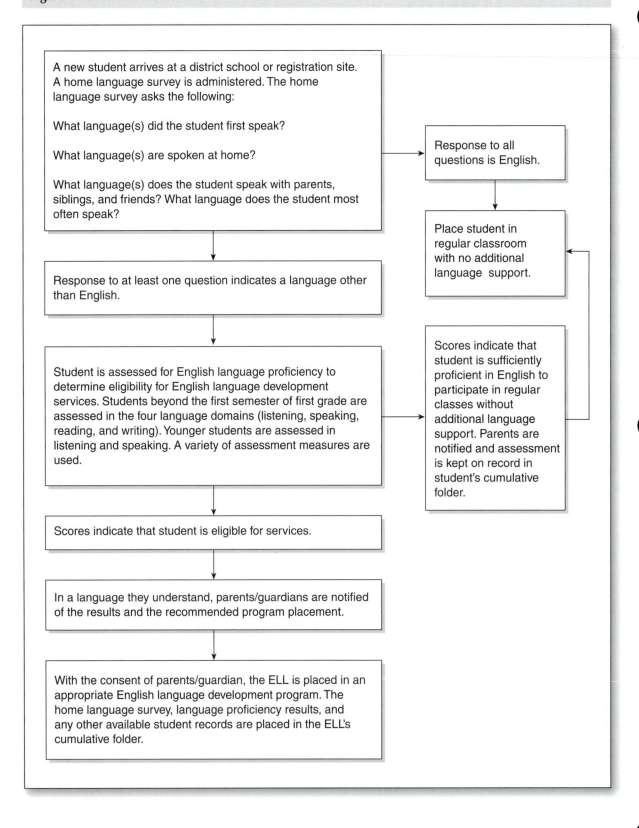

In Unit I, you were briefly introduced to Jorge Alvarado, a fourth grade student who was to be placed in Mrs. Joanne Allen's fourth grade classroom. The following paragraph illustrates the assessment process used with Jorge. (This is an example of high quality assessment. There are not always school personnel who speak the language of the ELL, and smaller school districts are less likely to have Parent Information Centers.)

When Jorge's family moved to the district, his parents called the school to inform them they wanted to register their nine-year-old son for classes. Based on school policy, the school secretary inquired about the languages spoken in the Alvarado home. Upon learning that the language spoken at home was Spanish, she referred the Alvarado family to the school's Parent Information Center, where staff spoke several languages, including Spanish. Here, a well-qualified staff person completed a home language survey with Mr. and Mrs. Alvarado. When Mr. and Mrs. Alvarado's responses indicated that Spanish was the language that Jorge first learned to speak and that he spoke Spanish at home with his parents and siblings, the staff person arranged for an English language proficiency assessment for Jorge. The assessment revealed that Jorge had English language proficiency at Level 3—*Developing*. These results were sent to the guidance office of Jorge's district school, and the school guidance counselor e-mailed Mrs. Allen the results of the home language survey and language assessment. Mrs. Allen's understanding of the initial intake assessment data for ELLs facilitated her ability to plan and implement appropriate and effective instruction for Jorge.

IMPLEMENTING THE STRATEGY

To review the placement data to determine the needs of an ELL, do the following:

1. Through appropriate channels (guidance, administration, etc.), access pertinent information from the ELL's cumulative folder to review report cards, the home language survey, and language proficiency testing in order to determine the ELL's proficiency level: Level 1: *Starting* (no English to ability to communicate basic needs), Level 2: *Emerging* (can communicate simple experiences), Level 3: *Developing* (is able to communicate familiar, simple, and academic experiences), Level 4: *Expanding* (can communicate concrete and abstract experiences), or Level 5: *Bridging* (communicates at nearly the level of a English-proficient student) (TESOL, 2006, p. 39). This knowledge facilitates discussions with the ESL teachers, other school specialists, and paraprofessionals who are assigned to the classroom.

2. Review the home language survey, which shows the languages the ELL speaks in different situations (with parents, siblings, and friends) and may, depending on the form developed by the district, contain other information regarding prior schooling. It may also indicate whether the parents understand English or if you will need to communicate with parents through an interpreter and provide translated notes and school notices. (Unit VIII of this book provides strategies for making connections and building relationships with parents.)

3. Review any records from previous schools for information about prior schooling and gaps in schooling. Knowing the level of education students have attained in

another language is important because, according to the theory of Common Underlying Proficiency, which is explained in the introduction of this book, concepts that have been learned in another language will transfer to English. ELLs who are educated at or near grade level in their primary languages will need instruction that builds academic language for the concepts that they have already learned. These students have a solid academic base on which to build, and teachers must make new content and concepts comprehensible so that ELLs continue to learn at grade level. Conversely ELLs who have gaps in their education will need to learn concepts in English—a language that is foreign to them. They will also need to develop academic English and continue to learn through English. (Units V, VI, and VII focus on strategies for building academic language for ELLs with various levels of English proficiency and prior schooling.)

4. Speak with the ESL specialist about the ELL's records. Inquire about the schedule for English language development services and develop a plan for providing instruction that is comprehensible and will develop academic English proficiency. (Unit II provides strategies for working with the ESL teacher and paraprofessionals.) ELLs with lower levels of proficiency will require greater amounts of language development instruction from the ESL specialist than will ELLs at higher proficiency levels. Request a native language tutor if the proficiency level of the ELL has been assessed as Level 1: *Starting* or Level 2: *Emerging,* or if the ELL is at a Level 3: *Developing* proficiency level but has significant gaps in her or his prior schooling.

STRATEGY IN ACTION

When Mrs. Allen reviewed the results from Jorge's language assessment, she learned that Jorge had English language proficiency that could be categorized as *Level 3: Developing,* meaning that he could understand and use language about familiar matters, had general and specific academic vocabulary, and could write in expanded sentences, yet would likely make oral and written language errors that would impede communication. A review of his report card showed that Jorge had successfully completed the third grade in the Dominican Republic, suggesting that he could complete grade-level work in his native language, Spanish.* This knowledge enabled Mrs. Allen to begin to plan instruction that would include Jorge in small and large group activities in meaningful and appropriate ways (described in Unit I), to differentiate assessments to ensure that Jorge could demonstrate his content-area knowledge apart from his language ability (described later in this section), to include strategies to make grade-level content comprehensible (described in Unit IV), and to implement strategies to build Jorge's academic vocabulary (described in Unit V).

When Mrs. Allen reviewed the home language survey, she discovered that neither Mr. nor Mrs. Alvarado spoke English, and therefore, they would need to receive school notices in Spanish.** Mrs. Allen contacted the school secretary to inform her that the Alvarado family would need copies of school notices in Spanish as well as in English. She also contacted the Parent Information Center to ask about the availability of an interpreter for the upcoming Open House. She sent an e-mail to the school's ESL specialist requesting a meeting to determine the type and amount of services that Jorge would receive from the ESL department and to work out a schedule for ESL services that would complement her classroom schedule.

*Like children who are native speakers of English, ELLs will differ in cognitive, social, and emotional development. They may have gaps in their schooling and may or may not require special education services.

**Providing translations is not usually a problem when the language spoken by the ELL is a language common to the region. When the language is more obscure, it is helpful to seek the support of community organizations that may be able to provide an interpreter to convey important information to parents.

REFLECTIONS

1. Think back to the description of ELLs in the introduction to this book. How will a review of the home language survey help you to know more about an incoming student? What information will it provide that you would not have otherwise? How might you discover more about an ELL than is provided in the intake assessment?

2. How will you use language assessment data to plan for instructional grouping and to plan instruction for a newly arriving ELL?

STRATEGY RESOURCES

1. The Office for Civil Rights guidelines and resources for assessing and instructing ELLs

   http://www.ed.gov/about/offices/list/ocr/ellresources.html

2. National Clearinghouse for English Language Acquisition and Language Instruction Programs newsletter, AccELLerate provides articles about assessment

   http://www.ncela.gwu.edu/accelerate/

Strategy

12

Planning Different Forms of Assessment

Teachers, administrators, and parents have long known that not all students learn in the same way. Some students appear to be visual learners, others may be auditory learners, and many students learn by doing; some students speak English as a primary language, whereas ELLs are in the process of acquiring academic English. Teachers strive to ensure that instruction is compatible with the learning styles, developmental levels, and language proficiencies of students. Assessment, an integral part of instruction, must also account for student differences in strengths and needs to enable all students to demonstrate conceptual knowledge, abilities, and skills.

THEORY AND/OR RESEARCH UNDERLYING THE STRATEGY

The student's assessment or the product that she or he produces should clearly demonstrate that the student has developed a deep understanding of the concepts that have been taught and the learning outcomes that have been established While exceptional writing, high-quality artwork, and skillful public speaking are all important skills that can be assessed, skills in these areas should not obscure a student's lack of conceptual understanding in the content areas. Conversely, lack of writing, artistic, or speaking skills should not interfere with ELLs or other students' ability to demonstrate conceptual knowledge and understandings. ELLs must be given opportunities to demonstrate their mastery of content-area learning outcomes apart from their proficiency in academic English. At least some of the time, all students should be allowed choice regarding the type of assessment they produce to demonstrate their growing understanding and mastery of ideas. When all students, not just ELLs, have some choice as to how they will best demonstrate conceptual understanding, student concerns about fairness in regard to workload and grades are diminished (Wiggins & McTighe, 2005).

Any assessment is simply a snapshot in time. A portfolio assessment, which includes student work, both self- and teacher-selected, provides a clearer and more comprehensive picture of student progress in content and language over time. ELLs, who are challenged to meet content-area learning outcomes as they acquire academic English, especially benefit from reviewing their progress in content and language over a semester's or year's time. Portfolios are discussed in more detail in Strategy 16, and resources for developing student portfolios are included at the end of this section.

IMPLEMENTING THE STRATEGY

1. Once you decide *what* is most important for students to know, think about *how* they will demonstrate their understanding or skill. For example, second grade students may demonstrate their understanding of summarizing and skill in summarizing non-fiction texts in written paragraphs. They can also demonstrate this skill by informally reporting to the teacher or a small group, preparing and audio recording an oral response, preparing an outline or a graphic organizer, or developing a PowerPoint presentation. (Eventually, all students will need to develop well-written paragraphs, but if summarization is the goal of instruction, students should be able to demonstrate their mastery of summarization apart from writing.)

2. Provide a choice of assessments, ensuring that each assessment, whether written, oral, visual, or multimedia, requires all students to demonstrate mastery of the content-area concept. An assessment that provides each student with a way to demonstrate mastery is a fair and equitable one. (Remember, *equitable* does not mean equal or the same.)

3. Consider the English language proficiency that students will need to access the instruction (e.g., What oral language proficiency and skills must they have to understand the concepts presented? What are the vocabulary demands of this concept? What words must the student know to understand the instruction? What is the level of the reading required to access the concept?).

4. Think about the English language proficiency that students will need to demonstrate their understanding of concepts. (Strategy 14 demonstrates how to differentiate assessments by English language proficiency levels. A graphic organizer is provided to facilitate the planning of steps 3 and 4.)

5. Design two rubrics—one for content and one for academic language. You may hold students accountable for both, but it is important to measure each separately. (Sample rubrics are illustrated by Mr. Christopher in the Strategy in Action section of this strategy.)

6. Design a content-area assessment rubric to ensure that ELLs and other students include key points to demonstrate their understanding. Include a rigorous understanding of conceptual knowledge in each rubric. Regardless of assessment form (written, visual, or multimedia), the rubric must ensure that ELLs are able to demonstrate content-area understanding.

7. On an ongoing basis, share assessment rubrics with colleagues for feedback; make changes when appropriate.

8. Pilot assessment rubrics with students and make changes based on results. Most rubrics can be adjusted and improved over time, and including students in this process involves them in the assessment of their own learning.

9. Explain each assessment option to students, ensuring that they understand the assessment requirements for content and for language.

Strategy in Action

Mr. Michael Christopher teaches English language arts and social studies in the sixth grade. When he first began teaching, he used the standard assessments found in the teacher's guide to assess his students. Now, nearly 10 years later, Mr. Christopher uses a variety of assessments that he has developed with colleagues to enable his students to demonstrate mastery of content-area learning outcomes. As Mr. Christopher explains, "There is no reason to have to develop all these assessments alone. It is too much for any one teacher. Sharing with colleagues improves all of our capacity to accurately assess our students." His assessments enable ELLs to demonstrate content-area mastery apart from English language proficiency and also ensure that ELLs continue to develop linguistic proficiency within the content areas. For example, Mr. Christopher and his fellow sixth grade teachers have determined that one of the concepts students must master in social studies is the understanding of the rights and responsibilities of citizenship. A unit from his state curriculum frameworks centers on the ways in which governmental officials are elected or appointed, and the connections between citizenship and the right and responsibility to vote. Mr. Christopher begins with the end in mind and carefully designs assessments that require ELLs and FEP learners to demonstrate their understanding of the rights and responsibilities of voting. He provides four choices of assessments to ensure that all students will be able to demonstrate their understanding apart from their ability to read or write well in academic English:

- Write a three-page research essay about voting as social responsibility, including the history of voting in the United States and women's and African American suffrage.

- Write a persuasive letter to convince people to vote, including their responsibility to vote and the history of women and African American citizens voting, including suffrage.

- Create a persuasive photo poster showing the right and responsibility of each citizen to vote, including the history of the fight for women and African Americans to gain the right to vote.

- Working in a small group of three or four students, create a written script for and video of a public service announcement about voting, including women's and African American suffrage. (Mr. Christopher recently used his supply budget to purchase two video cameras for $129.00 each. He makes these available to students.)

Each of these assignments requires ELLs and FEP learners to demonstrate their knowledge and understanding of the history of voting rights and the social responsibility to vote—the content-area learning outcomes of his social studies unit—yet each assignment requires different language proficiency and skills. Strategy 14 further illustrates how different types of assessments can be modified for ELLs at various proficiency levels. (There are times that Mr. Christopher also wants to reinforce students' abilities to write, speak, or present within the content area. When this is the case, Mr. Christopher may purposefully assign a specific assessment that measures these skills.)

Mr. Christopher designed content-area assessment rubric for each assessment option; the rubric for the essay is included in Table 12.1. The rubric for the poster is included with Strategy 14 (Table 14.2) poster (Table 14.2, in Strategy 14). Table 12.1 illustrates the content-area assessment for the writing assignment.

Mr. Christopher and his colleagues recognize the importance of academic language and writing in the content areas and therefore also provide an assessment rubric for the

Table 12.1	Content-Area Assessment Rubric—Essay	
Mastery	*Approaching*	*Needs Improvement*
Content includes voting history, women's suffrage, and African American suffrage, and the most important concepts and historical events. The student demonstrates an understanding of each important concept (and event) as it relates to voting as a responsibility and a right.	Content includes voting history, women's suffrage, and African American suffrage. The student demonstrates knowledge of each important concept. Concepts are somewhat related to the importance of voting as social responsibility. The student demonstrates some understanding of the interrelationship of events and of voting as a right and a responsibility.	Content does not include all three important topics (voting history, women's suffrage, or African American suffrage is missing). Concepts are somewhat related to the importance of voting as social responsibility. The student does not demonstrate an understanding of the interrelationship of events and voting as a right and a responsibility.

final draft of the written essay. Separating content and language enables Mr. Christopher's ELLs and fully English proficient students to demonstrate mastery of each without allowing academic language abilities to obscure content-area understanding or lack thereof. Table 12.2 shows rubric that Mr. Christopher has created for students who are at or near grade level. He evaluates the writing on elements that have been specifically

Table 12.2	Academic Writing Rubric for Final Draft of Essay	
Mastery	*Approaching*	*Needs Improvement*
Essay is written in student's own words, except the use of no more than a few important quotes to illustrate key points. The writing is organized and clear, and it contains transitions between ideas. There are few mechanical errors in grammar and spelling. All word wall words and words that were corrected in previous drafts are spelled correctly. Grammar rules that have been taught are applied correctly. Punctuation rules that have been taught are applied correctly.	Essay is written mostly in student's own words. There is some overuse of quotations. The writing is mostly clear and organized. All word wall words and words that were corrected in previous drafts are spelled correctly. Grammar rules that have been taught are mostly applied correctly. Punctuation rules that have been taught are mostly applied correctly.	Parts of the essay are written mostly in student's own words. Lack of organization and/or errors with mechanics interfere with meaning. More than a few errors with word wall words and words corrected in previous drafts. More than a few errors with grammar rules that have been taught and noted in previous drafts. More than a few errors with punctuation rules that have been taught and noted in previous drafts.

taught in the areas of overall organization of the writing, use of grammar, spelling, and vocabulary. Mr. Christopher knows that writing is developmental, and as students try more sophisticated structures, they will naturally make more errors. He encourages students to try out new constructions and use new words, and he does not penalize students for these grammatical, spelling, and vocabulary errors.

This rubric and rubrics for the poster (see Table 14.2, in Strategy 14) and the performance (see Table 14.3, in Strategy 14) assessments are differentiated for levels of English language proficiency in Strategy 14.

REFLECTIONS

1. How do Mr. Christopher's students benefit from his approach to assessment? How might your students (ELLs and FEP learners) benefit from differentiated assessment? Why do you think it is important to the progress of ELLs and other students to measure both conceptual understanding and English language proficiency?

2. What are the benefits to ELLs when teachers separate the measurement of content-area understanding from academic English language proficiency?

STRATEGY RESOURCES

The best discussion about learning outcomes is found in the following texts:

Wiggins, G., & McTighe, J. (1998). *Understanding by design.* Alexandria, VA: Association for Supervision and Curriculum Development.

Wiggins, G., & McTighe, J. (2005). *Understanding by design* (2nd ed.). Alexandria, VA: Association for Supervision and Curriculum Development.

Designing Content-Area and Language-Based Learning Outcomes and Objectives

Strategy
13

When teachers are clear about the learning outcomes that students will master as a result of instruction, they are able to create assessments to accurately measure each student's progress toward learning outcome mastery and to plan appropriate instructional experiences. By sharing learning outcomes with students prior to instruction, teachers help students to understand the expectations for learning, thereby providing all students with a measure to self-evaluate progress (Echevarria, Vogt, & Short, 2007; Heritage, 2007; Marzano, Pickering, & Pollock, 2001; Stiggins, 2005). ELLs, who are double burdened in learning both concepts and academic language, especially benefit from knowing what they are intended to learn, both in content and language. Sharing learning outcomes and lesson objectives with ELLs also serves to contextualize instruction, which builds comprehensibility. (Comprehensible instruction is discussed in Unit IV).

For each concept in an instructional unit, the teacher identifies one to three content-area outcomes and one to three language-learning outcomes. Based on the learning outcomes (what the student will know by the end of the instructional unit), the teacher plans lesson objectives. Figure 13.1 shows the relationship between concepts, unit learning outcomes, and lesson objectives.

THEORY AND/OR RESEARCH UNDERLYING THE STRATEGY

Content-area learning outcomes are derived from the concepts that all students must learn and understand, and they will be the same for each student—although, as Strategy 12 illustrated, students may demonstrate their mastery in different ways. ELLs, who must develop academic language proficiency as they learn content, will also need clear and appropriate learning outcomes for language. Setting clear language learning outcomes for FEP learners will also contribute to development of their content-area language skills (i.e., reading, writing, and speaking across the content areas). In addition, measuring language and content separately ensures that the two are not conflated—mastery in one can be measured apart from mastery (or lack thereof) in the other.

Figure 13.1 Unit Concepts, Unit Learning Outcomes, Lesson Objectives

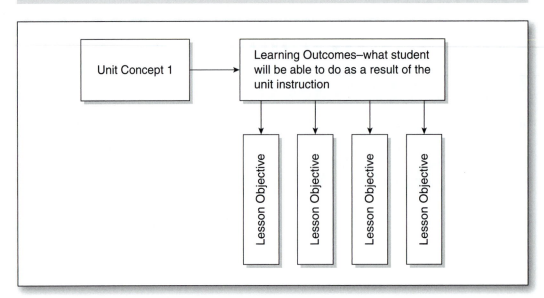

IMPLEMENTING THE STRATEGY

1. Think about the concepts in one content area that are essential for ELLs to truly understand as a result of instruction. (A lot of content is good to know and understand, much is important to know and understand, and some concepts are essential to know and understand.) (Wiggins & McTighe, 1998, 2005).

2. Discuss with colleagues the concepts that you have identified.

3. Once you have a clear understanding of the concepts that are necessary for all students to know, determine the content-area learning outcomes that students must master (e.g., early learners will identify numbers and understand one-to-one correspondence, etc.; fourth graders will make connections between their lives and the lives of children who lived in Colonial times; fifth graders will engage in inquiry demonstrating the steps of the scientific method, etc.).

4. As you plan lessons, write lesson objectives based on the learning outcomes you have identified.

5. Review the language proficiency levels of each ELL in the classroom based on the intake assessment, other available standardized assessments, samples of written work produced, and notes from your informal assessment of oral language proficiency. Establish language learning outcomes that are appropriate for the ELL's level of proficiency (e.g., first grade ELLs with *Starting* proficiency will participate in choral reading of the chorus of a story book following several repeated readings, fifth grade ELLs with *Emerging* proficiency levels will organize ideas by placing key words in graphic organizers, second grade ELLs with *Developing* proficiency levels will read a short story along with an audio recording of the story and then participate in a subsequent small group discussion). Table 4 in the introduction to this book provides a brief review of TESOL English language proficiency levels, and Table III.4 provides samples of assessment outcomes that are appropriate for ELLs at the five proficiency levels.

6. Create language objectives for each lesson based on the learning outcomes you have identified.

STRATEGY IN ACTION

Mrs. Lidia Clark, a third grade teacher, has set the following content-area learning outcome: Students will write a short report to share their observations of the terrariums they created as part of a science unit. She plans several lessons that integrate science and language arts. Each day, Mrs. Clark writes the lesson objectives on the whiteboard and reads through them with the class.

Days 1–3	Language Objective 1: We will record our observations of the terrarium in our science notebooks.
	Language Objective 2: We will discuss our written observations with our partners.
Day 4	Language Objective 1: We will use our observation data to complete the graphic organizer.
	Language Objective 2: We will share our graphic organizers with our partners.
Day 5	Language Objective 1: We will use our graphic organizers to write a rough draft of our observations.

Mrs. Clark establishes the following English language learning outcomes for Dinha (*Emerging* proficiency), Li (*Developing* proficiency), and Sophal (*Expanding* proficiency):

- Dinha will list the names of at least three items and write one word in English to describe each.

- Li will write about three items, spelling the words (on the word wall) correctly. She will also use capital letters and correct punctuation in her sentences.

- Sophal will complete the expository paragraph. He will correctly spell word wall words and the words from the third grade word list he learned previously this year, use correct punctuation, and vary the length of his sentences, including correctly written compound sentences where appropriate.

Each student in Mrs. Clark's classroom is learning how to write expository text, yet the language learning outcomes are differentiated according to English language proficiency levels.

Ms. Jenna Salmon, a first grade teacher, has determined that one learning outcome for all first grade students is making and confirming predictions about text. Among the strategies she uses to help students achieve this learning outcome are picture walks and conversations about the text they are reading. Ms. Salmon's learning outcomes and her objectives are the same. She writes these on chart paper and shares them with the class.

1. Today we will make predictions about *The Mitten.*

2. We will read with our groups to confirm our predictions.

Ms. Salmon has set the following language learning outcomes for two ELLs in her class:

- Mehmet, who has an *Expanding* level of proficiency, will make and share a prediction during a picture walk following a think-pair-share in which he first practices his language with his partner.

- Cha, who has a *Developing* level of proficiency, will accurately state a prediction during a small group reading session using a big book filled with illustrations (the third they have read in the series, which facilitates familiarity with the series characters and vocabulary).

REFLECTIONS

1. How is it helpful to plan both content-area and language-learning outcomes? Why must all students master the same content-area learning outcomes? Why is it important to differentiate language-learning outcomes?

2. Consider one content-area unit that you teach, and think of an ELL at each level of TESOL language proficiency (Table III.4). What language learning outcomes might you establish for each ELL?

STRATEGY RESOURCES

1. *Educate Interactive* provides a discussion of differentiated assessment and links to several useful websites.

   http://www.educateinteractive.org/best_practices/differentiated_assessments.html

2. 📑 *About.com: Special Education* provides useful articles about differentiated assessment.

   http://specialed.about.com/od/teacherstrategies/a/differentiated.htm

Planning Differentiated Assessment According to Language Proficiency

Strategy 14

S trategy 12 provided examples and steps for varying assessments by the type of work that ELLs and others will produce to demonstrate content-area understanding, and it provided a sample essay rubric that measured content-area knowledge and writing quality. ELLs and FEP learners will also benefit from assessment of academic language proficiency, which is the focus of Strategy 14. To plan appropriate language assessments, you should familiarize yourself with the broad characteristics of each level of English language proficiency: *Starting, Emerging, Developing, Expanding,* and *Bridging,* which were illustrated in Table III.4 on pages 71–72 of this book.

THEORY AND/OR RESEARCH UNDERLYING THE STRATEGY

Teachers adapt instruction to ensure that instructional language is accessible to ELLs and to implement assessments that enable ELLs to demonstrate content-area mastery apart from their language abilities. Appropriate assessments also enable ELLs to demonstrate growth in academic language proficiency (Gottlieb, 2006). For ELLs and their teachers to measure ongoing progress in academic English, assessments must be differentiated according to level of English language proficiency (Gottlieb, 2006).

IMPLEMENTING THE STRATEGY

To differentiate assessments according to English language proficiency, do the following:

1. Determine several types of assessments (e.g., written, oral, visual, multimedia) that will enable students to demonstrate content-area mastery (Strategy 12).

2. Review the indicators of the levels of proficiency: *Starting, Emerging, Developing, Expanding,* and *Bridging* (Table 4 in the Introduction to this book provides a broad overview of the levels; specific indicators are included in the first few pages of the following units: Unit V [vocabulary], Unit VI [oral language development], and Unit VII [reading and writing].)

3. Review the assessment ideas for each proficiency level (Table III.4 of this unit).

4. Adjust rubrics for each assessment option to ensure that ELLs are working at the high end of their proficiency levels (*Output + 1*).

STRATEGY IN ACTION

As illustrated in Strategy 13, Mr. Christopher has collaborated with colleagues to determine the content-area concepts that all students should know, and he has developed several assessments to measure student understanding (written essay, persuasive letter, photo poster with captions, performance video). He decides on the elements that must be included in each assessment to measure content-area mastery (See Table 12.1). He then reviews the language proficiency levels of the students in his class. He encourages students to choose the assessment in which they can best demonstrate their content-area knowledge and their ability to use academic language. He encourages ELLs with *Starting* and *Emerging* proficiency levels to consider the photo poster, which demonstrates understanding but requires less academic writing and speaking. Tables 14.1, 14.2, and 14.3 illustrate the language rubrics that Mr. Christopher has developed for various English proficiency levels.

Table 14.1	Sample Writing Mechanics Rubric for ELLs With *Expanding* Proficiency Level	
Mastery	*Approaching*	*Needs Improvement*
Essay is generally written in student's own words and conveys student's main points and ideas. The writing is logical at the essay, paragraph, and sentence levels (or the ELL can explain how he or she organized the paper.*) Mechanical errors do not interfere with meaning. Words on the word wall and words that the teacher provided corrections for in the first draft are spelled correctly. There is some variation in sentence structure. Simple sentences are written correctly.	Essay is generally written in student's own words. Student's main points and ideas are present. The writing is generally well organized, but inconsistencies exist and interfere with meaning. Mechanical errors do not interfere with meaning. Most words on the word wall and the words that the teacher or peer editor provided corrections for in the first draft are spelled correctly. Most simple sentences are written correctly.	There is a lack of organization (essay, paragraph, or sentence level), and the ELL cannot explain the organization of the paper. Organization interferes with meaning. Errors with mechanics interfere with meaning. Spelling errors exist with more than a few word wall words. Many errors in structure and punctuation of simple sentences.

* Writing styles are influenced by first language and culture. The ELL may have a first language or culture organizational style that differs from the linear style expected in U.S. classrooms. Although the ELL will need to learn a linear writing style as one way to express his or her ideas, this is a process, which is enhanced when teachers build on the writing style the ELL brings to the classroom.

As Table 14.1 illustrates, Mr. Christopher has specified that students show some variation in sentence structure to demonstrate mastery. He holds ELLs at this level accountable for what they have learned (simple sentence structure, word wall words, and words that have been corrected on previous drafts). He does not, however, penalize students for errors with more complex sentence structure. He knows that students will make errors when using more sophisticated structures in their writing. Therefore, he develops a rubric that sets clear standards and at the same time encourages language growth and academic risk taking.

Table 14.2 illustrates how Mr. Christopher has differentiated the photo poster according to six proficiency levels (from *Starting* to *Fully English proficient*).

Table 14.2	Differentiated Rubric for Mastery—Poster

Regarding content, posters at each language proficiency level must (1) contain an appropriate title; (2) illustrate at least four key events in history; (3) include a caption for each key event, with date(s) and a descriptor; and (4) include a slogan that explains the importance of voting. With regard to language, students at each level are responsible for correctly spelling key terms, which are posted on the unit bulletin board and prominently displayed in the classroom.

Starting	*Emerging*	*Developing*	*Expanding*	*Transitioning*	*Fully English Proficient*
			Content		
A one to two word descriptor is included with each key event. A simple slogan is included to show the importance of voting.	A simple sentence is included to describe each key event. A simple sentence is included to explain the importance of voting.	A sentence or two is used to describe each key event. One or two sentences also explain the importance of voting.	A two to three sentence paragraph describes each key event.	A two to four sentence paragraph describes each key event.	A two to four sentence paragraph describes each key event.
			Language		
No additional requirements	Capital letters are used to begin each sentence and the appropriate end mark is used to complete each sentence.	Simple sentences are grammatically correct. Correct punctuation is used.	Some variation in sentence structure. Sentences are grammatically correct. Punctuation is correct.	Sentence structure is varied. Sentences are grammatically correct. Punctuation is correct. No more than a few errors in spelling, including words that are not on word walls.	Sentence structure is varied. Sentences are grammatically correct. Punctuation is correct. Words are spelled correctly.

Table 14.3	Performance Presentation				
Students work in groups of three to four to complete the video-recorded performance presentation. All presentations are accompanied by credits that clearly show the names of students who completed research, wrote scripts, and edited scripts. The research documents and all versions of scripts (with dates) are submitted. Each student plays some part in the video itself. Each video includes a discussion of the history of voting and persuades viewers of their rights and responsibilities to vote.					
Starting	*Emerging*	*Developing*	*Expanding*	*Transitioning*	*Fully English Proficient*
No adjustments to content-area requirements					
Language					
Each student appears in the video in a meaningful way, although students' spoken parts vary in length and complexity. Some evidence of participation in the planning of the video is evident.	Video role includes brief sentences that may be read from a script. Some evidence of participation in the writing or editing of the script is evident.	Video role includes expanded sentences with clear pronunciation.* Some evidence of participation in the writing or editing of the script is evident.	Video role includes expanded sentences with clear pronunciation.* Clear evidence of participation in the writing or editing of the script is evident.	Same as expanding	Same as expanding.

* This does not suggest pronunciation without an accent.

REFLECTIONS

1. Review an assessment that you believe measures content-area mastery, then review the language descriptors for each proficiency level. Think about how you will make your assessment clearly accessible to ELLs at each proficiency level. What are the benefits of adjusting assessments and providing clear assessment rubrics for ELLs at various levels?

2. How might you differentiate rubrics for other students in your classroom who may not have grade-level language, reading, or writing skills?

3. What challenges do you think you might encounter when differentiating assessments?

STRATEGY RESOURCES

1. 📑 Organizing and Assessing in the Content Area Classroom (originally published in *TESOL Matters*)

   http://www.everythingesl.net/inservices/judith2.php

2. 🎬 Assessment of English Language Learners: Dr. Valdez Pierce discusses classroom strategies for assessing ELLs in this 45-minute webcast.

   http://www.colorincolorado.org/webcasts/assessment

Planning and Using Formative Assessment

Strategy
15

W ell implemented formative assessment provides both teachers and students with an ongoing data stream that enables them to judge the effectiveness of instruction and student learning. In discussing upper elementary and middle school students, Garrison (National Middle School Association, 2009) likens formative assessment to coaching a sport such as baseball. Teaching and learning form an instructional cycle. The coach sets learning outcomes for the week—one of these may be a specific play that she wants team members to execute. On the first day of practice, the coach explains the play and uses a variety of instructional materials to demonstrate it. Once she is sure that the players understand the play, she provides them with time to practice it. She observes as they practice and identifies the gaps between their level of practice and the learning outcome (Sadler, 1989). She provides ongoing feedback to help them understand their performance level and continues to observe. Based on observation data, the coach continues to provide feedback, and players learn to self-evaluate and self-correct. According to Heritage, Kim, Vendlinkski, and Herman (2009), formative assessment includes taking action "to close the gap based on the evidence" (p. 24) gathered and, at least at the middle school level and above, must involve students in data collecting and data analysis, and making adjustments to how they are learning (Heritage, 2009). Involving younger students in the formative assessment process helps them to develop a vision of learning.

In applying the coaching analogy analogy to the classroom, the teacher identifies a learning outcome, such as writing an expository paragraph, which he shares with students. He explains what an expository paragraph is and provides several exemplars. He provides students with practice objectives and time for supervised practice. He uses observations, drafts of student writing, and conferences to measure progress. Depending on the results of the formative assessments, the teacher may provide other exemplars or explicitly teach skills that students need. The instructional cycle continues with the teacher providing ongoing feedback to enable students to know how close they are to meeting the learning outcomes. Finally, it's game time—the students write and submit a final paragraph for formal assessment.

THEORY AND/OR RESEARCH UNDERLYING THE STRATEGY

Formative assessment has been shown to substantially improve student achievement—especially the achievement of low-achieving students (Stiggins, 2005). Experts in the field of second-language assessment (Gottlieb, 2006) support utilizing formative assessment with ELLs. Recently, World-Class Instructional Design and Assessment (WIDA, 2009), an organization that provides standards and assessments for teaching ELLs in 23 states, launched a project to improve formative assessment for ELLs across grade levels. Formative assessment should allow teachers, ELLs, and FEP learners to focus on the broad questions in Table 15.1.

Table 15.1 Formative Assessment—Guiding Questions	
Questions for Students	*Questions for Teachers*
Where am I going?	What is the learning outcome for the student?
Where am I now?	Where is she or he now?
How am I going to get there?	What instructional supports or scaffolds will I provide to take her or him there?

Source: Based on *Classroom Assessment for Student Learning: Doing It Right—Using It Well,* 2004, by R. J. Stiggins, J. A. Arter, A. Chappuis, & S. Chappuis. Portland, OR: Assessment Training Institute.

IMPLEMENTING THE STRATEGY

Formative assessment is considered to be part of a classroom culture rather than specific strategies or a checklist. Nonetheless, it is useful to have strategies (or tools) to gather assessment data.

1. Begin by clearly articulating a clear and specific content-area learning outcome, being specific about language modifications. (For example, in social studies for *Starting* proficiency, arrange the graphics on the time line and write the year that each event occurred; for *Emerging proficiency,* arrange the graphics on the time line and write the year that each event occurred and a simple sentence descriptor, etc.)

2. Prepare, distribute, review, and display a rubric showing how student work will be evaluated. Separate rubrics for ELLs can be distributed and reviewed individually. (Content will be the same; it is form or language that may differ.)

3. Make a three-column list that shows the knowledge and skills learners need to meet each learning outcome, the instructional strategies and materials you will use to help them develop knowledge and skills, and the formative assessments you will use to measure student progress as well as the effectiveness of your instruction. Some formative assessments that might be useful are shown in Table 15.2.

4. Decide what you will do with assessment data. If, for example, your observations of and subsequent conversation with Juan, a *Developing* ELL, reveal that Juan cannot complete a sequence of historical events because the reading level of the social studies text is too high, decide how you will use this data to change your instructional materials.

Table 15.2	Formative Assessments			
Assessment Tool	*Additional Considerations for ELLs*	*Grade Levels*	*Structure*	*Uses*
Structured/ systemic observation	None	PK–8	May be implemented with any size group, but is more easily implemented with small groups.	Reveals whether students are able to stay on task, level at which they can complete task, and if they need additional supports to do so.
Conferencing	Student may know more than he or she can express orally. If possible, use the ELL's first language with students who have *Starting* and *Beginning* proficiency levels.	PK–8	Small group or individual	Allows teacher to probe for understanding of concepts and misconceptions as well as learning styles and specific areas of difficulty.
Dipsticking	ELLs at lower proficiency levels may not understand for a variety of reasons or they may understand the concept, but not the prompt.	PK–8	Large group	Allows teacher to check general understanding and identify confusions while teaching.
Running records	None	Usually primary, but effective with older struggling readers.	Individual	Measures progress and indicates specific difficulties.
Tickets to leave	Modify language requirements (i.e., ELLs could write words, phrases, a simple sentence, or draw sketches).	4–8	Large group, but can be evaluated individually	Measures effectiveness of instruction and individual understanding.

STRATEGY IN ACTION

Here are some examples of formative assessment at work in a variety of regular education classrooms with ELLs learning with FEP learners. The examples are based on the formative assessments in Table 15.2.

1. Structured Systemic Observation

Ms. Kathleen Brideau, a middle school teacher, uses structured systematic observation to measure the progress of her students. She uses a rubric to measure the participation of ELLs and FEP learners in academic conversations during language arts and social studies blocks. (Sample rubrics are available in Tables 31.3 and 31.4 in Strategy 31 of this book.) Ms. Brideau circulates as her students discuss the question of the day. A quick glance around the room helps her to understand who is on task, and as she visits with different groups, she is able to use the formative assessment rubric to develop a clear picture of her students' language proficiency, their understanding of content, and the gaps in her instruction. This perspective enables her to clarify confusions and adjust her plans for the following day's instruction.

2. Conferencing

Friday is conference day in Mr. Gary Dinardo's middle school science class. While the larger class is completing work from the week, writing questions that they will submit to Mr. Dinardo at the end of the science period, or working on their independent projects, Mr. Dinardo calls students to his desk one at a time. They bring the work they have completed for the week, which enables Mr. Dinardo to ask them specific questions about their work, to explore their levels of understanding, and to monitor their language use; he takes careful notes during this time. Mr. Dinardo formally conferences with each student in his class at least every two weeks. In addition to building rapport and engaging students in one-to-one academic conversations, these conferences enable Mr. Dinardo to make vital instructional decisions.

3. Dipsticking

Mrs. Bourque regularly uses a technique known as *dipsticking* (Sahpier & Gower, 1997) as a formative assessment during instruction. At the beginning of each year, Mrs. Bourque spends a considerable amount of time building an inclusive classroom community. She has established a routine for ELLs and FEP learners to signal to her that they are "right on" with the instruction, "clear enough for now," or "confused." Mrs. Bourque does this with green, yellow, and red cards that students keep on their desk while Mrs. Bourque is teaching. Mrs. Bourque stops instruction at least every 10 minutes to ask students to hold up their cards. This quick, large-group formative assessment enables her to adjust her pacing and instruction. It also encourages students to monitor their understanding.

4. Running Records

Running records are the legacy of reading teacher, researcher, and author Dr. Marie Clay, the founder of Reading Recovery. Running records are formative assessments that show student progress over time. They also indicate how teachers need to adjust their instruction to meet the needs of students. Using running records, the reading progress of individual students can be measured fairly quickly and very frequently. With running records, teachers can measure a student's use of reading strategies, their self-monitoring, accuracy, errors, and self-correction. While running records are often a lower-grade phenomenon, they can also be effective in upper grades.

5. Ticket-to-Leave

The Ticket-to-Leave is a two- to five-minute activity conducted at the end of the class that provides students with a way to summarize their understanding of the lesson and content or to ask unanswered questions. Mr. Francis uses it regularly in his eighth grade math class. Oftentimes, he asks questions that have to do with the math content, such as "What would be the first step to solving this problem?" Other times, he encourages more open responses: "The most important thing I learned today was _____," and "One thing that still confuses me is _____." He dedicates time to review the language of the tickets-to-leave he uses most frequently to ensure that these are accessible to ELLs.

REFLECTIONS

1. What types of formative assessment might be most effective at your grade level and in your content area?

2. How would you adapt your instruction based on possible results from the formative assessments in the Strategy in Action section?

STRATEGY RESOURCES

1. [Podcast] Formative Assessment: Debunking the Myths and the Culture of Formative Assessment. In this two-part series, Kate Garrison from Measured Progress discusses the myths and culture of formative assessment in the classroom. (Running Times: Part I: 21:13, Part II: 21:38)

   http://www.nmsa.org/Publications/TodaysMiddleLevelEducator/tabid/1409/Default.aspx

2. 🗐 Formative and Summative Assessments in the Classroom (Garrison & Ehringhaus, 2007).

   http://www.nmsa.org/portals/0/pdf/publications/Web_Exclusive/Formative_Summative_Assessment.pdf

3. 📄 Key Strategies Brief: Five "Key Strategies" for Effective Formative Assessment, from the National Council of Teachers of Mathematics

   http://www.nctm.org/news/content.aspx?id=11474

4. The Concept of Formative Assessment. This paper, which is available online, provides research supporting the effects of formative assessment on student achievement.

   http://pareonline.net/getvn.asp?v=8&n=9

Strategy

16

Summative Assessments Including Portfolios

Regardless of how well-constructed any assessment may be, individual assessments only provide snapshots in time of student progress. Portfolio assessment, on the other hand, has the capacity to measure progress over time. The portfolio serves as an organizing tool for individual assessments and pieces of student work—a photo album that demonstrates growth and learning over time (Wiggins & McTighe, 1998, 2005). A portfolio is a useful and effective tool for capturing pre-instructional, formative, and summative assessments, and it provides a clear picture of student growth in content and language throughout instructional units. Not all student work goes into a portfolio, however. Rather, teachers guide students in learning to self-select various pieces of work (writings, illustrations, recordings, tests, etc.) that illustrate their progress toward mastering learning outcomes and, often throughout the school year and encourage students to discuss the elements of each piece of work that should be included in the portfolio.

THEORY AND/OR RESEARCH UNDERLYING THE STRATEGY

Assessing and analyzing student progress across time is particularly important in the evaluation of students who may struggle initially but make greater gains toward the end of the unit. This group of students is likely to include ELLs, who are continually developing academic language and therefore tend to perform better later in an instructional unit as their academic language develops (Freeman, Freeman, & Mercuri, 2002). The process of developing a portfolio also promotes self-regulation and self-efficacy because in selecting pieces for the portfolio, ELLs engage in thoughtful reflection and dialogue with their teachers (Bandura, 1977, 1986; Zimmerman & Ringle, 1981). Through this reflective dialogue, students learn to evaluate their work and their progress toward meeting learning outcomes. Thus, implementing portfolio assessment gradually shifts the locus of responsibility for learning from the teacher to the student.

IMPLEMENTING THE STRATEGY

1. Explain the unit learning outcomes to students, and display learning outcomes written in language that students will understand, using visuals and pictograms as appropriate for grade and proficiency levels. Refer to these often.

2. Explain to students that they will be evaluating their learning and will select some of their work to show what they are learning.

3. Using a think-aloud, model the process of selecting work for inclusion in the portfolio.

4. Engage students in reflective conversations about work that might be selected (What does each piece of work illustrate or demonstrate? Why should it be included? Why not?).

STRATEGY IN ACTION

Mrs. Allen's fourth grade students (ELLs and FEP learners) are learning about the diverse U.S. population as part of their social studies curriculum. Mrs. Allen plans an instructional unit that requires students to locate areas where Native American nations once flourished and areas where large populations of several immigrant groups have settled. This learning activity requires students to learn and use map skills (such as latitude and longitude), identify states and capitals, and learn about the area's geography (including climate, major physical features, and natural resources). Mrs. Allen also incorporates the major contributions of native American and immigrant populations, as well as background information about their countries of origin. Mrs. Allen explains the unit's content and language learning outcomes. The students will create a portfolio to demonstrate their learning as they work through the unit.

Unit Content Area Learning Outcomes:

1. Locate and describe geographical areas that were inhabited by at least three Native American nations (include latitude and longitude, names of current states and capital cities).

2. Describe the climate, major physical features, and natural resources of at least six areas within the United States, and explain why people originally settled there.

3. Compare and contrast the lives of Native American nations prior to and following colonization.

4. Describe the most significant contributions that major immigrant populations have made to the United States.

Unit Language Learning Outcomes:

5. Read about the population that you are researching (using books in the class and school library and the Internet), and keep a reading log.

6. Discuss your findings and make collaborative decisions in your small groups.

7. Write about the population that you are researching.

8. Create a media presentation to teach others about the population that you researched.

Based on the English proficiency levels of her students, Mrs. Allen adjusts rubrics for language outcomes. Mrs. Allen provides students with a checklist of types of items they must include in the portfolio and provides students with choice as to which items they include.

Mrs. Allen's Unit Portfolio List

1. Research log (a copy of a log is distributed with columns titled Date, Title of reading/audio/video, What I learned, and What I want to know).

2. Group work log (Date, What we did, What I learned)

3. One piece of written work of which you are most proud (with drafts, showing how you improved)

4. One drawing, map, or photo of a model that you created

5. Copy of the multimedia presentation

Students have choices regarding the materials they will read, listen to, or watch. They are also provided choice with regard to the written work and drawing that they include in the portfolio. Mrs. Allen conferences with students to help them make decisions about the items they will include in their portfolios. During conferences she and students are able to observe and assess language development content-area understanding and across time.

REFLECTIONS

1. Why do you think that portfolio assessment might be particularly valuable for measuring the progress of ELLs?

2. How does student choice regarding the items that are included in the portfolio improve student learning opportunities?

3. What instructional units that you teach will lend themselves to portfolio assessment, and what types of evidence could students include in the portfolio to demonstrate their language development and content-area understanding?

STRATEGY RESOURCES

Portfolio Assessment

1. The National Capital Language Resource Center (NCLRC) provides extensive information about the rationale, development, and implementation of portfolios. Developed for the foreign language classroom, guidelines and discussions are appropriate for developing portfolios for ELLs and other students in regular education classrooms.

   http://www.nclrc.org/portfolio/modules.html

2. Portfolio Assessment and English Language Learners

   http://www.cal.org/resources/Digest/0010assessment.html

Making Content Comprehensible

Native English speakers often have difficulty with new concepts. How do I help ELLs understand content at grade level if they do not speak the language well?

—Lusa, 6th-Grade Teacher in
an Inservice Professional Development Workshop

The question asked by Lusa is similar to those asked by pre- and inservice teachers at all grade levels and across content areas. If ELLs are to learn grade-level content, they must be able to understand the instruction that is delivered in content-area classrooms; teachers must present content in a way that is comprehensible to ELLs with varying levels of English language proficiency. The descriptors of each TESOL proficiency level (Level 1: *Starting*, Level 2: *Emerging*, Level 3: *Developing*, Level 4: *Expanding*, and Level 5: *Bridging*), which are included in Table 4 in the Introduction to this book, provide an understanding of approximate proficiency levels. (Sample performance indicators for various proficiency levels are also found in Units V [vocabulary], VI [academic language], and VII [reading and writing].) This unit provides strategies to make instructional materials more comprehensible to ELLs, thus providing **scaffolds** to grade-level instruction.

Scaffolding is most effective when instructional materials and presentations are comprehensible and just a little beyond the ELL's current ability level, thereby promoting ongoing development of English language proficiency (Krashen, 1982; Vygotsky, 1978). Instructional language that is too far above the language proficiency level of ELLs will result in frustration and impede learning. ELLs with lower levels of English language proficiency will need substantial linguistic scaffolding, including first language explanation (when available), videos, demonstrations, diagrams, graphic organizers, and extensive opportunities to check their understanding. Scaffolds are meant to be temporary—they form a bridge between the learner's

> A **scaffold** is any instructional device that provides support, enabling the learner to access concepts, strategies, or skills (or in this case, language) that he or she is not able to access independently. The notion of scaffolding comes from Vygotsky's Zone of Proximal Development. As the learner becomes more proficient with academic language, scaffolds are gradually removed.

current proficiency level and the targeted proficiency level. As ELLs' language proficiency increases, scaffolds are gradually removed and responsibility is released to students. This gradual removal of linguistic scaffolds and release of responsibility to ELLs is illustrated in Figure IV.1.

Figure IV.1 Scaffolding Comprehensible Input for Multiple Proficiency Levels

Level 5 Bridging—Provide visuals for clarity (in the same way these are provided to native English speakers). Responses approach that of native language speakers.

Level 4 Expanding—Provide ongoing scaffolding using visuals, especially when introducing new concepts. Encourage ELLs to respond in English with the understanding that they will make errors, but these will not interview with meaning.

Level 3 Developing—Provide content-area support in native language when necessary. Provide ongoing scaffolding using visuals described in Level 1 within small and large group settings, and individual scaffolding when necessary. Encourage ELLs to respond in English, understanding that they will make errors that sometimes impede communication.

Level 2 Emerging—Provide content-area support in native language when possible, and allow ELLs to respond in native language when necessary. Provide individual support and ongoing scaffolding using visuals as described in *Level 1*. Enable ELLs to respond with one-word responses and short phrases accompanied by visuals, graphics, or pictures.

Level 1 Starting—Provide content-area instruction in native language whenever possible, and encourage ELLs to respond in native language when they cannot respond in English. Provide additional individual support and scaffolding using few words that are accompanied by visuals (realia, photos, videos, etc.) and graphic organizers. Enable ELLs to respond using visuals, graphics, or pictures.

Realia refers to actual physical objects; for example, an apple that a student can hold, smell, and taste

Unit IV includes five strategies that will help you scaffold grade-level academic language and make content comprehensible to ELLs: Strategy 17, Providing Context for Instruction; Strategy 18, Connecting to and Expanding on ELLs' Background Knowledge; Strategy 19, Adjusting Speech and Using Realia, Videos, and Visuals to Build Comprehensibility; and Strategy 20, Finding and Creating Comprehensible Materials. The strategies presented in this unit are appropriate for ELLs with all proficiency levels.

What You Will Learn

Unit IV provides theory, research, vignettes, and strategies to help you do the following:

1. Understand the ways in which comprehensible input is consistent with TESOL standards.

2. Design instructional settings that provide context.

3. Develop instructional strategies for making grade-level content comprehensible to ELLs with varying levels of English language proficiency.

Comprehensible Input: Mrs. Fortin's Middle School Classroom

When students enter Mrs. Susan Fortin's middle school science classroom, they are clear about what to expect. Mrs. Fortin, who has been teaching for 11 years, has clear instructional routines for everything from placing the classroom agenda and objectives on the same place on the whiteboard to displaying photos that build context on bulletin boards, placing realia that demonstrate content on shelves and tables in prominent areas of the room, organizing students' materials in folders, and following clear routines for grouping and distributing and collecting materials. The organized flow of Mrs. Fortin's classroom enables even ELLs with *Starting* levels of proficiency to follow along as Mrs. Fortin reviews the lesson agenda and objectives, begins the lesson, and distributes materials. For example, Anna, an ELL who has a *Starting* level of proficiency, knows that when Mrs. Fortin distributes blue student folders, she will write in her science journal. She also knows that Mrs. Fortin will begin each class by referring to the left-hand side of the whiteboard to review the class agenda and learning objectives for content and language. Anna knows that Mrs. Fortin will leave the agenda and objectives on the whiteboard, so that she and the students can refer to them throughout the lesson. She also knows that Mrs. Fortin will post words that are important to the lesson and student-friendly definitions on the side word wall. Anna can expect Mrs. Fortin to use the same display table, located at the front of the room, to display any model or experiment to illustrate lesson concepts. Anna also knows both that Mrs. Fortin will stop instruction at least every 10 minutes to allow students to check for understanding with their partners and that she will clarify confusion with the large class, with small groups, or with individual students.

Even with these scaffolds, the language load is heavy for Anna. When she does become confused, she can rely on the context Mrs. Fortin provides to keep her grounded in the lesson until Mrs. Fortin is able to check in with her to provide additional scaffolding. Clear routines for group work allow Anna to know what to expect when students transition into small group work. Mrs. Fortin's classroom setting provides context for the ebb and flow of instruction, which frees ELLs, like Anna, to concentrate on academic language and content.

Mrs. Fortin knows that the structure she provides is important but insufficient for making complex content comprehensible. Students are learning complex concepts, and ELLs are learning these in a language they do not fully understand. The cognitive demands are heavy for all students, and they are heavier for ELLs. The more cognitively demanding a learning task is, the more important it is to provide appropriate linguistic scaffolds.

Cummins (2000) illustrated the types of language tasks that students experience and the importance of using context as scaffolds as learning tasks become more cognitively demanding.

Figure IV.2   Context-Embedded Versus Context-Reduced Language

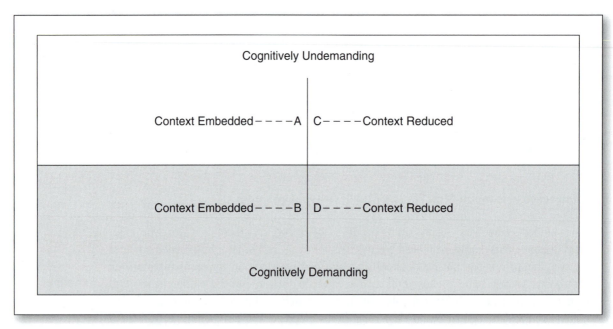

Source: From *Language, Power, and Pedagogy: Bilingual Children in the Crossfire,* 2000, by J. Crawford. Buffalo, NY: Multilingual Matters.

Quadrants A and C, found in the upper half of the model, represent content that is social or more casual in nature. This is the language that ELLs develop within a year or two. A face-to-face conversation about a casual known topic is represented by Quadrant A. Quadrant C represents cognitively undemanding communication as well, but in Quadrant C the context is reduced. A phone conversation about a casual topic is an example of Quadrant C. Quadrants B and D represent cognitively demanding topics, such as the topics commonly encountered in classroom instruction. Quadrant D represents a lecture without visual information or a text without supporting structures, such as illustrations, boldface text, or callouts. The content in Quadrant B is also demanding, but is supported with scaffolds. For example, the begins teacher lecture with a three-minute video clip, and then provides two minutes for students to think-pair-share or time for a KWL activity. The teacher also introduces new vocabulary, keeps this vocabulary on the whiteboard, and refers to it as she speaks. She paraphrases difficult language structures, and she provides time for students to debrief every eight to ten minutes. Although teachers cannot make content less cognitively demanding, they can ensure that the content is presented in context with scaffolding (Quadrant B), rather than without context (Quadrant D).

Mrs. Fortin's Lesson

Knowing that ELLs at varying levels of English language proficiency will need differentiated scaffolding to understand content, Mrs. Fortin ensures that she taps into ELLs' background knowledge, connects instruction to previous learning, and uses tools such as graphic organizers to build comprehensibility. She knows, too, that unlike FEP learners, ELLs cannot fill in the white spaces that exist between words when listening, which results in words blurring together and decreasing comprehensibility. For this reason, she is careful to focus on the rate and clarity of her speech: not unnaturally slow or stressed, but clear. As she presents content, she often uses graphic organizers to build context. She also uses realia, videos, photos, and graphics to make content understandable for ELLs in her classroom. When Mrs. Fortin assigns reading, she often assigns simplified readings based on the language proficiency level of her students. Mrs. Fortin uses models IV.1 and IV.2 to help her plan appropriately scaffolded instruction and instructional materials for ELLs at various levels of language proficiency. The strategies in this unit are consistent with Mrs. Fortin's planning and instruction.

Strategies 17 through 20 offer ways to provide context for cognitively demanding instruction. These strategies are consistent with TESOL standards for teachers and students.

Table IV.1	TESOL Standards for Teachers

Domain 3: Planning, Implementing, and Managing Instruction

3.a.2. Create supportive, accepting classroom environments. *(p. 45)*

3.a.3. Plan differentiated learning experiences based on assessment of students' English and L1 [first language] proficiency, learning styles, and prior formal educational experiences and knowledge. *(pp.45–46)*

3.a.5. Plan for instruction that embeds assessment, includes scaffolding, and provides reteaching when necessary for individuals and small groups to successfully meet learning objectives. *(p. 46)*

Using Resources and Technology Effectively in ESL and Content Instruction

3.c.1. Select, adapt, and use culturally responsive, age-appropriate, and linguistically accessible materials. *(p. 55)*

3.c.2. Select materials and other resources that are appropriate to students' developing language and content-area abilities, including appropriate use of L1 [first language]. *(p. 55)*

3.c.3. Employ a variety of materials for language learning, including books, visual aids, props, and realia. *(p. 56)*

3.c.4. Use technological resources (e.g., web, software, computers, and related devices) to enhance language and content-area instruction for ELLs. *(p. 56)*

Source: TESOL Teacher Standards Tables: TESOL (2010). *TESOL/NCATE Standards for the Recognition of Initial ESOL Programs in P–12 ESL Teacher Education,* Alexandria, VA: TESOL.

Complicating the task of providing the appropriate level of comprehensible input is the fact that, in addition to differing in language proficiency, ELLs differ in the amount and quality of their previous schooling and their overall academic knowledge. For example, it is one thing to make instruction in two-digit multiplication comprehensible to ELLs who have learned to multiply. ELLs without this understanding must be taught the prerequisite skills in a comprehensible manner. When, for whatever reason, ELLs do not have background knowledge and schemata in an instructional area, teachers must build this background knowledge just as they would for any student in the classroom who required concepts, strategies, or skills. The difference is that teachers must build this background knowledge in a way that makes both language and content comprehensible. Whenever possible, ELLs who have lower levels of English proficiency (*Starting* or *Emerging*) and who are not educated at or near grade level should receive this remedial instruction in a language that they understand. Knowing the concepts that ELLs understand and can apply requires ongoing assessment, as is detailed in Unit III.

STRATEGY RESOURCE

1. 📄 *Teaching Diverse Learners: Equity and Excellence for All,* from Brown University, provides research and strategies for practice for making content comprehensible. Guidance is provided for eight broad categories for sheltering instruction.

http://www.alliance.brown.edu/tdl/tl-strategies/mc-principles.shtml

Strategy

Providing Context for Instruction

17

As discussed in Unit I of this book, routines in instructional settings provide an overall structure that enables students to know what to expect in the classroom. Having clear routines facilitates the instructional and social ebb and flow of the classroom for all students (ELLs and FEP learners). For ELLs, who are struggling to understand the language of the classroom, these routines provide the comprehensibility necessary to scaffold the development of social and academic language. An integral component of these routines is the explicit use of clearly articulated lesson objectives. Content-area and language objectives should be written on the whiteboard or in another prominent place in the classroom, reviewed with students at the beginning of the lesson, referred to during the lesson, and reviewed again during the lesson wrap-up.

THEORY AND/OR RESEARCH UNDERLYING THE STRATEGY

Clear instructional routines provide broad context for classroom instruction. This context frees ELLs to focus on academic instruction and facilitates the development of social and academic language. Contextualizing lessons with clear objectives for content and language promotes the development academic language (Echevarria et al., 2003). Providing clear learning objectives (content and language) enables all students to understand what they should learn as a result of the lesson—and to notice the gap between what they currently know and what they will know (Stiggins, 2005). Reviewing objectives with students at the end of the lesson enables them to monitor what they have learned—measuring the difference between what they have learned and what they need to learn (Stiggins, 2005).

IMPLEMENTING THE STRATEGY

1. Decide on the content and language objectives* for each lesson, and ensure that these are written in a place that is readily visible to students. (Consider writing content-area objectives in one color and language objectives in another.) Review

the objectives with students at the beginning of the lesson, and then refer to objectives both during the lesson and in the lesson wrap up.

*Content and language objectives are derived from the instructional unit's learning outcomes (described in Unit III).

2. Consider ways to make the planned instructional activities consistent. This consistency enables ELLs to focus their attention on the language of the lesson, rather than on classroom activity. For example, use one color of notebooks for writing activities, another for students' mathematics work, and colored index cards for word analysis tasks. Use graphic organizers to build comprehensibility, and be clear about explicit structures for group work.

3. Organize and label boxes and storage areas for all necessary materials, and make this organizational structure explicit to students. Placing materials in the same places and consistently referring to these by the same names provides context so that ELLs with *Starting* and *Developing* levels of English language proficiency can connect the names of materials to the objects.

4. Place instructional models and examples (realia) in one place so that students know where to look for them.

5. Consider your expectations for homework and classwork, how you will make these expectations explicit, and where you will post visual reminders of these expectations. Keep these posted in the same place, using the same print type and color.

6. Decide on the expected roles for group members and outcomes for group work, make these explicit, use visuals (cards or charts), and check for understanding before moving on.

STRATEGY IN ACTION

Grade 2

A second grade teacher, Mrs. Kleine, begins her vocabulary lesson by calling students to the reading center at the front of her classroom. Mrs. Kleine has worked with her students to establish and maintain clear routines for behavior in the classroom (discussed in Unit I of this book). Students know that they come to the reading center by rows when Mrs. Kleine calls them, that they come quietly, fill available seats, and then wait quietly for all children and Mrs. Kleine to be seated. Once Mrs. Kleine is seated in her chair, the students know to turn their eyes and bodies toward her and give her their full attention.

Mrs. Kleine has also established clear instructional routines, which are evident throughout her lesson. She begins this vocabulary lesson by building on students' prior knowledge and reminding them of the new vocabulary words they learned that week. She calls on individual students to offer one vocabulary word each. She then calls on student volunteers to give meanings for each of these words using their own words. Once Mrs. Kleine has activated student knowledge, she launches into the lesson by telling students the content and language objectives, which she prints on the easel as she speaks: "The content objective for our language arts class is to define and *illustrate* (she underlines illustrate as she speaks and says, 'that means to draw') one vocabulary word we learned this week. Your language objectives are (1) to *discuss* this word with your partner, (2) to *agree* on a definition for the word, and (3) to *write* a sentence for the word."

She tells students that they will meet the objectives in pairs and then explains the roles of each pair member: "Alisa will scribe, and Ana will draw, but first they must collaborate to decide on the definition of the word, come up with an original sentence for the word, and create an illustration for this sentence. They can help each other with spelling and word choice." Once Mrs. Kleine is certain that students understand the objectives, she provides a different word to each pair of students. Students are told that they will have until 9:00 to complete the activity (25 minutes).

Students meet in pairs to complete the learning task; ELLs are paired with FEP learners, and each student knows the expected outcome of the activity and his or her role in this outcome. All students are engaged. At the end of the lesson, Mrs. Kleine brings students back to the center at the front of the room. Again, they come in an organized fashion. Mrs. Kleine asks students to hold up their illustrations and sentences, and she asks for volunteers to share their work. After several students share their word, sentence, and drawing, Mrs. Kleine reviews each objective with the students: "Boys and girls, let's review the objectives." Again, Mrs. Kleine reads through each objective and asks, "Did we meet this objective?" She waits while students respond, and then she checks for understanding.

Grade 4

Ms. Juliana Chou, a fourth grade teacher, posts a daily agenda on the right-hand side of her whiteboard, where it does not interfere with other instructional uses of the whiteboard. Each morning, she reviews the agenda, and she calls students' attention to it throughout the day as they transition from one lesson to the next. Ms. Chou contextualizes each lesson by connecting it to previous lessons or materials learned. Reviewing the agenda and making connections to the previous day's learning take only a few minutes at the beginning of each lesson, and they provide context for ELLs and FEP learners.

On this day, Ms. Chou's schedule looks like this.

Daily Agenda, Tuesday, December 2

8:20	Scrambled sentences
8:30	Morning meeting (greeting in different languages)
8:45	Literacy block—See literacy wall
10:00	Recess
10:15	Large group literacy lesson
11:15	Mathematics lesson with Ms. Chou and teams
12:15	Lunch
1:00	Transition: Independent reading
1:15–1:50	Social Studies: Maps—latitude and longitude (packet)
1:55–2:45	Science experiment sheets—team work and meetings with Mrs. Chou

Anchor: If you finish your work, read your book or complete a card from the challenge box.

Ms. Chou's carefully planned schedule provides a clear routine for transitioning between lessons and for introducing new lessons. Ms. Chou points to each new content area as she explains that it is time to transition to another subject, and she thus provides broad context for the lesson to be learned. Once Ms. Chou ensures that students have transitioned, she is ready to begin using the same predictable lesson sequence:

1. Review what was learned the previous day by asking students to report out, checking that students understand the context for the lesson—where it fits into the instruction.

2. Introduce the content-area and language objectives for the lesson, which are written on the flip chart—one color for content, one for language.

3. Teach the lesson using visuals, graphics, and pause-think-pair activities to check understanding. (Mrs. Chou never teaches longer than 10 minutes without using a one-minute pause-think-pair to allow students to check their understanding.)

4. Provide practice (with some opportunities for small groups or pairs so that students can practice language as well as content).

5. Assess understanding and ability to apply concepts or skills.

6. Wrap up the lesson by reviewing objectives to help students match what they have learned with what they should have learned—the lesson objectives.

REFLECTIONS

1. How do Mrs. Kleine and Mrs. Chou ensure context-rich instructional settings? How will these settings benefit ELLs at each proficiency level?

2. Specifically, how might you provide a context-rich instructional setting for your content area and grade level?

Connecting to and Expanding on ELLs' Background Knowledge

Strategy 18

Connecting to and expanding on the background knowledge that ELLs bring to the classroom is another way to contextualize instruction and to prepare all students for meaningful learning. In earlier grades, teachers tend to build background knowledge by providing real-world multisensory experiences, including field trips, hands-on learning, realia, and visuals. These multisensory experiences, followed by discussion, looking at pictures, and reading about similar experiences help to build background knowledge (Marzano, 2004).

Research tells us that students from majority middle-class homes frequently have background experiences that are well matched to classroom learning (Marzano, 2004). ELLs come from a variety of cultures and backgrounds. Due to their parents' inability to speak English, a disproportionate number of ELLs live in poverty. Likely, whether the ELLs in your classroom were born and raised in the United States or have just arrived from other countries, the background knowledge and **schemata** they bring to the classroom are different from those of middle-class majority students. This is particularly true for ELLs who have not been able to access curriculum because of language barriers or ELLs who have limited education. ELLs who are educated in other countries may have different background knowledge as well (e.g., limited knowledge of U.S. history).

As teachers, we know that all students come to the classroom with rich funds of knowledge (González, Moll, & Amanti, 2005). We also know that for students to be academically successful in U.S. schools, they must develop background knowledge required in U.S. classrooms and then build on this knowledge. It is much easier for students to learn new concepts and skills when they can integrate these new experiences with their background knowledge (Marzano, 2004).

> **Schemata:** the plural of schema, it refers to the elaborate and meaningful mental network that organizes and stores mental representations of concepts (Anderson, 1977).

THEORY AND/OR RESEARCH UNDERLYING THE STRATEGY

The importance of activating (or building) background knowledge is based on schema theory (Anderson, 1977). Our schemata (mental representations of concepts) help us to make sense of new content, vocabulary, and language structures. As Marzano (2004) wrote: "What students *already know* about the content is one of the strongest indicators of how well they will learn new information relative to the content" (p. 1). Our ability to store new information is directly related to the information we already have stored—the schemata we have developed (Marzano, 2004). Teachers may have to build the schemata of ELLs and other students prior to teaching so that they will have the background knowledge necessary to understand new concepts. Background knowledge can be developed through authentic or vicarious experiences and discussions (Marzano, 2004).

IMPLEMENTING THE STRATEGY

1. When introducing a new concept, do not assume that ELLs have the necessary background knowledge; FEP learners in the class may not have this knowledge either.

2. Although firsthand experiences that involve multiple senses, such as field trips, may be the richest way to build background knowledge, limited resources in terms of time and money make it impossible to build all background knowledge in this way. Virtual experiences, such as watching and discussing videos, storytelling, reading, enacting, and role playing, also build background knowledge.

3. Once you introduce a topic (with visuals, realia, and primary language support if available), use a group KWL to determine the background knowledge that ELLs bring to the lesson.

4. If there are ELLs who speak the same language, place them together in groups to complete the KWL. The goal here is not to build English language proficiency, but rather to uncover prior content-area knowledge.

5. Complete the KWL in the large group. Each student's experiences will serve to scaffold background knowledge for other students.

6. Develop background knowledge through actual field trips, videos, images, texts, and rich small group discussions that will enable ELLs and other students to process this knowledge, thus deepening their schemata. For example, if you will teach about biodiversity in shoreline habitats, and students have never been to the shore, it will be necessary to either take the students to the shore or to show video of at least one shoreline and its biodiversity.

7. If you have instructional materials in the primary language of an ELL with proficiency levels of *Developing* or below, provide this material to the ELL.

STRATEGY IN ACTION

Grade 7: Science

Mr. Parker is teaching students about wildlife populations, ecosystems, and the diversity and adaptability of organisms. He also wants to teach his ELL and FEP learners about engaging in scientific inquiry. Mr. Parker usually begins his class with a story about an animal that he saw on the way to school that day. He uses a combination of pictures he has downloaded from the Internet that he displays using his LCD projector. He also uses gestures and paraphrasing to make the stories comprehensible to students. Mr. Parker uses a variety of picture books as well as other supplemental materials to build his students' background knowledge about animals, their habitats, and behaviors. To provide students with firsthand experience about wildlife habitats and wildlife monitoring, he has registered his class for a monitoring project called *RoadKill* (http://roadkill.edutel.com/rkprotocol.html). As part of the *RoadKill* project, students and teachers throughout the United States monitor road kill found in their communities and enter these data into a national database. Monitoring road kill helps students to understand the population of wild animals in their communities, animal habitat, and the conflict between humans and nature as humans build and use roads within wildlife corridors. Mr. Parker's students develop background knowledge by "doing" science.

Grade 5: Social Studies

Mrs. Alencastro is teaching social studies to her class of fifth graders, comprised of 15 FEP learners and five ELLs with English proficiency levels ranging from *Developing* to *Transitioning*. Mrs. Alencastro is teaching about the American Revolution and has just begun a unit in which she will teach about the multiple perspectives held by the colonists. To help students make connections, Ms. Alencastro taps into their knowledge of multiple perspectives. She knows that most of the boys and girls in her class spend recess time in gender-similar groups, so for a 10-minute lead-in activity, she pairs boys with girls to compare their accounts of recess. Each pair completes a similarities and differences graphic organizer. As Mrs. Alencastro has predicted, the pairs do not have the same accounts about recess. She uses students' experiences to introduce the word *perspectives* and explains that they will be considering multiple perspectives in this history lesson. She writes content and language objectives on the board and reviews them with students.

Student Language Objectives:

1. Work with your partner to discuss similarities and differences in perspectives.

2. Read about perspectives with your partner.

3. Complete the graphic organizer with your partner.

Building on students' background knowledge, Mrs. Alencastro conducts a KWL about the perspectives of the colonists. She first allows students to share their ideas in pairs and then has students report to the larger group. She records their responses. She tells them that they will try to understand the different perspectives of some everyday people who might have lived during prerevolutionary times.

With the large group, Mrs. Alencastro introduces young fictional adults from the time leading up to the American Revolution. She provides her students with a description of each character's economic status, gender, and so on. Mrs. Alencastro and students engage in a discussion of the likely perspectives of each character. Once they have discussed several characters and several perspectives, Mrs. Alencastro asks each student to work with her or his partner. She provides each student in each pair with a character and a description of the character's gender, economic status, and family background. She tries to ensure that, within each pair, two perspectives on the events leading up to the American Revolution will be presented. Mrs. Alencastro allows students time to use the materials she has compiled for this lesson, which include excerpts from websites she has vetted, children's books, picture books, and audio books. After students read excerpts from their reading materials, they complete a graphic organizer showing similarities and differences. (Carol Hurst's children's literature site has recommendations for children's literature at various reading levels that can be used in U.S. history. It can be accessed at http://www.carolhurst.com/index.html.)

Ms. Chou's Fourth Grade Social Studies Class

Ms. Chou always begins the class with a review of the previous day's lesson objectives. In this way, Ms. Chou activates students' knowledge and explicitly links the previous day's lesson to the present day's lesson, providing context for new content. Today, she begins her social studies lesson by reviewing map skills. She reminds students that they learned that using lines of latitude enables them to locate their state and city on a map. As she talks, she writes the word *latitude* on the whiteboard, pronouncing it clearly. She provides a point of latitude and asks students to work in pairs to identify places on their maps that are on that line of latitude. After briefly checking for understanding, she asks students to complete another example individually. Again, she checks for understanding. Ms. Chou observes that all students except Angela, a FEP learner, and Xuan, an ELL with *Developing* proficiency who speaks Mandarin as a first language, have found their locations correctly. This formative assessment tells Ms. Chou that nearly all her students are ready to move forward, and it prompts her to meet briefly with Angela and Xuan to explain that she will work with them as a small group once she has presented the lesson. She moves on to introduce the day's lesson on latitude. She writes the lesson objectives for the day on the board, saying them aloud as she writes. As always, Ms. Chou writes the content-area objective in blue and the language objective in red.

Mr. Clark's Eighth Grade Science

Mr. Clark begins his unit on space science by building background knowledge with a video, which he introduces with visuals and presents in 10-minute segments. Every 10 minutes, Mr. Clark stops the video and has students work in a three-minute pause-think-share where they share one thing they have learned or noticed, one question they have, and one thing they want to know more about. Both the visuals and the time to pause-think-share increase the comprehensibility of this experience and build background knowledge. His students are grouped heterogeneously with regard to English language proficiency so that they can support one another.

REFLECTIONS

1. How does each teacher check for and build on background knowledge?

2. Think about an instructional unit that you will teach. How will you gauge the background knowledge of the ELLs and other students in your classroom, and how will you build background knowledge?

Adjusting Speech and Using Realia, Video, and Visuals to Build Comprehensibility

Strategy 19

As teachers, we know that students have to understand instruction to learn content. ELLs also must understand the language of instruction in order to develop academic language proficiency. There are several ways to make language more understandable or comprehensible to ELLs and FEP learners in the regular classroom. Strategy 19 considers three areas for building comprehensibility: voice, visuals, and time for processing.

Teachers should be aware of the pace and tempo of their speech and should speak clearly and slowly, but not unnaturally so. It is important to use the academic vocabulary that ELLs will have to master, such as the words *analyze, hypothesize,* or *critique,* and it is equally important to make this vocabulary comprehensible by paraphrasing so that ELLs have access to these academic words. For example, "Today we are going to hypothesize; we are going to guess based on what we know. . . ." Speech is also more understandable when it is accompanied by visuals of some sort.

Realia, video, photos, graphics, and graphic organizers can be useful in improving the comprehensibility of presentations. They provide critical scaffolds for ELLs, who are learning the language while they are learning the content. Words also serve as visuals that make speech and presentations more comprehensible. ELLs benefit when teachers briefly present new vocabulary prior to instruction, write the vocabulary on the whiteboard, and refer to this visual representation of words as they use them in their speech.

ELLs and other students need time to process academic speech and the content of the lecture. Teacher-talk should be limited to 10-minute intervals with time for quick think-pair-share activities to allow ELLs and FEP this to process content.

THEORY AND/OR RESEARCH UNDERLYING THE STRATEGY

Primary speakers of a language speak rather quickly. The speech of English speakers is sprinkled with reductions, such as "didja," "couldja," and "wouldja," with idioms, such as "to pitch in," "a steal," "ahead of time," and "Achilles heel," and with ellipses, such as "He is taller than I" (am tall) and "That is heavier . . ." (than this is heavy). FEP learners are able to hear the white spaces between the words, easily understand idioms, and fill in any words that are missing. In addition, they use their background knowledge of English to fill in missing sounds. ELLs are less likely to be able to process spoken English efficiently. They must have the necessary vocabulary to understand spoken language; researchers suggest that speakers must understand 90% to 95% of the vocabulary to access meaning while listening (Nation & Waring, 1998). They must also process the sounds or the phonology of English and process English syntax and grammar. Academic listening is exhausting for ELLs at all levels, and particularly for ELLs who lack background knowledge about the topic and have levels of English language proficiency below *Developing*.

IMPLEMENTING THE STRATEGY

Preparing for the Lecture

1. Begin planning early so that you have time to collect appropriate materials.

2. Review the most important concepts for the lesson, and think, "Which concepts will be most difficult for students to understand?"

3. Review the language that students must understand to access the lesson. Determine which words might be difficult for ELLs think, "What visuals can I use to make these key words understandable?"

4. Keep in mind that the nearer to the real thing the better. Plan a field trip or bring in an object or model if possible.

5. Review the material that you will present verbally and look for vocabulary that may be challenging. Do not limit this to terms that all students must know. The academic word list (AWL) (Coxhead, 2000) provides one list of words appropriate for middle and secondary school that are common across content areas and therefore words that students should know. The Academic Word List is available at http://www.uefap.com/vocab/select/awl.htm. (This is provided as a link in the Resource Section of Unit V.)

6. Make lists of the words that will can quickly review with students prior to the lesson.

7. Define the words in student-friendly language, using only one definition. Use the definition that fits the way the word will be used in the lecture. (Writing student-friendly definitions is more difficult than it seems; prepare these prior to the lesson.)

8. Locate or create visuals that will make the lecture more comprehensible; for example, maps, photos, graphic organizers, diagrams, hands-on material, or models. The Internet is a particularly good source of visuals and virtual experiences, such as the *National Library of Virtual Manipulatives*. Another excellent source is picture books.

9. Prepare materials so that they are readily accessible as you lecture. The best materials are of little value if you cannot find them!

10. Plan for logical stops within the lecture or lesson, not to exceed 10-minute intervals, so that students can process what they have learned and formulate questions they may have.

During the Lecture

1. If a field trip has been part of the experience, build on that at the beginning of the lesson. Discussing the field trip experience will help to store this experience in permanent memory, building rich background knowledge.

2. *Briefly* introduce new words. The goal in this lesson is to make language comprehensible, not to provide rich vocabulary instruction.

3. Write each word on the board or overhead, accompanied by the student-friendly definition you developed. Keep these visible, and refer to them throughout the lesson.

4. Be aware of your enunciation and tempo as you speak.

5. Use visuals as appropriate. Depending on the content, students may manipulate or examine models in small groups.

6. Supply students with graphic organizers and project the same graphic organizer using the overhead projector. Complete the graphic organizer with students as you speak.

7. Check for understanding as you speak—*thumbs-up or thumbs-down* or *red card, green card* works well as a formative assessment of student understanding and of your instruction. If you have access to electronic clickers, this is an excellent way to use them. Students can show the gesture *thumbs-up* or *thumbs-down* in response to your prompt (asking them if they understand). Alternatively, you can ask students to show you thumbs-down whenever they are confused. With *red card, green card,* students have both cards at their desks and use them similarly to *thumbs-up* or *thumbs-down.*

8. Stop at least every 10 minutes to provide students with time for a two-minute debriefing with a partner. During this time, the partially completed graphic organizer provides additional context for ELLs.

STRATEGY IN ACTION

Grade 3: Science

Mrs. Marcia Bourque teaches third grade in a regular education classroom. Much of her science class is dedicated to engaging students in inquiry and hands-on exploration, which is consistent with her district's science program and is a good source of comprehensible input for ELLs. There are four ELLs in this classroom: three ELLs who speak Spanish as a primary language and who have proficiency levels of *Developing* and above, and one primary speaker of Arabic, who has an *Emerging* level of English language proficiency. Mrs. Bourque is beginning a unit on changing physical properties, which is part of the district's science curriculum. She has decided that she will review the three stages of matter; students who were in the district the previous year, including one ELL with a *Transitioning* level of proficiency, were taught the three stages as part of the regular second grade science curriculum. Mrs. Bourque intends to check everyone's background knowledge with an informal KWL. She is, however, most concerned about Adam, who speaks Arabic; he was not in U.S. schools the previous year, and his English is quite limited.

Mrs. Bourque prepared for this lesson by bringing a variety of objects, including large plastic tubs for catching liquids that will be poured; several different shaped containers; clear juice; a ½ pint of milk; two jugs of water, one clear and another colored with red food

Graphic organizers are a way of visually arranging concepts and content.

- Cause-effect diagram: Used to show the relationship between cause and effect
- Concept map: Shows multiple traits related to a concept or a word
- Cycle diagram: Illustrates how events are related to one another cyclically
- Flow chart: Shows events with possible multiple outcomes at various decision points
- KWL: Used to activate background knowledge, stimulate inquiry, and record and measure learning
- T-chart: Used to identify two facets of a topic, such as fact and opinion, pros and cons, etc.

Source: From *Teaching English Language Learners: Content and Language in Middle and Secondary Mainstream Classrooms* (p. 179), by M. Colombo and D. Furbush, 2009, Thousand Oaks, CA: Sage.

coloring; and enough balloons for each pair of students. She has set up stations in the room.

Mrs. Bourque also reviewed key vocabulary with the ESL teacher, Ms. Willis, who assured her that *solid, liquid,* and *gas* will be very comprehensible to the Spanish-speaking ELLs because the words are cognates. Mrs. Bourque had intended to discuss the vocabulary with Mr. Ali, the Arabic tutor who provided three hours of classroom services for Adam. Normally, Mr. Ali would have a copy of Mrs. Bourque's graphic organizer, and she would supply the Arabic translation of the key word next to the English word. Unfortunately, Mr. Ali has been out sick this week.

Mrs. Bourque will teach changing states of matter by having students observe these stages in water, which she believes will enable her to show Adam the different states of matter. She shares this idea with Ms. Willis, who agrees that the demonstration will make the content comprehensible.

Mrs. Bourque begins the lesson by activating student knowledge of three states of matter: solids, liquids, and gasses. She writes the words on the board and tells students that they will write definitions together, but first they will engage in a KWL to find out what they remember. Mrs. Bourque knows that the affective filters of her ELLs are lessened when they have the opportunity to try out their language in a small group, so she provides three minutes for students to work in pairs and groups of three to determine what they know about each stage of matter. Mrs. Bourque then has the students come back together in a large group and report out as she writes their responses on a KWL sheet. A few students demonstrate a depth of understanding, most students remember the concept to some degree, and several students, including Adam, appear very confused.

She provides students with a **graphic organizer** (Figure 19.1). They review the first three statements in a large group. She then pairs students intentionally, ensuring that Adam is with Billy, an FEP learner who works well with other students and who demonstrated his understanding of the stages of matter. The student pairs use the graphic organizer to write as many examples as they can for each stage. Each student's job is to ensure that the other student understands.

Student Language Objectives:

1. Tell your partner as many examples of stages of matter as you can.

2. Listen carefully to your partner.

3. Record the examples that you and your partner have listed.

Figure 19.1 Graphic Organizer

Properties of Matter
1. All matter takes up space.
2. All matter has mass.
3. Properties are constantly changing.

Solid	Liquid	Gas

Mrs. Bourque provides students with 15 minutes and then has them come back together as a large group. She checks understanding using *red and green* cards. (Students display the green card to indicate understanding and the red card to indicate confusion.)

Mrs. Bourque tells students that they will transition to the day's lesson. They will begin by learning and practicing the vocabulary words, and will complete the lesson the following day with an experiment. She introduces the key vocabulary: *freezing, melting, boiling point, demonstrate, observe, thermometer*. Students write these and the student-friendly definitions in their science notebooks.

Grade 7: Science

Mr. Paul Smith is teaching a unit that includes lessons on erosion. He is in an inner-city environment, and thus, it is difficult to provide a firsthand example via a field trip. He has constructed a landforms model in a large plastic tub. Approximately half of his landform is covered with sod, and the other half is without. He allows some students to use a watering can to simulate heavy rainfall, while other students observe the landform for changes. He follows up with videos he has found on YouTube that show erosion in various areas. He then assigns reading and group discussion work. Students have ongoing access to a YouTube video he has downloaded, and he has photos of landforms in various stages of erosion. He uses a graphic organizer to facilitate students' reading and understanding.

Student Language Objectives

1. Read your handout about erosion for understanding. Ask your partner for clarification if you do not understand something.

2. Explain erosion to your partner.

Grade 6: Math

Ms. Fournier teaches sixth grade math. According to Ms. Fournier, equations often confuse both ELLs and FEP learners. To improve comprehensibility of content for all students and to ensure that ELLs have access to concepts apart from language, Ms. Fournier uses a balance scale to demonstrate solving equations, and she then provides scales to pairs of students so they can practice solving equations.

REFLECTIONS

1. Review the planning process of Mrs. Willis and Mrs. Bourque. Why was their planning so critical to the success of their lesson?

2. Think about a unit that you teach. What materials would help to make the unit content comprehensible to ELLs at proficiency levels *Starting* through *Transitioning?* How would you begin to find these materials? Revisit Unit I. Why is it important to develop a system for collecting and storing materials? What system do you think might work for you? (See proficiency levels in tables 4 and III.4.)

Strategy

20

Finding and Creating Comprehensible Materials

Regardless of grade level, every student needs access to text that is comprehensible. Text structures that are too difficult or that have too many words that ELLs do not understand are unusable for young students who are learning to read and inaccessible for older students who are reading to learn. The purposes of Strategy 20 are to help you to find text that students can read and to make existing text more accessible with audio recordings, simplifications, and glossing.

Theory and/or Research Underlying the Strategy

In early grades, as students begin to make sense of text and to develop an understanding of sound-symbol relationships, they do so with text that includes language that is congruent with their oral proficiency. As a simple example, an ELL cannot match the letter **c** to the sound /k/ when presented with a picture of a cat if the word *cat* is not in the ELL's **mental lexicon**.

Mental lexicon: the vocabulary knowledge we carry in our minds.

The ELL may know the word for *cat* in Spanish (gato), and therefore, he or she knows the concept of the word *cat*. The letter **c** and the sound /k/ are confusing when the ELL is thinking *gato*.

This principle holds true for older readers as well. ELLs must know between 95% and 98% of the words in a text in order to learn new words from reading the text. They must know at least 90% to 95% of the words in the text to even comprehend; what they are reading when ELLs are trying to read text in which more than 10% of the words are unknown, they are reading at a frustration level.

Implementing the Strategy

1. Review the English language proficiency levels of ELLs in your classroom.

2. Review the performance indicators for reading and writing in tables VII.4 and VII.5 in Unit VII of this book. ELLs will need text that is aligned as closely as possible with these performance indicators.

3. When teaching ELLs to read, including teaching symbol-sound relationships, make sure to use words that are in ELLs' mental lexicon—words they know.

4. Consider using picture books that are accurate and make complex content accessible. Picture books are often used in lower grades, but they frequently remain an untapped resource for the middle grades. If you use picture books, make them available as reference sources for all students—ELLs should not be the only students in the classroom who use the picture books. Carol Hurst's children's literature site provides excellent suggestions for using children's books in the content areas. This and other user-friendly sites are included in the Strategy Resources section.

5. Review content-area textbooks, which are typically very dense. Select specific passages that contain information that ELLs must know to participate in instruction. Copy the pages, highlight the words, and gloss in margins. Help ELLs access text structure: If the textbook lists five ideas, write *five ideas* in the margin and then number each idea within the text. (If you cannot make copies or mark texts, consider using sticky notes for this purpose.)

6. Some textbooks contain a chapter lead-in with the main ideas of the chapter listed. Unpack the main idea and rewrite this for ELLs. For example, in a chapter labeled the "War of 1812," one textbook features a callout box with the main idea. While this callout box appears to be useful for ELLs, the language of the main idea is dense and the structure is likely to be confusing. Making the structure of the sentence more linear makes it longer, but it also improves its comprehensibility. See Figure 20.1.

7. Consider **leveled books** to make content comprehensible.

8. Use the Internet to find images, simplified text, and free translation software. While software-generated translations are frequently imperfect, translations may help to make concepts comprehensible to middle and upper grade ELLs who can read in their own languages and have proficiency levels from *Starting* to *Emerging*—ELLs will still need to learn the English for concepts.

9. Make multiple reading resources available to all students in the classroom.

10. Keep student-generated summaries of text as reading materials for the classroom.

11. Maintain a listening center; audio record or have students audio record key portions of text. Make these available to all students as part of the classroom library.

> *Leveled books* are books that are written at different reading levels, enabling teachers to match the level of a book to the reading level of the student.

Strategy in Action

Mr. Collins unpacks his eighth grade history text for ELLs and many of the FEP learners in his history course. Figure 20.1 demonstrates how he accomplishes this.

For numbers 1 through 4, page numbers could be included to link each number to the expanded discussion and to images.

Figure 20.1   Unpacking Complex Text Structures

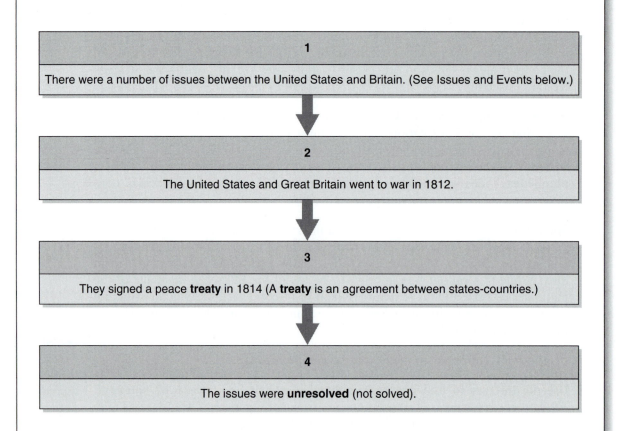

"The United States and Britain went to war in 1812 over a number of issues that remained unresolved by the peace treaty they signed two years later" (Ritchie, 2001, p. 124).

1

There were a number of issues between the United States and Britain. (See Issues and Events below.)

2

The United States and Great Britain went to war in 1812.

3

They signed a peace **treaty** in 1814 (A **treaty** is an agreement between states-countries.)

4

The issues were **unresolved** (not solved).

Issues and Events

1. There was a war between the British and the French.
2. The United States provided supplies to the British and to the French.
3. The British and the French tried to stop the United States from providing supplies to the other side.
4. They violated (went against) the United States' freedom to use the seas and oceans.
5. British soldiers left British ships because the United States paid them more and treated them better.
6. The British went on to U.S. ships to take their men back.
7. The United States thought its rights were violated (not respected).
8. In 1807, the United States passed a law that forbade (did not allow) U.S. ships to go to foreign ports (land where ships go).
9. A U.S. ship attacked a British ship.
10. The United States declared war on great Britain.

REFLECTION

- Consider one unit that you teach and the reading materials you generally use for that unit. How might you make the reading for this unit more comprehensible to ELLs at each proficiency level?

STRATEGY RESOURCES

1. 📄 Carol Hurst's site for using children's books in the content areas contains recommendations for students of all ages.

   http://www.carolhurst.com/index.html

2. 📄 Database to search for leveled books by Books First, a nonprofit group

   http://www.leveler.booksfirst.org/

3. 📄 Waring's reading levels

   http://www.robwaring.org/er/ER_info/checking_learners_level.htm

4. 📄 Leveled readers are available in most content areas from a variety of publishers. A search for leveled readers and specific content areas will yield several publishers in each content area. I have not reviewed these specifically and therefore cannot recommend a specific series.

5. 📄 Lists of picture books that can be used for teaching all content areas and grade levels by content area

   http://www.lebanon.k12.mo.us/profdev/picturethis_20050406.pdf

6. 📄 The *Teach With Picture Book* blog site provides useful recommendations for using storybooks for teaching content-area topics.

   http://teachwithpicturebooks.blogspot.com/

7. 📄 Susan Hall has published a series of user-friendly books to help educators teach literacy devices using picture storybooks, including *Using Picture Storybooks to Teach Literacy Devices: Recommended Books for Children and Young Adults, Volume 2, Volume 3,* and *Volume 4* (publisher: Libraries Unlimited).

UNIT V

Strategies for Developing Vocabulary

There are so many words English language learners need to learn that I can't teach all of them. How do I decide which words to teach, and when do I find the time to teach them?

—Grade 5 Teacher

The number of words that a student knows matters! Vocabulary size is related to comprehension and conceptual understanding, and it is a predictor of reading ability and overall academic achievement (Stahl & Nagy, 2006). Children who speak English as a first language enter kindergarten with a vocabulary of 3,000 to 5,000 English words, and they add approximately 2,000 to 3,000 additional words per year (Stahl & Nagy, 2006). In contrast, English language learners (ELLs) enter schools knowing far fewer words in English, and they must develop English vocabulary as they learn content-area concepts. The limited English vocabularies of ELLs interfere with their ability to read, access content-area text, and learn content (Francis, Rivera, Lesaux, Kieffer, & Rivera, 2006).

One of the greatest challenges for ELLs (and other students who enter school with underdeveloped English vocabularies) is the sheer number of words they must master in order to access content and demonstrate content-area understanding. In this regard, ELLs are constantly trying to catch up with their FEP peers.

The relationship between vocabulary and reading is a circular one. Growth in vocabulary is connected to extensive reading, and high-level vocabularies make reading more comprehensible and enjoyable to students. Thus, students who enter school with large vocabularies are likely to comprehend more when they read, enjoy reading more, read widely, and further develop their vocabularies through reading. On the other hand, students who enter schools with limited vocabularies are more likely to struggle to comprehend written text, read poorly, and read less, thus limiting opportunities for vocabulary development.

Similar to FEP learners, when ELLs repeatedly encounter the same academic vocabulary and phrases in texts, they will likely acquire these words and structures (Schmitt, 2008). To acquire vocabulary through reading, however, ELLs (and FEP learners) must know approximately 98% of running words in the text (Nation, 2001, 2008). High-interest, leveled readers (discussed in Unit IV and VII) help ELLs to develop vocabulary, yet they do not contain many of the academic words that ELLs will need to know. Therefore, it is highly unlikely that reading alone will result in grade-level academic vocabulary growth for ELLs.

FEP learners who cannot yet read at grade level have been shown to learn vocabulary through read-alouds at the same rate as capable readers learn vocabulary through written text (Stahl, Richeck, & Vandivier, 1991). ELLs, too, are likely to acquire vocabulary through read-alouds; however, they must know at least 90% to 95% of the words they hear in order to learn new words from oral input. And ELLs are not always capable of hearing the white spaces between the words, sometimes making even known words unintelligible. The opportunity to learn from oral text is increased when visuals are used to make the text more comprehensible.

Explicit and effective vocabulary instruction is crucial for school success for ELLs and other students (Beck & McKeown, 2007; Marzano, 2004). Yet ineffective traditional methods for teaching vocabulary, such as looking up words in dictionaries, writing words multiple times, and using words in sentences prior to elaborate instruction, have resulted in vocabulary instruction being overlooked in many classrooms (Biemiller, 2000; Carlo, August, & Snow, 2005).

Effective instruction is key! Vocabulary can be effectively taught by presenting each word in student-friendly language, enabling students to make connections between the new word and their world knowledge, and providing meaningful activities that require students to use the word in authentic conversation.

Because there are so many words to teach and there is not time to provide rich instruction for all of these, a multifaceted approach to vocabulary development is warranted. One three-pronged approach includes (1) introducing key words prior to instruction, (2) providing rich instruction for words that represent concepts and for words that build the precision of vocabulary, and (3) implementing review activities that require students to think about words and their meanings (Beck, McKeown, & Kucan, 2002; Graves, 2010).

The focus of Unit V is the use of classroom strategies to build academic vocabulary for ELLs. The unit begins with a description of the process of vocabulary learning and then provides six instructional strategies for developing vocabulary, beginning with Strategy 21: Developing Survival Language for *Starting* and *Emerging* Proficiency, Strategy 22: Selecting Academic Vocabulary for Instruction, Strategy 23: Providing Robust Vocabulary Instruction for Tier 2 Words, Strategy 24: Word Analysis: Building Vocabulary With Word Parts (Tiers 1, 2, 3), Strategy 25: Semantic Mapping (Works Well for Tier 3 Words), Strategy 26: Using Quick Prereading and Review Strategies, and Strategy 27: Interactive Word Walls. Each strategy in this unit is accompanied by a *Strategy in Action* section and *Reflections* exercises.

WHAT YOU WILL LEARN

Unit V provides theory, research, vignettes, and strategies to help you do the following:

1. Understand the importance of building academic vocabulary in all content areas.

2. Develop strategies to select vocabulary for rich instruction.

3. Develop multiple strategies for building vocabulary for ELLs at different proficiency levels.

4. Develop strategies for helping ELLs to become independent vocabulary learners.

WHAT IT MEANS TO KNOW A WORD

Students who already have a fairly extensive English vocabulary may quickly gain a sense of a word when they encounter it while reading or listening, but a full understanding of a word's meaning and the ability to use a word with precision requires multiple and varied encounters with the word (Beck et al., 2002; Stahl & Nagy, 2006). Knowing a word is a multifaceted process that consists of knowing the words used with it (collocations), the word's multiple meanings (polysemy), the word's connotations, and the appropriateness of the word's use (Nation, 2001, 2008). Knowledge of a word can be measured on a continuum from no knowledge to a rich and decontextualized knowledge, as shown in Table V.1.

Table V.1	Knowing a Word			
No Knowledge	*General Sense of the Word*	*Context-Bound Knowledge*	*Knowledge of, but Inability to Readily Use the Word in Communication*	*Rich, Decontextualized Knowledge of the Word*
"I have no idea what this word means."	"I think *ignite* has something to do with starting a fire."	"I know *ignite* relates to the Bunsen burner in science, but I don't know what it means when people use it outside of science class."	"I think ignite means to get it going" when 'to ignite the imagination' is encountered in text."	"The movie ignited my interest in world history."

Source: Adapted from *Bringing Words to Life: Robust Vocabulary Instruction* (p. 10), by I. S. Beck, M. G. McKeown, and L. Kucan, 2002, New York: Guilford Press.

LEARNING WORDS

To learn any new word, the learner must notice and attend to the word, have multiple and intermittent opportunities to retrieve the word (generally thought to be about 12), and then have the opportunity to use the word creatively and generatively (Beck et al., 2002; Nation, 2001; Stahl & Nagy, 2006). This is illustrated in the following example of Maritza, a seventh grade ELL with *Expanding* English language proficiency.

While reading, Maritza encounters the word *parallel*. She notices that this is a word she does not know and attends to this word by recognizing that she does not know its meaning. She may look back to the beginning of the sentence or complete the sentence in an attempt to uncover the meaning of the word. Eventually, she determines the meaning of the word, either independently or with the help of a teacher or peer. During the next few weeks, she encounters the word several more times while reading and while listening to her teacher's instruction. These repetitions provide her with multiple opportunities to retrieve the word. Each time Maritza retrieves the word, the context is slightly different (e.g., parallel thoughts, structures, lines, bars, etc.), and each of these retrievals is likely to deepen Maritza's knowledge of the word. Ongoing opportunities to use the word creatively in focused academic discussions and in writing will further expose Maritza to multiple meanings of the word (Beck et al., 2002), which is likely to further increase her knowledge of this word (Nation, 2001).

Maritza is an example of an ELL who has background knowledge of the concepts underlying the word *parallel*. ELLs who have interrupted or limited schooling in their first languages will need to learn the concepts that underlie many new words as well as the words themselves. Unlike Maritza, ELLs who cannot yet read in English will not encounter academic words in their reading, which makes direct classroom instruction of vocabulary even more critical.

The strategies presented in Unit V are aligned with TESOL standards for teachers (Table V.2) and TESOL Standards for Students (vocabulary) for proficiency levels from *Starting* (Level 1) to *Bridging* (Level 5). Table V.3 illustrates performance indicators for each standard at each proficiency level (TESOL, 2006). The performance indicators are purposefully generic, and you are encouraged to apply these as appropriate for social and academic communication at the grade level you teach.

Table V.2	TESOL Standards for Teachers

Domain 1: Language

1.a.2. Apply knowledge of phonology (the sound system), morphology (the structure of words), syntax (phrase and sentence structure), semantics (word/sentence meaning), and pragmatics (the effect of context on language) to help ELLs develop oral, reading, and writing skills (including mechanics) in English. (p. 29)

1.a.4. Demonstrate proficiency in English and serve as a good language model for ELLs. (p. 31)

1.b.5. Understand and apply knowledge of the role of individual learner variables in the process of learning English. (p. 37)

Source: TESOL Teacher Standards Tables: TESOL (2010). *TESOL/NCATE Standards for the Recognition of Initial TESOL Programs in P–12 ESL Teacher Education*, Alexandria, VA: TESOL.

| Table V.3 | Vocabulary Performance Indicators (Based on TESOL) |

Standard 1: ELLs use vocabulary to communicate for social and instructional purposes.

Level 1—Starting: Objects, photos, drawings, and gestures are necessary to make everyday words comprehensible. Once ELLs feel comfortable, they begin by speaking simple words and mix these with gestures to convey meaning. They follow one-step directions, respond to routine social communication (greetings, goodbyes, introductions, etc.), and use short and formulaic phrases and sentences to communicate needs.

Level 2—Emerging: Although visuals and gestures remain important, ELLs understand simple and often repeated words and phrases. They follow directions with multiple steps when these are accompanied by visuals and gestures.

Level 3—Developing: In small group settings, ELLs use vocabulary to tell about daily and social events. They begin to differentiate vocabulary depending on the audience (teachers, peers). They recognize and respond to common idioms and slang (at grade level) used in speech.

Level 4—Expanding: ELLs use vocabulary to elaborate on daily and social events. When reminded by teacher or others, they are able to adjust vocabulary for various audiences and appropriately use idioms and slang to participate in conversations.

Level 5—Bridging: ELLs use appropriate vocabulary in role plays and presentations and when communicating with various audiences in different contexts (both in speech and in writing). They understand and use idioms, slang, nuances, and sarcasm appropriately.

Standards 2–5: ELLs will use vocabulary to communicate across the content areas.

Level 1—Starting: Using visuals and gestures, ELLs identify new grade-level words that have been explicitly taught, practice saying target words with a partner, match pictures with target words, and label maps, graphs, models, and other visuals with content-area words that have been explicitly taught.

Level 2—Emerging: As described in Level 1, with gradually decreasing levels of visual support, ELLs use target words in longer phrases and novel constructions.

Level 3—Developing: ELLs use target words in constructions that are continually more complex and unique, in comparative phrases (as appropriate to words), and to describe events (personal or from classroom stories). They identify affixes in target words, and they can use more than one meaning of targeted words (e.g., riverbank, bank where money is deposited, to bank [save] money, to bank on it [count on it]). They use target words with a growing amount of precision (i.e., exhausted rather than tired, satisfied rather than happy).

Level 4—Expanding: ELLs explain multiple meanings of target words and use specialized words (e.g., multiply, describe, analyze) correctly. They begin to use appropriate transition words (finally, then, therefore, etc.) and targeted vocabulary in sentences, paragraphs, short essays, personal essays, logs, journals, descriptions, and so on; and they edit writing for appropriate word choices.

Level 5—Bridging: ELLs appropriately use vocabulary words in presentations and in written stories, narratives, lab reports, explanations, and research reports.

Source: Adapted from *PreK–12 English Language Proficiency Standards* (pp. 47–97), by TESOL, 2006, Alexandria, VA: Author.

STRATEGY RESOURCE

ReadWriteThink provides general information and lessons for developing vocabulary.

http://www.readwritethink.org

Developing Survival Language for Starting and Emerging Proficiency Levels

Strategy

21

ELLs who are new arrivals and speak little to no English will clearly benefit from placement in bilingual settings where use of their primary languages creates a bridge to their understanding of academic English. However, when there are too few students in a district to offer a bilingual program, newcomers' classes, which often include native language tutors to explain grade-level instruction, can also be beneficial. These special services are particularly important for ELLs who are at *Starting* and *Emerging* proficiency levels and who have gaps in their schooling, including limited literacy in their first language.

At times, ELLs with *Starting* and *Emerging* levels of English proficiency are placed in regular classrooms with little or no support. This placement presents a very difficult situation for ELLs and for the teachers who teach them. When this placement occurs, teachers, paraprofessionals, and other students can help to support ELLs by creating a classroom climate that is accepting and by teaching survival vocabulary.

THEORY AND/OR RESEARCH UNDERLYING THE STRATEGY

Teachers who create a welcoming classroom climate with a focus on language help make ELLs more comfortable, which in turn lowers ELLs' affective filters and makes language acquisition more likely. Affective filters (Krashen, 1982) are discussed in the introduction to this book.

ELLs who have *Starting* or *Emerging* levels of English proficiency are likely to experience a **silent period,** which is perfectly normal (Krashen, 1982, 1985). The length of the silent period depends on the personality and disposition of the ELL, the way in which she or he acquires language, and the quality of the instructional setting; it may extend from a few days to several months. During this period, teachers should maintain a supportive and welcoming environment and should not pressure ELLs to speak.

During the silent period ELLs, will absorb language and benefit from ongoing comprehensible exposure to English. Total Physical Response (TPR) (Asher, 2009) can be used to teach simple verbs and verb phrases such as *open, close, pick up, put down, write, draw, read, listen,* and so on. TPR is somewhat similar to the game *Charades,* in that the teacher or peer models the behavior (standing up, opening a book, closing a

> A **silent period** is a time when ELLs take in language via comprehensible input but do not yet speak.

door) that matches the phrase to be learned. It differs from *Charades* in that there is no guessing; the teacher or student says the phrase (e.g., "I am standing up," "I am opening the book") as he or she models the behavior. ELLs then mimic the behavior (e.g., standing up, sitting down, or opening the door) as they repeat the target phrases. Labels and word cards can be used effectively for ELLs who read or who are emergent readers.

Strategy 21 is consistent with TESOL Standard 1 (Social Language) for ELLs with English proficiency levels from *Starting* to *Emerging*.

IMPLEMENTING THE STRATEGY

This strategy is presented in two parts: Steps 1 through 8 focus on preparing other students in the classroom for the arrival of the ELL, and Steps 9 through 16 concentrate on working with the ELL.

Part I. Prior to the arrival of ELLs with
English proficiency levels from Starting to Emerging

1. Engage students in the class to make a list of school-based, survival words that all students must know. Be sure the list includes nouns for places such as the gym, bathroom, cafeteria, nurse's office, and playground; nouns for people, such as the teacher, principal, nurse, and bus driver; nouns for things such as a book, notebook, pencil, pen, and bus; and verbs that denote processes such as forming a line, obtaining lunch, playing at recess, or completing homework.

2. Prepare labels with English words for items that are in the classroom.

3. Make a word card for each survival word, placing the written word on one side and a pictorial representation on the other (Shore, 2005). Teachers, paraprofessionals, and, depending on grade level, students can prepare word cards.

4. Store the words in a box that the ELL can easily access for practice (Shore, 2005), or use book rings to secure sets of words for each student so he or she can easily practice them at school and at home (Colombo & Fontaine, 2009).

5. Using age-appropriate language, explain the silent stage to other students in the classroom so that they will understand why the ELL may not speak and will not try to pressure the ELL to speak (i.e., "When someone is first learning another language, he might understand you, but may not be able to speak," or "It's often very difficult for someone who is learning English to speak at first—she will when she is ready.").

6. Using age-appropriate language, explain the role of affective filter in acquiring English (i.e., "Remember the first time you went to [name a situation] and you felt a little unsure of yourself and you needed people to be supportive of you . . . .").

7. Label objects in the room, and when possible, add the word in the ELL's native language to the label.

8. Demonstrate the concept of TPR to students with verbal phrases such as *open the book, close the book, pick up the pen, open the door,* and so on.

Part II. When the ELL arrives

9. Have each student show the ELL a labeled object, pronouncing the English word as she does so. If the ELL appears comfortable doing so, ask her to teach the identified words in her native language to other students in the classroom. This validates the ELL's language and builds community.

10. Teach words to ELLs using word cards with a word in English on one side and an illustration on the reverse. (Teachers, paraprofessionals, and students can present cards to ELLs.) If ELLs are able to read and write in their native language, they can write the word in their native language on the reverse side of the card.

11. Provide ELLs with time to practice survival words and phrases purposefully with native English speakers (e.g., "Where is the office, the line for the bus, the cafeteria?").

12. Honor the silent stage. ELLs will speak when they are ready. To pressure them to speak raises their affective filter, may cause trauma, and will likely delay the acquisition of English.

13. Use and have other students in the classroom use TPR when appropriate (Asher, 2009).

14. As ELLs acquire more vocabulary, add additional words (a few words at a time) to the word boxes or word rings.

15. Provide ELLs time to think and process language before they respond. It is helpful to allow the ELL to speak to his or her buddy and check understanding before he or she tries to speak to a larger group. This reduces the affective filter and enhances language acquisition.

16. Encourage ELLs to use their native language in the classroom. This demonstrates respect for the ELL's native language and is particularly helpful if there is a student, tutor, or paraprofessional who can interpret.

STRATEGY IN ACTION

When Mr. Colón received notification that Sara—a 12-year-old girl from Iraq who, according to the guidance counselor, "spoke almost no English at all,"—had registered for school and would be placed in his seventh grade homeroom, he set about preparing for Sara's arrival.

Student Language Objective: Develop basic vocabulary for social communication

Using Strategy 4 in Unit I of this text, Mr. Colón helped students learn something about Sara's background and home country and about the difficulty that students like Sara might experience when moving to a new country and culture. He also assigned a buddy for Sara. He asked his students to imagine themselves in school in another country where they did not understand the language and provided 10 minutes for students to collaborate in groups of four to brainstorm elements of the process of getting to school and getting around the school building, both inside and out. Mr. Colón explained the following:

> The things we do every day become routines. When we are working with routines, we forget all the steps that we follow. To help Sara learn the routines and the words for each part of a routine, we need to think these through carefully.

At the end of the 10-minute brainstorming session, one student in each group reported to the class and Mr. Colón recorded student responses on the whiteboard, underlining key words, such as *office, bathroom sheet, lunch, book,* and *pen*. He then distributed strips of oak tag on which students created labels for the objects they identified. They then labeled objects within the classroom. Since no one in the class spoke Arabic, students were unable to add Arabic translations to the labels. However, after Sara had settled in and developed rapport with her buddy, Mr. Colón invited students to point to the labeled objects, read the words in English, and ask Sara to supply the word in Arabic. Mr. Colón carefully observed Sara's comfort level. Sara added the Arabic translation to word labels and students were able to see the difference in the writing systems. Sara said the word in Arabic and the students repeated it, thus giving value to multilingualism within the classroom.

Sara's buddy sat next to her in homeroom and in each content-area classroom. She used TPR to make phrases such as *open the book, write your name,* and so on comprehensible and to build Sara's survival language.

REFLECTIONS

1. How is including all students in teaching Sara conducive to Sara's language acquisition and conducive to English-speaking students' knowledge and social skills? How do native-language students and Sara benefit from the experience?

2. How is it likely that the classroom climate created by Mr. Colón will contribute to Sara's acquisition of English? Why?

STRATEGY RESOURCES

1. TPR: A review of the principles underlying TPR, and other articles about the TPR process for language learning

   http://www.tpr-world.com/Merchant2/merchant.mvc?Screen=CTGY&Category_Code=200

2. "About.com: English as a Second Language" provides 20 key points for teaching beginners.

   http://esl.about.com/od/teachingbeginners/a/ab_beg_intro.htm

Strategy

22

THEORY AND/OR RESEARCH UNDERLYING THE STRATEGY

Robust vocabulary instruction, when used as one strategy in a multistrategy program to develop vocabulary, will substantially improve the verbal ability (Beck et al., 2002) of ELLs and FEP learners. Explicit attention to learning new words builds more than target vocabulary (Feldman & Kinsella, 2003; Kinsella, 2005). During discussions about target vocabulary words, ELLs and FEP learners generate other words and constructions that serve to further expand their vocabularies.

With a limited amount of time and the vast number of words that students need to learn, one problem teachers confront is how to choose the academic words for rich instruction. The focus of Strategy 21 is the selection of academic words that merit the time necessary for rich vocabulary instruction.

Graves (2010) suggested that teachers consider the following questions when choosing vocabulary words for rich instruction:

- Is the word important to understanding the text?
- Does the word represent a specific concept that students must know?
- Can students use text context or structural analysis to determine the meaning of the word?
- Can study of this word enhance students' structural analysis or dictionary skills?
- Is the word useful beyond the present reading selection?
- Will learning this word spark students' interest in learning words?

Researchers who study vocabulary development primarily with native English speakers, such as Beck et al. (2002) and Stahl and Nagy (2006), and researchers who focus on vocabulary development for ELLs, such as Nation (2001, 2008) and Schmitt (2008), divide words into three major categories. Beck et al. (2002) refer to these as tiers, a descriptor used throughout this book.

Tier 1 Words

Tier 1 words are frequently and commonly encountered in social situations (high-frequency words): Examples include words like *clock, and, say,* and *about.* ELLs and other students are likely to be exposed to Tier 1 words in classrooms that provide time for student interaction and discussion and in normal conversations with English-speaking peers. Survival language instruction for ELLs who have *Starting* and *Emerging* levels of English proficiency will also include some of the most common Tier 1 words.

Based on their observations and assessments of ELLs, teachers should provide explicit instruction for the Tier 1 words that ELLs do not know. Depending on the ELL's level of English language proficiency, she or he will benefit from multiple intermittent exposures, modeling and scaffolding in small groups, and strategies for self-study, such as vocabulary notebooks, word cards, word rings, and so on, in order to comprehend and use Tier 1 words correctly.

Tier 2 Words

Tier 2 words are not commonly used in social conversation, but they are encountered frequently in academic settings; words such as *abandon, contribute, fund,* and *define* are examples of Tier 2 words.

Most students in the classroom will benefit from rich instruction in Tier 2 words. One source for locating Tier 2 words for older students is the Academic Word List (AWL), which consists of 570 words found in texts across the content areas. It is available online at http://www.uefap.com/vocab/select/awl.htm (Coxhead, 2000). Another way to choose Tier 2 words that are appropriate for teaching ELLs and FEP learners at different grade levels relies on the expertise of the teacher, who knows the words that students will need in order to talk about grade-level content and age-appropriate interests. Beck et al. (2002) suggested that teachers choose words for which students already know the word concept and that offer "more precise and mature" (p. 16) ways of expressing the concept. For example, young children, regardless of previous experiences and educational opportunities, are likely to know the word and concept for *tired*, and thus, teaching the word *exhausted* would provide them with a more precise way of expressing this concept.

Expertise enables teachers to identify the academic words that regularly appear in content-area texts and discussions—the words that ELLs must comprehend and use (e.g., *analyze, interpret, involve, structure, period, theory, context, establish, principle, percent, variable, proceed, significant, process, source*). Teachers who are familiar with content-area texts also are able to identify the words most often used in these texts to signal text structures, such as the following:

- Description—*for instance, for example*
- Compare and contrast—*however, similarly, otherwise*
- Time sequence—*during, following, meanwhile, initially*
- Cause and effect—*therefore, consequently, as a result of*
- Generalization—*consequently, in conclusion, generally*

The focus of Strategy 23 is robust instruction for teaching Tier 2 words.

Tier 3 Words

Tier 3 is comprised of two types of words: (1) technical words and terms, such as *metaphor, inverse,* and *ionic,* that are typically glossed in textbooks and taught to all students as part of content-area instruction, and (2) words that are important to the meaning of a passage, but encountered so infrequently that they are best defined for students during reading or lecturing.

Strategy 25, Semantic Mapping, is effective in teaching vocabulary words and terms and their underlying concepts. Semantic mapping helps ELLs to build connections between words, and as a result they learn new words more quickly and deeply because new words are connected to what they know. Strategy 25 is appropriate for ELLs at all English language proficiency levels.

Implementing the Strategy

Steps 1 through 4 of this strategy are based on the findings from *Text Talk,* a project developed to enhance students' vocabularies through reading aloud (Beck et al., 2002; Beck & McKeown, 2007), which is consistent with effective instruction for ELLs. In *Text Talk,* teachers select sophisticated vocabulary words from high-interest trade books with age-appropriate themes to enhance students' vocabularies.

1. Select grade-appropriate high-interest trade books to read to ELLs and other students in the classroom. For this strategy, it is important that vocabulary is *not* limited to the reading level of the student. (ELLs must be able to understand 90%–95% of vocabulary; they do not need to be able to read it.)

2. Peruse trade books for words that ELLs and other students are unlikely to know, but with concepts they are likely to know and use in everyday conversation; for example, *nauseating, prefer, hesitant,* or *hesitate*—found in the first chapter of *Anastasia Krupnik* (Lowry, 1981).

3. Review concepts presented in leveled readers or picture books that you read to the class. Young children, for example, may read *The Very Hungry Caterpillar* (Carle, 1987). The concept of *hungry* can be extended with new vocabulary words such as *famished* or *ravenous.*

4. Explore themes and concepts presented in basal reader selections, and consider words that will help students to discuss the themes or concepts you identify. For example, Theme 1 in Harcourt's Trophies Series for Grade 3 is *Something Special.* Each reading selection in this theme features a character who has a quality or qualities that make her or him special. The vocabulary words *quality/qualities, characteristics,* and *unusual,* while not necessarily found in the reading selections, can be taught as part of an extended discussion of the reading.

5. Review expository text (and content units) for vocabulary words that students will likely encounter in subsequent chapters and in other content-area classes, such as *accurate, adjust, communicate, compound, interpret, interpretation, method,* and *presume* (all found in the AWL).

6. Consider providing rich instruction for words that students ask about after they encounter the words while reading, watching television, listening to the radio, or conversing with others. These words are appropriate for rich instruction if they are likely to be encountered frequently in academic contexts.

Strategy in Action

Grade 3

Mrs. Wilmot reads big books to her third grade students to build their vocabularies. As she prepares to read *Anansi the Spider: A Tale From the Ashanti* (McDermott, 1987), she considers how she might extend the vocabulary of ELLs and FEP learners with this reading. Mrs. Wilmot decides that one word students will encounter and that will enrich their vocabularies is *collaborate.* She reviews the checklist (Table 22.1) to ensure that collaborate is a good word-choice candidate.

Table 22.1	Criteria for Identifying Tier 2 Words

1. Words are used by mature language learners and appear with regularity across content areas.

2. Words can be used in a variety of contexts and promote connections to other words and concepts.

3. Words for which students understand the underlying concept but cannot describe the concept with specificity and precision.

Source: Bringing Words to Life: Robust Vocabulary Instruction (p. 19), by I. S. Beck, M. G. McKeown, and L. Kucan, 2002, New York: Guilford Press.

She thinks the following:

1. It is a word used by mature language learners and appears with regularity across content areas.

2. It promotes connections to other words, such as cooperate. She confirms that collaborate is a word that students will use in a variety of social and academic contexts. She knows, for example, that her students will later complete a social studies unit that includes the words *collaboration* and *cooperation.*

3. She believes that ELLs and others know the concept behind the word *collaborate,* but she strongly doubts that they could use this word appropriately, flexibly, and with precision (as indicated in Table 22.1).

4. Mrs. Wilmot decides that *collaborate* is a word for which she will provide rich instruction.

Grade 6

Mr. Peter Collins regularly reviews his sixth grade science curriculum and textbook to identify words for which he should provide rich vocabulary instruction, in addition to the glossed terms that he will teach as part of the content. He is preparing to begin a unit on the solar system. Based on the three criteria outlined in Table 22.1, Mr. Collins has identified the following words: *survive* (*survival*) and *investigate* (*investigation*). Neither of these words is glossed in the sixth grade science text, and yet both are important for ELLs to know well enough to use precisely throughout the sixth grade science program and in other content areas. Mr. Collins decides that he will informally assess ELLs' abilities to understand and use these words. Depending on the results of this informal assessment, he may provide rich word instruction.

Grade 5

Ms. Sarah Clark, a fifth grade English language arts teacher, tries to balance the words she will teach by including words self-selected by students along with the words she has selected. By including student-selected words, she extends vocabulary study beyond the classroom and makes instruction more relevant to students. Ms. Clark selects trade books that are available as audio recordings to provide increased comprehensibilty for the four ELLs in her classroom. She previews each trade book for vocabulary words that lend themselves to rich instruction, following the checklist in Table 22.1: The word is widely used by mature speakers, it makes connections to other words, and students know the concept that underlies the word. She identifies the words *unique, proud, casual (casually), puzzled, discourage (discouraging),* and *educate.* She also encourages ELLs and FEP learners to bring words they have seen in newspapers or magazines or heard while watching the evening news to class. She posts these student-generated words on a wall that is prominent within the classroom. She shares the word selection criteria (Table 22.1) with all students in the classroom so that they can begin to select words that are most appropriate for word study. Using the selection criteria, this week, she and the students review the student-generated words and decide together on four words that they will learn during the week. (The ratio of teacher-selected to student-generated words may vary from week to week.) Once students have made selections, Ms. Clark places a star next to each of the selected words and highlights each word in yellow.

REFLECTIONS

1. How does each of the teachers increase the likelihood of selecting vocabulary words that will substantially improve students' vocabularies?

2. Review your curriculum and reading materials for students. If you will provide rich instruction for 10 words each week, which words will you select for week 1, week 2, and so on? How do these words meet the criteria for rich instruction?

3. How does sharing the selection criteria help students understand the value of word study? How might it help them to become independent vocabulary learners?

STRATEGY RESOURCES

1. "Selecting Vocabulary Words to Teach English Language Learners," from Colorín Colorado

   http://www.colorincolorado.org/educators/content/vocabulary

2. 📄 Kinsella (2005), *Preparing for Effective Vocabulary Instruction.* A publication of Aiming High: A Countrywide Commitment to Close the Achievement Gap for English Learners

    http://www.scoe.org/docs/ah/AH_kinsella1.pdf

3. 📄 Beck, I., McKeown, M., & Kucan, L., "Choosing Words to Teach" (Chapter 2 from *Bringing Words to Life: Robust Vocabulary Instruction*)

    http://web1.d25.k12.id.us/home/title1/download/choosingwords.pdf

Providing Robust Vocabulary Instruction for Tier 2 Words

Strategy 23

Once teachers have selected Tier 2 words, they are ready to plan rich vocabulary instruction, Robust Vocabulary Instruction (Beck et al., 2002) is one effective strategy for teaching Tier 2 words, and consists of three steps: 1) Define each word using age-appropriate, child-friendly language, 2) provide direct instruction, and 3) ensure multiple opportunities for ELLs and native English–speaking students to use the word in meaningful conversation. This conversation expands ELLs' ability to use words and English constructions. (Beck et al., 2002)

THEORY AND/OR RESEARCH UNDERLYING THE STRATEGY

Explicit vocabulary instruction is critical to students' academic success (Beck & McKeown, 2007; Marzano, 2004). Robust instruction, which helps ELLs and FEP learners to use academic language with increasing precision is recommended for Tier 2 words—the words that are commonly found in academic language, but used less often in social conversation (Beck & McKeown, 2007).

IMPLEMENTING THE STRATEGY

1. Review the words you have selected to extend reading (especially useful for developing vocabulary in English language arts for ELLs and FEP learners who do not read at grade level), words from reading (especially useful for content-area reading), and words that students have brought to the classroom.

2. Trim the list to approximately 10 words so that ELLs and FEP learners can use the words appropriately in authentic conversations and make connections

between these and other words. Learning only 10 Tier 2 words and their corresponding word families each school week will result in a vocabulary gain of 400 word families each year, thus substantially improving vocabulary (Beck et al., 2002). Remember, students will acquire other words and language structures while they are actively learning new target words.

3. If the new word will extend a concept or theme from the reading, *first read the story to provide context* and then introduce the word. If the word appears in student reading, *introduce and define the word prior to reading* to improve student comprehension of the passage.

4. Write each word on a whiteboard, a word wall, or an oak tag strip.

5. Call students' attention to the written word and say the word aloud so that ELLs and FEP learners know how to pronounce the word. (Words that are pronounceable are easier for students to learn [Nation, 2009].)

6. Ask all students to repeat the word.

7. Define each word in student-friendly language. It is not necessary to provide every possible meaning of the word; rather, define the word as it is used in context.

8. Add this written definition to the word and have students copy the definition onto word cards or into a vocabulary journal.

9. Use the word in a meaningful sentence that extends the reading. For example, "Anansi's sons used their skills to save their father. They *collaborated* to save their father."

10. Introduce words in the same word family in meaningful contexts: "They were collaborative; it was their collaboration that made them successful."

11. Ask students to use the word in meaningful sentences to extend their understanding of the word. For example, "John and I collaborated to write our story about heroes."

12. Post words on the board so students can see each word, its configuration, and its spelling.

13. Revisit words throughout the week so that students have multiple opportunities to retrieve and use the words in conversation and in written work.

Strategy in Action

Ms. Wilmot reads *Anansi the Spider* with children. In this Ashanti tale, each of Anansi's sons does his part to save Anansi, and through the sons' collaboration, Anansi is saved. The tale provides context for the word *collaborate*. Following the reading, Ms. Wilmot introduces the word *collaborate*.

Student Language Objectives:

1. Listen to the story *Anansi the Spider*.

2. Discuss the meaning of the word *collaboration*.

3. Use the word collaboration *in your own conversation*.

Ms. Wilmot shows her students the written word, pronounces it and asks all students to repeat it. She tells students that *collaborate* means working together to achieve something, and asks students what each son in the tale did to save Anansi. (His son, See Trouble, knew Anansi was in danger; his son, Road Builder, created a road so that all the sons could travel to rescue him; the son, River Drinker, stopped the fish that swallowed Anansi, etc.) Ms. Wilmot elicits that each son did one thing to save Ananzi. Ms. Wilmot explains, "Yes, they collaborated to save their father." She then provides examples of *collaborate* to which she thinks students will relate, and to make these clear to the ELLs in her class, she uses visuals and realia:

- She points to the poster of class rules that she and students decided on collaboratively and tells students, "Remember when we established rules for the class? I didn't decide on the rules and no one student decided on the rules. We collaborated; we worked together, to set the rules."

- She holds up one of the bilingual (English-Portuguese class books, which were written and illustrated by four students in the classroom and bound by the school librarian. Ms. Wilmot asks, "How did you collaborate to complete this book?" Maria offers, "We collaborated by making a plan, and then Anna wrote some in English, and I wrote some in Portuguese." "What collaboration!" Ms. Wilmot scaffolds. "I collaborated with them too," adds David. He points to specific pages in the book: "I did this drawing, and then I did the drawing of the classroom on the next page."

After providing several other examples that extend the use of the word *collaboration* beyond the tale of *Anansi*, Ms. Wilmot asks students if they can think of times when they have worked collaboratively at home or at school. Knowing that the affective filters of ELLs are lower if they can share with a partner before sharing with the larger class, Ms. Wilmot places students in pairs and asks each to share a time when he or she was collaborative. After a few minutes of discussing in pairs, several students, including ELLs, are encouraged to share their examples. Then, Ms. Wilmot again calls students' attention to the word, pronounces it, and has students repeat it. She posts the word on the class vocabulary wall and writes the definition next to it. She solicits words from the same family from students and writes these on cards that she places under the word: *collaborated, collaboration, collaborating.* Students take out their vocabulary card rings; they write *collaborate, collaborated, collaboration,* and *collaborating* on one side and a definition of collaborate on the other.

Ms. Wilmot knows that students will need many encounters with the new word before it becomes part of their vocabulary, so she is careful to use the word and solicit students' use of the word frequently throughout the week: Edy, Carlo, and Anna *collaborated* on the playground to decide on the rules for a game; Sandi, Maria, and Freddy *collaborated* to complete a difficult problem from the math box; and two parents and Ms. Wilmot *collaborated* to plan family story night. Ms. Wilmot will keep the word on the wall during the year and ensure that she and students use it regularly and appropriately so that they have ongoing and intermittent exposure to the word, which will result in their using words in this word family with precision.

Other Grades

Mrs. Beland, a first grade teacher, teaches the word *cooperate* based on the class's reading of *Anansi the Spider,* using the same process as Ms. Wilmot. Mr. Peter Collins and Ms. Sarah Clark use a similar process for introducing, discussing, and reinforcing content-area and student self-selected vocabulary words.

Reflections

1. What are some of the advantages of building vocabulary by extending a story?

2. Think of some of the Tier 2 words that would be useful for ELLs and other students in your class to learn well and to use with precision. How will you introduce these words, provide practice using them, and ensure multiple and intermittent retrievals of them?

Strategy Resource

📰 🎬 Reading Rockets features a research-based article for teaching vocabulary.

http://www.readingrockets.org/teaching/reading101/vocabulary

Word Analysis: Building Vocabulary With Word Parts (Tiers 1, 2, 3)

Strategy 24

One way for ELLs and FEP learners to increase their vocabulary is to analyze newly encountered words by breaking them into manageable parts (prefixes, roots, suffixes) and by building words from word parts. In some ways, analyzing word parts seems intuitive. In fact, at a very young age, children develop an understanding of the internal structure of words. Children as young as four are able to make and apply morphological generalizations (add *s* to make a noun plural, *ed* for past tense, etc.) (Berko, 1958). Although many native speakers of English demonstrate the ability to make morphological generalizations at a young age, students who have difficulty with reading often do not continue to develop this skill, and ELLs will need to learn how to analyze words in English. Thus, learning to analyze words is useful to many students in the regular education classroom.

Word analysis builds students' understanding of Latin and Greek roots, which account for over 50% of the polysyllabic words in academic texts (Feldman & Kinsella, 2003; Stahl et al., 1991). Table 24.1 (Stahl et al., 1991) illustrates some common Latin and Greek roots that students in upper elementary and middle school will encounter.

Word analysis is most effective for ELLs with proficiency levels of *Developing* and above, and after they have learned a number of polysyllabic words as unanalyzed wholes (Nation, 2001).Word analysis must be both meaningful and contextual, and it must be quick paced, and enjoyable to students. It is of little benefit to provide ELLs with long lists of word parts to memorize.

Teaching root words in meaningful context and providing ELLs with practice identifying roots and analyzing roots meanings builds ELLs' vocabulary knowledge and use. Calling attention to Latin and Greek roots is useful for ELLs who speak Romance languages, which share Latin and Greek roots with English words.

Knowing the most common prefixes and suffixes builds knowledge of word families. Seventy percent of English words with prefixes begin with *un, re, in, im, il, ir, dis, en, em, non*; 80% of English words with suffixes end with *s, es, ed, ing, ly, ion, tion, ation, ition,* or *er/or* (Stahl & Nagy, 2006, p. 166). Suffixes may be particularly important because, in addition to creating new words, they enable students to understand and interpret the language used in informational text (Nagy, 2010). (Unit VII in this book focuses on second language reading and writing.)

Table 24.1	Common Latin and Greek Roots Encountered in Content-Area Instruction		
Root	Meaning	Origin	Examples
aud	hear	Latin	audio, audition
astro	star	Greek	astrology, astronaut
bio	life	Greek	biography, biology
dict	speak, tell	Latin	dictate
geo	earth	Greek	geology, geography
meter	measure	Greek	thermometer
min	small, little	Latin	minimum
mit, mis	send	Latin	mission, transmit, remit, missile
ped	foot	Latin	pedestrian, pedal, pedestal
phono	sound	Greek	microphone
port	carry	Latin	transport, portable
scrib, cript	write	Latin	scribble, manuscript, inscription
spect	see	Latin	inspect, spectator, respect
struct	build, form	Latin	construction, destruct, instruct

Source: From *Vocabulary Development,* by S. Stahl, 1999, Brookline MA: Brookline Books.

An effective way to teach prefixes and suffixes is to have students work deductively. For example, the prefix *un* can be taught by presenting students with a list of commonly used words containing *un*. Students work as detectives in pairs or in small groups to identify the prefix, root, and suffix and to infer the meaning of the prefix or suffix from the words they have analyzed (Nation, 2001). This is illustrated with the example of *un* in Table 24.2.

Table 24.2	Word Detectives—Analysis			
Word	Prefix	Prefix Meaning	Root Word	Word Meaning
Unhappy	un	not	happy	not happy
Untrue	un	not	true	not true
Unreal	un	not	real	not real
Undone	un	not	done	not done
Unfair	un	not	fair	not fair

Source: Adapted from *Learning Vocabulary in Another Language,* by I. S. P. Nation, 2001, Cambridge, UK: Cambridge University Press.

Based on their expertise, teachers should decide which prefixes and suffixes are most appropriate for their grade levels, content areas, and the English proficiency levels of their students. Ongoing and engaging practice making words and breaking multisyllabic words apart builds ELLs' word analysis skills. This three-part strategy (prefixes/suffixes, root words, multisyllabic words) is consistent with TESOL Standards 1 through 5 and proficiency levels *Developing* through *Transitioning*. It works well as a regular filler between instructional activities and is engaging and enjoyable for ELLs and other students.

THEORY AND/OR RESEARCH UNDERLYING THE STRATEGY

When ELLs and FEP learners know the most common prefixes and suffixes, they are able to decode and build multisyllabic words (Nation, 2001, 2008; Stahl & Nagy, 2006). Learning suffixes may be especially important because, in addition to helping ELLs to create new words, fluency with suffixes also enables students to interpret greater amounts of language used in informational text (Nagy, 2010). The ability to manipulate the components of multisyllabic words has been used to help struggling readers to access text and to improve their spelling and writing (Cunningham & Hall, 1998).

IMPLEMENTING THE STRATEGY

1. Choose root words that are meaningful to students (content-area words, commonly used academic words) and affixes that are found in content area reading materials.

2. Introduce one root word, one prefix, or one suffix at a time and in context.

Part 1. Teaching Affixes

1. Choose a prefix (or suffix) that your students should know, such as *anti, a,* or *dis.* The prefix should come from a unit of study. For example, a story that students are reading features the words *disengaged* and *disinterested,* a science chapter discusses abiotic features in the rainforest, or a social studies unit focuses on antislavery proponents.*

2. Create a word detective chart (such as in Table 24.2), listing multiple examples of words that contain the target affix.

3. Provide students with a few minutes within small groups to deductively define the affix.

---

*For younger students: Present the prefix *un* by animatedly providing examples: *unhappy, unbelievable, untrue, unfair.* Allow students to infer that *un* means *not.* Place a card with *un = not* written on it on the class word wall. Have students work in small groups to generate other examples. (With younger students, teacher and students chant together the affix, its spelling, the word, and its meaning: *un, u-n, un, unfair, not fair.* Cunningham and Hall [1998] recommend chanting for students of all ages!)

4. Write the meaning of the affix provided by students on the whiteboard, and solicit other examples of words that use the affix.

5. Provide students with the word detective chart and have them work in pairs to complete.

6. Circulate and check charts for student understanding—call on student pairs to share their responses.

Extension: Create an affix wheel. During vocabulary or transition time, spin the wheel and let students work in pairs to generate as many words (and word meanings) as possible.

Part II. Implementing the Strategy: Teaching Roots

1. Choose root words that are meaningful to students, and introduce words in context. For example, in a fifth grade science unit on weather, the terms *thermometer, barometer, anemometer,* and *meteorologist* appear in the text and are frequently used during classroom hands-on activities. Because students will encounter these words frequently and must know their meaning, it is useful to teach the root *meter.* Connections can be made to math class, where students use meter sticks to measure the perimeter of the room.

2. Provide students with a sample word (*thermometer*), the root (*meter*) and the meaning of the root (*to measure*).

3. Generate a list of other words with the same root. *Thermometer, barometer,* and *anemometer* are glossed on the first two pages of the science text. In this example, the teacher provides everyday definitions of *therm* (a measure of heat), *baro* (pressure), and *anemo* (wind). The focus is on learning that *meter* refers to measurement.

Part III. Implementing the Strategy: Working With Multisyllabic Words

1. Make lists or ask students to make lists of multisyllabic words they encounter in their reading, in class, and outside of class.

2. Have students work with the word detective sheet to analyze words on the list.

3. Make word cards by printing multisyllabic words on heavy paper or oak tag and then cutting the words into parts (e.g., dis taste ful, beauty(i) ful, un truth ful) (Cunningham & Hall, 1998).

4. Place word parts in small envelopes, which can be stored in a vocabulary resource box.

5. Provide students with time to build words using the word-part cards during 15-minute segments of class. (This can also be done as a game in which pairs or groups of students compete to make, define, and use the most words in a given period of time.)

STRATEGY IN ACTION

Mr. Collins introduces the reading for his sixth grade unit on biospheres by reviewing (and teaching) the root word *bio.*

Student Language Objectives:

1. Make words using word parts.

2. Use word wall words correctly.

Students collaborate in small groups to generate words that have *bio* as a root (*biosphere, biography, biographer, biology, biologist, bionic,* etc.) and to define these words without dictionaries. Mr. Collins then asks the students to use each word in context. He provides time for each group to share their words, the meanings, and the ways in which they use each word in context. Mr. Collins's students engage in word part analysis during the last 15 minutes of science class each Friday. He has found this activity to be effective with ELLs and with FEP learners; it is easy to implement and stresses to students the importance of word study. He teaches affixes one at a time, using the process described in Step 1 of *Implementing the Strategy*. He has created and maintained a word wall with the words he has taught, and he regularly reviews these words. He expects students to use these word wall words with increasing degrees of precision.

When Mr. Collins teaches an affix, he posts it on the classroom small word wall. (Strategy 27 provides ways to create, maintain, and use word walls.) Often, during word analysis time, he provides students with three to five words. In small groups, students generate as many words as possible by adding affixes posted on the word wall to these words. This is a quick-paced activity—one minute to generate new words, a few minutes for each group to report out the words they have generated, and three to five minutes for each group to create and share a meaningful sentence that features the word used with precision. For example, *investigate* yields *investigated, investigates, investigator, investigation,* and *investigating.* Meaningful and precise sentences are ones such as "When we *investigated* the ways that levers work, we did an experiment that showed that levers make work easier."

Grade 4

Mrs. Nancy Clark provides her fourth grade students with short lists of multisyllabic words featuring familiar root words and the affixes she has taught in class (i.e., *unavailable, unhappiness, sadness*) and a graphic organizer, such as the one shown in Table 24.3. In small groups, students break words into parts and identify the meaning of each prefix and suffix. They then determine the meaning of the multisyllabic word and use the word in context. The purpose of this word detective game is to help ELLs and FEP learners to develop skills that will enable them to build vocabulary through word parts.

Table 24.3	Word Parts						
Word	Prefix	Prefix Meaning	Root Word	Suffix	Suffix Meaning	Word Meaning

Grade 1

Mrs. Beland uses word parts to build on the *sparkle words* that her students have collected. As part of *sparkle words,* students bring words to the class that they have heard outside of school. Mrs. Beland places these words on the *sparkle word wall,* defines the words in child-friendly language, purposefully uses the words in meaningful context throughout the week, and encourages students to use the words in their discussions. She then teaches students how to analyze the polysyllabic *sparkle words* using a word detective table.

Student Language Objectives:

1. Bring sparkle words to class.

2. Use sparkle words in your own sentence during the week.

3. Find the parts in sparkle words.

Reflections

1. How does helping students to analyze words build their vocabulary?

2. How might the ability to analyze words improve reading comprehension?

3. Think about your content area. What root words, prefixes, and suffixes are most important for students to (1) understand, (2) be able to use, and (3) be able to manipulate to form new words?

Semantic Mapping (Works Well for Tier 3 Words)

Strategy 25

Semantic mapping, an instructional strategy that can be traced to Johnson and Pearson (1984, as cited in Stahl & Vancil, 1986), is an effective strategy to build concept and word knowledge for ELLs because it engages them in academic discussions supported by comprehensible input. It provides rich and deep instruction for teaching words as well as for teaching underlying concepts. In addition to promoting vocabulary development, semantic mapping features the added benefits of activating and building knowledge prior to reading and other instructional activities. It is the rich discussion that is involved in the creation of semantic maps that makes it so effective for vocabulary learning (Stahl & Nagy, 2006; Stahl & Vancil, 1986).

THEORY AND/OR RESEARCH UNDERLYING THE STRATEGY

Semantic mapping engages ELLs and FEP learners in meaningful academic conversations about words, and it therefore supports overall oral language while building proficiency with specific vocabulary words. The development of academic language fosters overall literacy development (August & Shanahan, 2006) as well as greater conceptual understanding (Michaels, O'Connor, & Resnick, 2007). Thus, academic language proficiency contributes to the overall academic success of ELLs in learning content (Francis et al., 2006).

IMPLEMENTING THE STRATEGY

1. Identify a target word or term that students will encounter and need to know for an upcoming reading or classroom activity, and write it on the whiteboard. For example, in an upcoming unit about the weather, a teacher knows that students will need to know the meaning of the word *meteorology*.

2. Together with students, brainstorm words related to that target word. For example, the teacher writes the target word *meteorology* in the center of the whiteboard. Students then brainstorm words such as *weather, forecaster, news, weather person, radar, thermometer, barometer, storms, sunny,* and so on. (Build comprehension by explaining and discussing words that students do not seem to know [Stahl & Nagy, 2006].)

149

3. Once a comprehensive list (or wheel, see Figure 25.1) of related words has been generated, ask students to decide how they will categorize these words. With the meteorology example, *weather* might be a category that includes *storms* and *sunny*. Measurement tools might be a category that includes *thermometer* and *barometer*, and so on.

4. Next, students discuss the words and arrange categories with words on a semantic map. This should be a teacher-guided activity until students understand how to use this strategy; then it can also be completed in small groups. It should always be a discussion-based activity.

5. Have students read the selection or engage in the learning activity.

6. Guide students in a discussion about the reading (or activity), and add to the map as appropriate.

Figure 25.1   Fourth Grade Student-Generated Wheel and Categories From Ruby Bridges Unit

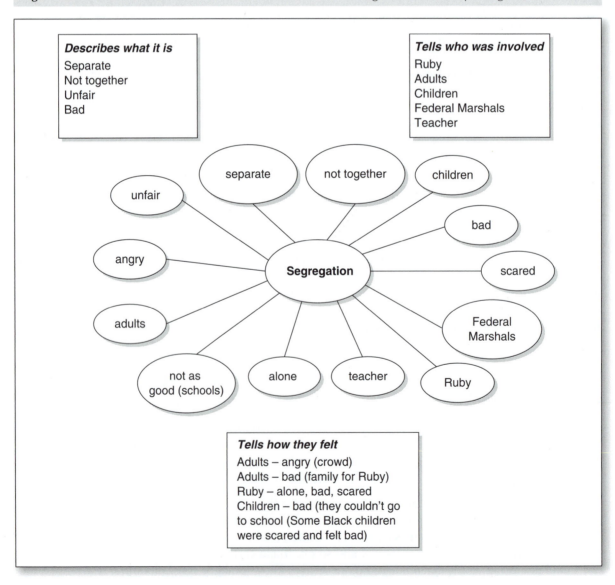

Describes what it is
Separate
Not together
Unfair
Bad

Tells who was involved
Ruby
Adults
Children
Federal Marshals
Teacher

Tells how they felt
Adults – angry (crowd)
Adults – bad (family for Ruby)
Ruby – alone, bad, scared
Children – bad (they couldn't go to school (Some Black children were scared and felt bad)

STRATEGY IN ACTION

Mr. Peterson regularly creates semantic maps with his students. Initially, he used whole-group lessons to guide students through each step of the process. Students now understand the process and are able to work more autonomously within their groups. Mr. Peterson's eighth grade students are about to begin an instructional unit about the Earth, which includes the geosphere, atmosphere, hydrosphere, and biosphere. The first section of their text (and supplementary comprehensible reading) is based on the geosphere. This is clearly a concept and term that all students must know in order to make sense of the instructional unit. Mr. Peterson has introduced the word *geosphere* and has used an apple as a metaphor for the layers of the geosphere. ELLs and FEP learners have worked together in groups of four; each group has cut open an apple to examine its layers. Today, Mr. Peterson focuses on the Earth's crust—the skin of the apple.

Mr. Peterson writes *crust* in the center of the whiteboard. He says the word aloud and asks students to repeat it. He tells students that this is a word with multiple meanings. Many students recognize *crust* as the outer layer of bread. Mr. Peterson then assigns students to work in groups of four for 10 minutes to generate as many relevant words as possible. They are encouraged to use their books, supplementary materials, photos, and models to generate a list of words that are related to the Earth's crust. Students begin working immediately, collaborating within their groups, turning pages of their text, studying the models and the photos, and writing lists of words. After 10 minutes, Mr. Peterson asks students to stop and to prepare to share the words each group has generated.

He calls on groups one at a time. A spokesperson from each group shares three words, which Mr. Peterson writes on the whiteboard. Students must listen attentively and attend to the whiteboard so that they do not repeat words. Collectively, students generate the list shown in Table 25.1.

Table 25.1	Student-Generated Vocabulary
Rocks	dirt
Desert	mountains
Erosion	erosion from water
Sand	forests
Erosion from wind	farmlands
Prairies	plants
Trees	grass
People live there	animals live there

As a student in each group reports the words, Mr. Peterson checks for understanding and explains any word that students do not know. He then asks student to work in their groups for five minutes to decide how they might classify the words—that is, the categories they might use. Figure 25.2 illustrates the categories and the words that students have placed in each category.

(For ELLs with proficiency levels *Starting* through *Developing,* the use of pictures will make each word comprehensible. Pictures will also be effective for early grades and for preliterate ELLs at any grade level.)

Figure 25.2   Semantic Map—Crust

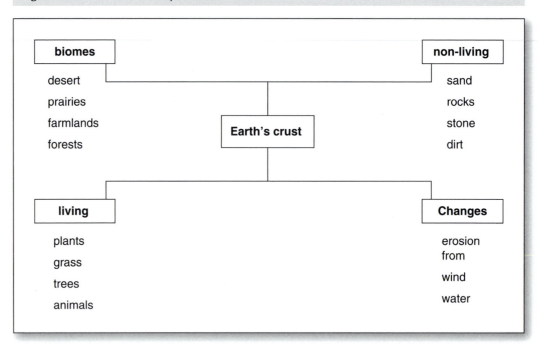

A variation on semantic mapping is the Frayer model (Frayer, Frederick, & Klausmeier, 1969), which is designed to be completed within small heterogeneous groups. Similar to semantic mapping, the Frayer model's strength is that it promotes discussion about words and concepts between ELLs and native English speakers. Through this discussion, vocabulary words and concepts are elaborated upon and deepened.

In the Frayer model, teachers provide students with a word or term that represents a concept. Using a variation of the Frayer model provided by Stahl and Nagy (2006), students and their teacher discuss what the word is, what it is like, and examples and nonexamples. Figure 25.3 illustrates this model.

Figure 25.3   Variation of Frayer Model—Revolution

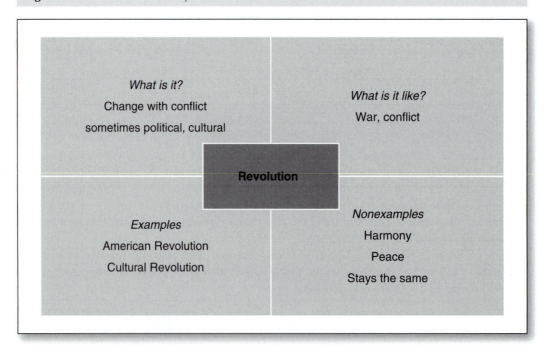

REFLECTIONS

1. How is semantic mapping useful for teaching both new words and underlying concepts?

2. How would you use the Frayer model to teach and reinforce a concept for your content area?

3. What words in your content area might you teach with semantic mapping?

Strategy 26

Using Quick Prereading and Review Strategies

T here is not time to teach all the words that students must understand to comprehend readings and lessons. In an article written for *The Reading Teacher,* Richek (2005) presented several ways to promote vocabulary understanding and development. Strategy 26 is actually comprised of two quick (20 minutes and under) strategies. The first, Semantic Expressions, is used for prereading or prior to listening; the second, Connect Two, is a review activity. Both Semantic Expressions and Connect Two engage ELLs in interactive academic discussions with the teacher and with other students.

THEORY AND/OR RESEARCH UNDERLYING THE STRATEGY

Semantic Impressions is a 20-minute activity for previewing words. It was piloted and tested with elementary school ELLs, and it resulted in an increase in targeted vocabulary (Richek, 2005). In addition, it promotes depth of understanding because ELLs use new words in their own stories. Connect Two (Richek, 2005), a vocabulary review, includes interactive discussion about words and about text that was read by, or read aloud to, ELLs and other students. Because the level of the reading material determines the words that are woven into Semantic Expressions and Connect Two, these strategies are appropriate for all age groups, reading levels, and English proficiency levels. (ELLs with lower levels of English proficiency will need increased scaffolding. Please see Table V.3.)

IMPLEMENTING THE STRATEGY

Semantic Impressions

Preview students' reading (or a story that will be read aloud) for words that are essential: Richek (2005) suggests 5 to 20 words. The following implementation is adapted from Richek (2005, p. 416):

1. Write the words on the whiteboard in the order they are found in the story.

2. Explain to students that they will create a meaningful story using the words.

3. Briefly explain the meaning of each word and check for understanding.

4. Present and discuss three rules that students must follow: (1) the words must be used in order, (2) words that have been used may be used again, and (3) the form of words can be changed, including plurals, tenses, and parts of speech.

5. Provide students with time to discuss the words in small heterogeneous English-language proficiency groups.

6. Ask students to begin to create the story.

7. As students give sentences or phrases with the words, write these on the whiteboard next to the list of words. (The list of words stays visible throughout the lesson.)

8. Guide students to create a narrative that makes sense.

9. Once the story is complete, you may edit it with students.

10. Read the published story with students.

STRATEGY IN ACTION

Student Language Objectives:

1. Discuss the meaning of each word on the board within your group.

2. Write a paragraph using all the words on the board.

To introduce *Cloudy With a Chance of Meatballs* (Barrett, 1978) for a reading lesson, Richek (2005) chose the following words and phrases:

1. pancakes

2. weather

3. rain

4. snow

5. prediction

6. sanitation department

7. took a turn for the worse

8. damaged

9. abandon

10. new land

11. supermarket

Source: Reprinted with permission: Richek, M.A. (2005). Words are wonderful: Interactive, time-efficient strategies to teach meaning vocabulary. *The Reading Teacher, 58*(5), 414–423. doi:10.1598/RT.58.5.1

The story in Table 26.1 was created collaboratively by a class of third grade ELLs.

Table 26.1	Day of Snow

Yesterday I woke up at 5 a.m. and I ate pancakes. That morning the weather was very cold. It was so cold that the rain became ice and snow covered the streets. The weather prediction was wrong because they had predicted a sunny day. The pancakes didn't fill me, so I was still hungry. I called the sanitation department to move the snow so I could go out and buy food. The weather took a turn for the worse so the sanitation department got stuck in the snow. Their truck's motor was damaged by the snow, so they had to abandon it. A day later, the snow melted. When the snow melted, the place looked like a new land. I was very happy because I could go to the supermarket.

Source: Reprinted with permission: Richek, M.A. (2005). Words are wonderful: Interactive, time-efficient strategies to teach meaning vocabulary. *The Reading Teacher, 58*(5), 414–423. doi:10.1598/RT.58.5.1

IMPLEMENTING THE STRATEGY

Connect Two

Connect Two (Richek, 2005) is a review strategy that students can complete in small groups. Again, the teacher chooses words that are central to understanding the text that students will read. These words are displayed and discussed prior to reading. Words, along with photos or images and student-friendly definitions, remain on the classroom word walls. Connect Two challenges students to make connections between words.

1. Select approximately 20 words that are important to the content-area reading.

2. Place the words in two columns (approximately 10 words in each column).

3. Working in pairs or small groups, students must find something that a word from column 1 has in common with a word from column 2. (As references, students may use their textbooks, supplementary leveled reading, graphic organizers generated during the unit of study, and the word wall with photos and images.)

4. Students must connect the words and explain their thinking.

STRATEGY IN ACTION

Mr. John Rogers's eighth grade class recently completed a chapter about the events leading to the U.S. Civil War. Mr. Rogers taught the words in Table 26.2. Then, each student in the class became an expert on one word (Richek, 2005), learning all she or he could about the word and creating a small 5 × 8-inch poster with the word, its definition, and any photos or drawings to illustrate the word.

Student Language Objectives:

1. Become an expert on one word.

2. Write the word's definition in your own words.

3. Illustrate the word.

Table 26.2	Connect Two Words
emancipate	slaveholder
conflict	run away
slavery	bondage
adequate labor	personal liberty
territories	dispute
settle	liberate
enslaved	controversy
criticize	citizens

The posters are displayed around the word wall. At the end of the week, ELLs and other students collaborate in a Connect Two activity.

Some connections made by students include the following:

- *Settle* and *dispute:* "What they have in common is that people work to settle disputes."

- *Conflict* and *dispute:* "Both show disagreement about something. A conflict is more serious than a dispute."

- *Enslaved* and *liberate:* "Enslaved and liberated are opposites because to enslave is to make someone a slave and to liberate someone is to set them free."

- *Slavery* and *slaveholder:* "The connection is that slavery kept African Americans as slaves who were owned by slaveholders."

REFLECTIONS

1. What are some of the ways that prereading and review strategies are helpful to ELLs?

2. Review the reading that students will complete in one unit that you teach. Select a chapter or a story, and then select 10 to 20 words that students can use in a Semantic Impression. How will this be useful to ELLs?

3. What words would you select for review?

4. What other pre- and postreading vocabulary strategies do you think would be useful to the ELLs in your classroom?

Strategy

27

Interactive Word Walls

Interactive word walls are a must in a mixed ability classroom, and are effective for building spelling and reading skills as well as for developing vocabulary. Word walls for commonly used words (Tier 1) that frequently are misspelled or confused by ELLs and FEP learners provide students with a reference, such as *too, to,* and *two, their* and *there, then* and *than, here* and *hear,* and so on. Word walls also provide an excellent venue for displaying Tier 2 words, many of which are on the Academic Word List (AWL), including words such as *analyze, distribute, estimate, identify, factor, principle,* and *theory.* Word walls can also be used for word parts, showing the most common root words and affixes that students will encounter during the school year.

THEORY AND/OR RESEARCH UNDERLYING THE STRATEGY

Students need multiple and intermittent exposures to a word in order to learn it (McKeown, Beck, Omanson, & Pople, 1985). To know a word in depth, students need to understand the multiple contexts in which the word can be used (Beck et al., 2002) and attach a visual image to the word (Pressley, Levin, & McDaniel, cited in Harmon, Wood, Hedrick, Vintinner, & Willeford, 2009). Word walls have been shown to be very effective in deepening word knowledge, especially when students are provided some choice regarding the words (Strategy 22), when words have been taught using rich instruction (Strategies 23, 24, and 25), and when a visual or image accompanies each word (Harmon et al., 2009).

IMPLEMENTING THE STRATEGY

1. Dedicate a place (or several places) in the classroom to word walls: One word wall might contain commonly misspelled or misused words, such as homonyms (*to, too, two,* etc.), another might contain words chosen and taught for rich instruction, and a third might contain word parts (commonly used roots, prefixes, and affixes [see Strategy 24]).

2. Write or have students write the selected word on colored card stock. Using colors that students associate with the word helps students make connections with the word (Harmon et al., 2009).

3. For word cards, supply or have students supply an image, such as a photo, symbol, or drawing, and discuss how the image is associated with the word.

4. For roots and affixes, provide clear examples of how each is used, and display these on the board.

5. Refer to the word wall during discussions and instruction.

6. Instruct ELLs and other students to use the word wall in discussions and in writing.

7. Hold ELLs with proficiency levels of *Developing* and higher accountable for using word wall words correctly.

Extension: Developing Word Cards From Word Walls

While some words may be present on a classroom word wall throughout the better part of the year, words will change. ELLs and FEP learners should be encouraged to use word cards for word wall words. Students can copy the word on one side of the card with a drawing and multiple examples of the word in use on the reverse. Practicing with word cards provides ELLs with ongoing opportunities for word retrieval, which in turn strengthens students' word knowledge. Nation (2001) noted that word cards provide several advantages: They are an efficient use of time and energy, they provide ELLs with word meanings that may be more useful than dictionary meanings, and they foster independent learning by giving ELLs complete control over the number of retrievals they make. Nation recommended that ELLs use small (2 inches × 3 inches) index cards for portability.

STRATEGY IN ACTION

Grade 2

As part of her vocabulary instruction, Mrs. Wilmot asks students to work in pairs to create a 5 x 8-inch poster for each of the vocabulary words she teaches each week. Each pair is responsible for one word, and draws a picture and writes a sentence to accompany their word. After Mrs. Wilmot has reviewed the completed posters for accuracy, she has each pair present their word and their sentence. Words are then displayed on the class word wall for easy reference.

Grade 4

Mrs. Allen has several word walls in her fourth grade classroom: One is dedicated to general vocabulary words, another to terms students have learned in the content areas, and one is dedicated to words that most FEP learners know (and ELLs are often still learning) but often misspell, including homophones such as *to, too,* and *two, there* and *their, threw* and *through,* and words commonly confused in their written form, such as *then* and *than* and *are* and *our.* Mrs. Allen has chosen these words based on an assessment of the writing of ELLs and FEP learners. She introduces each word before posting it on the word wall by displaying, defining, and explaining when to use the word. She encourages

ELLs to define the words in their first languages and writes (or has ELLs write) this definition on the board. She has the ELL pronounce the word and has the class repeat the pronunciation. She then generates examples of the word use with students. For example for the word *their,* students and Mrs. Allen generated *their room, their car, their ball,* and so on. Mrs. Allen wrote the phrases on the whiteboard. When she decided that students (ELLs and FEP learners) had generated a sufficient number of phrases to show their understanding, she called for a raise of hands to decide which phrase would be placed on the word wall to accompany the word.

Each word on Mrs. Allen's word wall is accompanied by a phrase, symbol, or image that helps students remember its meaning. For example, two is accompanied by the number 2, to has a picture of a boy walking and the phrase *to the park,* too has a picture of the boy and his little sister and the phrase *His sister is going too (also).* Mrs. Allen has arranged the words in alphabetical order so that students can easily locate the correct spelling of a word that they would like to use in their writing. She also calls students' attention to the word wall when they are editing their writing.

Grade 6

Mr. Collins uses one of the word walls in his classroom to post root words. His students engage in word part analysis during the last 15 minutes of science class each Friday. He teaches word roots, such as *bio,* and creates a web of all the words that ELLs and FEP learners have generated in small groups: *biosphere, biography, biographer, biology, biologist, bionic.* Mr. Collins writes the student-generated definition next to each word.

REFLECTION

- How will interactive word walls benefit ELLs and FEP learners as they acquire content-area vocabulary and read and write in the content areas?

STRATEGY RESOURCES

1. TheSchoolBell.com website provides an overview of the benefits of using interactive word walls and several links to useful activities.

   http://www.theschoolbell.com/Links/word_walls/words.html

2. Word wall activities for middle and secondary grades

   http://www.markville.ss.yrdsb.edu.on.ca/mm/oise2005/bestpractice/wordwall.htm

3. Word walls in the mathematics classroom

   http://www.broward.k12.fl.us/studentsupport/ese/PDF/MathWordWall.pdf

UNIT VI

Strategies for Developing Academic Language

The students in my classroom are so diverse. Some of them are above grade level and need to be challenged, others are trying to catch up. ELLs in my room are struggling to learn English and the subject area, and there is so much content to cover . . . so much for them to learn. How do I possibly find time to build oral language?

—Middle School Teacher

ELLs in U.S. schools acquire social oral language within a year or two. Once they are socially proficient and can make themselves understood, many ELLs reach a plateau, and do not continue to develop the academic language necessary for success in school. Yet it is oral academic language that is linked to literacy development (August & Shanahan, 2006) and to the development of conceptual understanding (Michaels et al., 2007). In fact, proficiency with academic language is one of the most important factors in content-area learning for ELLs (Francis et al., 2006). Ongoing participation in academic conversations provides practice in both listening to and speaking academic language, and it has been shown to increase content-area understanding and language development in students from diverse cultural, socioeconomic, and linguistic backgrounds (Michaels et al., 2007).

Regularly including academic conversations in the classroom provides ELLs with the opportunity to comprehend vocabulary and language structures, to try out new vocabulary and structures with their teachers and peers, and to receive immediate feedback regarding the comprehensibility of their language use. Academic conversations promote **communicative competence**—a hallmark of language development (Hymes, 1972).

> *Communicative Competence:* Receptive and productive language proficiency develops as a result of meaningful **communication** in the target language.

161

Despite the known benefits of academic conversations, these conversations are the exception in many classrooms, where teacher-focused Initiation-Response-Evaluation (IRE) all too often remains the norm. In IRE, the teacher asks a question with a known answer, a student responds, and the teacher evaluates the response: for example, *Who can name three causes of the American Revolution?* Contrast this with a question that might spawn an academic discussion: for example, *How did the perspectives of the colonists and of Great Britain on the events leading to the American Revolution differ?* Both questions require students to access and use factual information about the Revolution. The second question is also likely to encourage students to engage in conversation to explore events and multiple perspectives about these events in greater depth. Even in classrooms where academic discussions occur, ELLs are often not fully included in these discussions. Questions presented to ELLs often require less complex thinking, less use of language, and fewer expectations for high-level responses (Fisher, Frey, & Rothenberg, 2008). This is especially concerning given that many middle class, majority culture students will enter schools with access to academic discourse, whereas many students from monetarily poor families and families for whom English is not the first language are likely to need ongoing support and scaffolds in the classroom in order to develop academic language and academic discourse structures (Michaels et al., 2007). Schools may represent the only opportunity for ELLs to be engaged in rich English language that builds oral expression and vocabulary.

> **Phonemes:** the sounds of English; **morphemes:** (word forms) the smallest units of meaning in English, including prefixes and suffixes; **syntax:** the structure of phrases and sentences; **prosody:** the appropriate volume, tone, and emphasis; **fluency:** speaking with appropriate speed, accuracy, and expression; **semantics:** meaning at the word, phrase, and sentence level.

Developing academic oral language proficiency is a complex and multifaceted process for ELLs, and it involves proficiency with *phonemes, morphemes, syntax, prosody, fluency,* and *semantics.* Effective instruction provides ongoing practice with the sounds and phrasing of English as well as practice listening to and speaking structured academic language. This instruction must be comprehensible and include the ongoing use of visuals, realia, gesturing, video, and, when possible, clarification in an ELL's primary language. (See Table VI.2 for a description of accommodations that ELLs will need at each proficiency level.) Knowing that oral language proficiency is a key factor in language and academic success for ELLs, the focus of this unit is strategies teachers can use to enhance the oral proficiency of ELLs (Strategies 28 and 29) and to build structured academic conversations within their classrooms for ELLs at various proficiency levels (Strategies 30 and 31).

The strategies provided are aligned with TESOL standards (Table VI.1) and performance indicators for ELLs at all proficiency levels (Table VI.2).

WHAT YOU WILL LEARN

Unit VI provides theory, research, vignettes, and strategies to help you do the following:

1. Understand the importance of developing academic oral language in the classroom.

2. Understand the connections between oral language and reading.

3. Learn how to develop classroom communities that foster academic conversations.

4. Learn strategies for developing the academic oral language proficiency of ELLs.

Table VI.1	TESOL Standards for Teachers

Domain 1: Language

1.a.2. *Apply knowledge of phonology (the sound system), morphology (the structure of words), syntax (phrase and sentence structure), semantics (word/sentence meaning),* and *pragmatics (the effect of content on language)* to help ELLs develop oral, reading, and writing skills (including mechanics) in English. (p.30)

1.b.4. Understand and apply knowledge of sociocultural, psychological and political variables to facilitate the process of learning English. (p. 37)

Domain 3: Planning, Implementing, and Managing Instruction

3.a.1. Plan standards-based ESL and content instruction. (p. 45)

3.a.3. Plan differentiated learning experiences based on assessment of students' English and L1 [first language] proficiency, learning styles and prior formal educational experiences and knowledge. (pp. 45–46)

3.b.2. Incorporate activities, tasks, and assignments that develop authentic uses of language, as students learn academic vocabulary and content-area material. (p. 49)

3.b.3. Provide activities and materials that integrate listening, speaking, reading, and writing. (p. 50)

3.b.4. Develop students' listening skills for a variety of academic and social purposes. (p. 50)

3.b.5. Develop students' speaking skills for a variety of academic and social purposes. (p. 50)

Domain 4: Assessment

4.a.4. Demonstrate understanding of the advantages and limitations of assessments, including accommodations for ELLs. (p. 60)

4.c.5. Use a variety of rubrics to assess ELLs' language development in classroom settings. (pp. 67–68)

Source: TESOL Teacher Standards Tables: TESOL (2010). *TESOL/NCATE Standards for the Recognition of Initial ESOL Programs in P–12 ESL Teacher Education.* Alexandria, VA: TESOL.

Strategy 28: Choral Reading and Strategy 29: Building Oral Language With Read-Alouds and Picture Books, which are often used to build reading abilities, are also effective for developing oral language proficiency. These strategies promote oral proficiency with English phonemes, morphemes, syntax, prosody, semantics, and fluency. Choral reading helps to build an atmosphere of participation within the classroom. It is an enjoyable, low-risk activity that lowers ELLs' affective filters, engages them in oral language, and builds academic oral language proficiency.

Table VI.2 Oral Proficiency With Academic Language

Based on TESOL Performance Indicators Assuming Ongoing Appropriate Instruction

TESOL Standards 1–5: ELLs engage in focused social and academic conversations to share ideas, intercultural understanding, knowledge, skills, and concepts in instructional settings and across content areas.

Level 1—Starting: With the support of scaffolds, such as photos, illustrations, graphics, drawings, maps, and other visuals that build comprehensibility, and by using gestures and some native language, ELLs engage in academic conversations in pairs and/or small groups to share knowledge. ELLs respond to one-step commands, match survival vocabulary words with pictures, identify mathematical symbols, practice saying illustrated words with partners, match descriptive words with models/diagrams, identify parts of a story, and state personal preferences.

ELLs also respond to nonverbal communication in pairs and small group settings, describe self, give directions with support from peers or teacher, and communicate with phrases with the support of bilingual and/or picture dictionaries.

Level 2—Beginning: ELLs engage in academic conversations using the scaffolds (described in Level 1). They use short phrases/sentences comprised of general language and targeted academic words to share knowledge of concepts, respond to formulaic questions, and describe steps in solving problems. ELLs at Level 2 also respond to one- to two-step commands, ask questions, tell about everyday events, and share simple information in small groups.

Level 3—Developing: While support scaffolds remain important, ELLs are able to engage in two-way tasks that require processing of verbal language. For example, they are able to manipulate maps, diagrams, or objects in response to clear directions. With visual cues, ELLs are able to describe processes and historical events and use words in more than one context (branch of government, tree branch, department store branch).

Level 4—Expanding: While they continue to benefit from all types of visuals and clarifications of complex speech, ELLs communicate with an increasing level of complexity. They comprehend grade-appropriate nuances and participate in two-way discussions (e.g., compare/contrast, perform verses developed with classmate(s), monitor and discuss steps in a process), follow multistep directions, and use examples with details to elaborate.

Level 5—Bridging: ELLs interpret, make, and share inferences from oral stories, videos, and multimedia presentations. They explain ideas, processes, procedures, and multiple perspectives using grade-level vocabulary, phrases, and technical language. ELLs summarize information, respond to hypothetical situations, explain relationships and implications, give clear examples to support statements and arguments, and synthesize information provided by various speakers. In addition, they understand and respond to sarcasm and nuances.

Source: Adapted from TESOL Performance Indicators (2006, pp. 47–97). TESOL. (2006). *PreK–12 English language proficiency standards.* Alexandria, VA: Author.

Strategy

Choral Reading

28

As a teacher of middle school ELLs, Ms. Goguen often used choral reading to build social and academic oral language. One paper that she found particularly useful for supporting choral reading was published in *The Reading Teacher* (McCauley & McCauley, 1992). Strategy 28 is based on this work.

THEORY AND/OR RESEARCH UNDERLYING THE STRATEGY

Choral reading is included in this unit because it effectively supports the development of oral language fluency by providing repeated practice in a safe environment where potential errors are masked by multiple voices. This safety net encourages ELLs to feel comfortable in trying out new language structures and in making mistakes, both of which are likely to expand vocabulary, increase language proficiency, and contribute to overall understanding. The repetition inherent in choral reading promotes the development of syntax, syntactic phrasing, and fluency with language patterns. The use of gestures and cues provides a good source of comprehensible input for ELLs of all ages. Choral reading also promotes communicative competence and overall language ability in ELLs of all proficiency levels. Acting out words in a poem or story in choral reading is consistent with Total Physical Response (TPR) (Asher, 1965), which has been shown to facilitate language acquisition especially with ELLs with lower levels of English proficiency.

IMPLEMENTING THE STRATEGY

1. Find a poem or story that is relatively short and engaging and that deals with topics that are familiar and relatable. (Jack Prelutsky's poems are effective for choral reading. ELLs in Ms. Goguen's class enjoyed these poems, were engaged in instruction, and repeated the stanzas fluently with appropriate syntax, prosody, and clear pronunciation.)

2. Choose poems in which you can include actions and motion to convey meaning. Prelutsky's "Be Glad Your Nose Is on Your Face" is one that works well with lower middle school, as is "The New Kid on the Block" (Prelutsky, 1984).

3. Divide the poem into parts for different groups of students in the class. Heterogeneous grouping for language proficiency levels works well here.

4. Include visuals and acting out parts to make the meaning of the poem accessible to ELLs and to increase the opportunity to learn new structures through TPR.

5. Copy the poem on chart paper or project it using a document camera or overhead projector.

6. Introduce the poem with visuals, graphics, and gestures. Talk about the language in the poem.

7. Read the poem with expression using the visuals, graphics, gestures, and so on.

8. Hand out copies to students.

9. Read the poem slowly as ELLs and FEP learners read along.

10. Gradually increase the pace of the reading, adding the visuals and gestures.

11. Assign lines to groups of students once they appear to understand the poem.

12. Practice reading the poem with the assigned lines.

Choral reading is appropriate for elementary through secondary grades when used as one component to develop fluency, intonation, and pronunciation. The key to adapting choral reading to upper grades is to choose more sophisticated readings and multicultural readings, including rhymes, limericks, Indian chants, and *bombas*, which are Afro–Puerto Rican songs that are associated with plantation work (O'Shea, McQuiston, & McCollin, n.d.). Parts of content-area text books and study guides can also be scripted for choral reading.

Strategy in Action

Language Arts

When using Jack Prelutsky's poems in a combined fifth and sixth grade, mixed language English proficiency classroom, Ms. Goguen printed each poem on an 8 × 10 sheet and using the overhead projector, displayed it for the entire class. She also prepared copies for students, highlighting each stanza in a different color: yellow, pink, blue, and green. She laminated them so that she did not have to recreate the materials each year.

Ms. Goguen began by reading the poem with feeling. She checked for word understanding and discussed the meaning of the lines briefly with students. She then read through the poem again with feeling. (She often had at least one or two students with lower levels of English language proficiency. When this occurred, she allowed other students who spoke their primary language to explain the poem to them. Primary language tutors, if available, could also assist in making the poem comprehensible.)

Mrs. Goguen grouped students heterogeneously with regard to English language proficiency. Students in each group then practiced reading their stanza together. ELLs with lower proficiency levels had the advantage of repeating their lines with the support of ELLs with higher proficiency levels. Once students had practiced several times, they read their stanzas aloud to the larger class. McCauley and McCauley (1992) also suggested adding drama by including an aside, which works well in this poem and provides exposure to terms used in plays and theater. Students reading the aside lean forward as though they are sharing a secret with the audience. Here this is illustrated using "Be Glad Your Nose Is on Your Face" (Prelutsky, 1984). The poem consists of five stanzas; three are included in the example that follows.

Student Language Objective:

1. Read or recite the poem together, paying attention to rhythm, rhyme, and the sounds of language.

   Group 1: Be glad your nose is on your face,
   not pasted in some other place,

   *Group 2: (as an aside): For if it were where it is not,
   you might dislike your nose a lot.*

   Group 3: Your nose would be a source of dread
   Were it attached atop your head,

   *Group 4: (as an aside): It soon would drive you to despair,
   forever tickled by your hair.*

Text copyright © 1984 by Jack Prelutsky.

Regardless of English language proficiency level, students participate enthusiastically in reading poems in a choral reading group. Because their voices are not heard alone, they are comfortable speaking aloud and trying to pronounce English sounds and words. Hearing the poem enables them to repeat it fluently with appropriate prosody.

Other sources for poems include anything written by Prelutsky, who has published over three dozen books, Shel Silverstein's poems for children, and Judith Viorst's "If I Were in Charge of the World" (1981) (recommended by McCauley & McCauley, 1992). Science and social studies texts can also be scripted and used for read-alouds.

Choral (Antiphonal) Reading in Science

Mr. Clark uses choral reading in his eighth grade science class. He began to do so by taking simple science passages and scripting them. He uses illustrations from the science text as prompts and to provide comprehensible input. Here is an example of a quick choral reading script he used with four groups of students, which include FEP learners and ELLs. He developed the script based on his physical science text, *Physical Science* (McLaughlin, Thompson, & Zike, 2008).

Student Language Objectives:

1. Pronounce words from science correctly.

2. Use language to help you remember science terms and concepts.

Students Together: *Different Forms of Energy*

Group 1: *Turn on an electric light*   Group 2: *Your dark room becomes bright.*

Group 3: *Turn on your TV*   Group 4: *A show is there to see.*

Together: *Energy moves from one place to another. Energy moves from one place to another.*

Energy has different forms.

Group 1: *Electrical*   Group 2: *Chemical*

Group 3: *Radiant*   Group 4: *Thermal*

Mr. Clark showed students how he adapted the text as scripts, modeled this process using an overhead projector, and then provided practice for students to write short scripts in teams. Students are often assigned writing scripts to extract the most important information from a text and set this information in an engaging format. Mr. Clark has found that ELLs' confidence in using academic language has grown and that their pronunciation and comprehension has improved. He stores student-generated scripts and prompts with his materials for each teaching unit so that he can use them in future years.

Choral Reading in Social Studies

In preparing a unit on the American Revolution, Ms. Penny works with students to prepare a poem for two voices, one voice representing the perspectives of the Patriots and the second voice representing the perspectives of the Loyalists. She guides students in developing the poem, which helps them to learn content as they develop language. She then divides the class into two heterogeneous groups, who stand at opposite ends of the room, and engages them in reading the poem chorally, each side reading one voice. Through this reading, students become accustomed to using the language of social studies.

Student Language Objectives:

1. Develop a poem for two voices.

2. Use language to build understanding of perspectives.

Assessment

Teacher observation is one way to formatively assess the progress of an ELL or FEP learner in choral reading activities. A simple file for each student kept electronically or in an assessment book enables teachers and students to see progress in academic language. A sample is shown in Table 28.1.

| Table 28.1 | Assessing Progress in Oral Language |

Student Name: Sayra D.

Date	Reading	Appears to understand the reading when it is first read 1–5	Appears to understand the reading with multiple repetitions and visuals 1–5	Participates in choral reading 1–5	Oral Language 1–5				Oral Proficiency Level—based on TESOL indicators 1–5
					Pronunciation	Syntax	Prosody	Fluency	
4/8	The Butterfly	1	3	3	4	2	2	1	3

REFLECTIONS

1. How does choral reading promote English language oral proficiency for ELLs at each proficiency level?

2. Take a passage from a text that you use—an interesting reading passage or a section of a science, social studies, or mathematics text—and create a choral script for the students in your class. Try your script out with a colleague and then with a group of students. Reflect on what worked well and what you might adjust.

STRATEGY RESOURCES

1. 📄 Recommendations from Reading Rockets

   Reading Rockets provides an overview of the benefits of choral reading and descriptions of choral reading in use in the content areas of language arts, science, and social studies. In addition, it provides a list of suggested books for conducting choral reading with younger students.

   http://www.readingrockets.org/strategies/choral_reading

2. 📄 Choral Reading in Science

   A choral reading lesson from ReadWriteThink that combines poetry and science

   http://www.readwritethink.org/classroom-resources/lesson-plans/multipurpose-poetry-introducing-science-69.html?tab=4#tabs

The Basics of Matter (Log into Teacher Tube to set up a free account): A choral reading demonstration

http://www.teachertube.com/members/viewVideo.php?video_id=19517

3. 🎬 Choral Reading in Social Studies—Like the Molave

A demonstration of choral reading with older students in an ESL setting

http://www.youtube.com/watch?v=vOEuQwR-YWU

4. 📄 Choral Reading in English Language Arts for Older Students

This ReadWriteThink lesson includes a classroom video of a choral reading of Shakespeare from student-made scripts.

http://www.readwritethink.org/classroom-resources/lesson-plans/constructing-understanding-through-choral-1121.html

Building Oral Language With Read-Alouds and Picture Books

Strategy 29

Reading aloud to students of all ages has the potential to expose them to academic vocabulary and language structures that, because of their reading level in English, they would not ordinarily be able to access themselves. Read-alouds and picture books make language more comprehensible and enable ELLs and FEP learners to hear and use rich language structures to derive meaning from books and engage in discussions about books. Read-alouds also provide a springboard for academic conversations, which promote greater content-area understanding than students are able to generate on their own (Albright, 2002). Engaging students in a read-aloud involves both careful planning and thoughtful implementation (Campbell, 2001; Goldenberg, 1992).

THEORY AND/OR RESEARCH UNDERLYING THE STRATEGY

Read-alouds are included in this unit because they support the development of oral language fluency through repeated practice in a safe environment where potential errors are masked by multiple voices. In this environment, ELLs are comfortable trying out new language structures, a practice that is likely to increase overall English language proficiency. Building oral language through read-alouds is consistent with the Zone of Proximal Development (ZPD) (Vygotsky, 1978) because ELLs first listen to the passage as it is read by the teacher, which provides a model for pronunciation, phrasing, prosody, and fluency and provides access to words and structures they could not access independently. They then practice these structures with more capable peers. The academic conversations that are integral to read-alouds serve to scaffold and extend language.

IMPLEMENTING THE STRATEGY

Planning

1. Choose high-quality literature that will appeal to the age and interests of ELLs and other students.

2. Read through the materials carefully to select an excerpt that will be meaningful and engaging to students. Content-area picture books can be effective in supplementing instruction for older students (Allbright, 2002).

3. Find or prepare resources (if any) that will build comprehensibility—big books, photos, artifacts, video, realia.

4. Decide how you will introduce the book or the written material and how you will tap into student interests. For example, to introduce a science reading about the phases of the moon, begin by sharing your observations of the changing appearance of the moon (shape and location.) In social studies, introduce *The Butterfly* (Polacco, 2000) with a lead-in about friendship. For older students, prior to reading a short passage from *The Outsiders* (Hinton, 1967), ask students about why they think youth join gangs.

5. Generate questions that will engage students in discussion. For example, while reading *Lyddie* (Paterson, 1991), ask students if they have stood up for something they believed was right, and provide time for them to discuss.

6. Prepare vocabulary words that students will need as part of this discussion. Print these on oak tag or colored cards so they can be displayed on the word wall.

7. Decide how you will wrap up the session. How will you extend the discussion? Will students discuss the story using the key vocabulary words and then write or illustrate the story? Will they present their writing to the class?

Implementing Read-Alouds With Students

1. Create a setting that is appropriate for the age of the students. Younger students can come to the reading center or reading corner. Older students may move their desks into a horseshoe or other pattern that ensures all students can see the visuals (big book, photos, realia, etc.).

2. For older children, begin with a guiding and provocative question first and then conduct the read aloud.

3. Perform the reading (Campbell, 2001) with expression, adjusting the pace according to the lines being read—and being careful not to read too quickly—pause for effect and emphasis.

4. Stop from time to time to share what you are thinking as you read. This will extend and develop language from the text. It also models critical reading.

5. Engage students by asking them to respond to the reading and the questions posed, providing pictures and graphics and allowing ELLs with lower levels of English proficiency to use pictures and gestures to respond.

Source: Adapted from *Read-Alouds With Young Children*, by R. Campbell, 2001, Newark, DE: International Reading Association; *The Read-Aloud Handbook* (4th ed.), by J. Trelease, 1995, New York: Penguin.

STRATEGY IN ACTION

Because read-alouds are often part of the typical early childhood and early elementary grades, this section illustrates the implementation of read-alouds for students in fourth grade and middle school.

Social Studies

As part of a seventh grade unit on Latin America, teacher-researcher Lettie Albright (2002) used picture books to supplement the classroom text. Albright read one of these books, *Discovering the Inca Ice Maiden: My Adventures on Ampato* (Reinhard, 1998) aloud to students. She chose this book because it was relevant to the unit, accurate, and well-written. She prepared questions that tapped into students' background knowledge and the content of the unit. She began with starter questions such as "What can you tell me about [topic]?" "Why might we want to read this book?" and "What do you think this book might be about?" (Albright, 2002, p. 422). As she read, she called students' attention to pictures in the book to stimulate their critical thinking and to engage them in academic discussion about the content. Examples of questions she used include "Does this remind you of anything you've read in your textbook or discussed in class?" "What do you think will happen next?" and "Do you think this is important and why?" (Albright, 2002, p. 422).

Facilitate the meaningful participation of ELLs using a think-pair-share and allowing ELLs at proficiency levels from *Starting* to *Developing* to make notes in their primary languages as they make connections to pictures and to point out pictures in their text that correspond to pictures in the picture book will

For sources for content-area picture books, please see the following (the first three were recommended by Albright, 2002):

1. The National Council for the Social Studies publishes an annual list of children's trade books that are notable in the field of social studies. The book lists are released in the National Council of Social Studies April/May publication. Lists from 2000 to 2009 are available from http://www.socialstudies.org/notable.

2. Each year, the National Science Teachers Association publishes lists of outstanding science trade books for students. The lists are published in March each year and are available from http://www.nsta.org/publications/ostb/ostb2000.aspx.

3. The National Council for the Teachers of English publishes an annual list of outstanding nonfiction for children. The 2010 outstanding award winners are listed at http://www.ncte.org/awards/orbispictus.

4. The California Department of Education has a comprehensible and searchable site for literature in mathematics and science, which is available from http://www .http://www.cde.ca.gov/ci/sc/ll/ap/searchlist.asp.

Science

Ms. Allen uses the picture book *A Drop of Water* (Wick, 1997) to introduce the properties of water and the water cycle. She begins by telling students that before school she turned on her shower and water came out just as it always does. She asks students if they know where the water in their homes comes from. After a few students share their ideas, Ms. Allen introduces the book and the content and language objectives for the lesson—the language objectives are included here.

Student Language Objectives:

1. Listen to the reading of the book and the new vocabulary words.

2. Participate in the discussion about the book.

3. Use the new words and language structures to describe the pictures in the book.

Ms. Allen has printed the vocabulary words on cards: *substance, molecules, surface tension,* and *adhesion*. She reviews these word cards with students. She has also prepared sentence frames to scaffold students' use of some of the difficult science language structures: passive voice, hedging, and nonliving subjects. She distributes handouts with the new vocabulary and sentence frames, which provide scaffolds to academic discussions.

Ms. Allen guides students through the book, discussing each picture. She emphasizes the structure of the book. For example, knowing that science often uses passive voice, which is difficult for ELLs, Ms. Allen reads, "If a drop of water is added to a jar of still water, and the water in the jar is not stirred, where will the new drop go?" (p. 18). Then, using the illustration, she has students say and complete the sentence frame, "If a drop of water is added to a jar of still water, it. . . ."

After Ms. Allen and her students complete the read-aloud, students work in small groups to prepare their own statements to describe each page of the book. Each group then shares their writing.

Table 29.1 provides one rubric that might be used to measure the language progress of ELLs as they participate in read-alouds.

Table 29.1	Assessing Language in Read-Alouds								
Student Name: Ana M.									
					Oral Language 1–5				
Date	Reading	Is attentive to the reading 1–5	Is attentive to the discussion 1–5	Contributes to the discussion in a way that suggests he/ she understands. 1–5	Uses target vocabulary	Contributes to discussion	Creates novel constructions	Is syntactically accurate	Oral Proficiency Level—based on TESOL indicators
9/21	*The Butterfly*	5	4	2	2	2	1	2	3
9/28	*A Drop of Water*								

Another way to assess student understanding is through a cloze test. In a cloze test, teachers create sentences, leaving out key words for students to complete. The cloze test was originally designed by Taylor (1953; cited in Nation, 2009) to measure readability. A reliable cloze test contains approximately 50 blanks, which are placed systematically—every five words or so (Nation, 2009). The cloze provides a quick informal way of checking student understanding. In an oral activity, the cloze should be completed orally. The purpose of the structured observation and the cloze test is to monitor English language development, not to assign a grade based on developmental levels.

REFLECTIONS

1. How does Ms. Allen use picture books to help students understand the water cycle and to build the academic language necessary for them to express conceptual understanding? What content-area unit that you teach could be enriched with high-quality picture books?

2. Conduct a search at NCTE or at the California Department of Education (in the Reference Section), and select picture books that would be appropriate for the next unit you will teach. What guiding questions will you use to facilitate academic conversation? How will you facilitate the participation of ELLs at various proficiency levels?

3. How do systematic observation protocols and clear record keeping enable you to measure the oral language development of ELLs? How would sharing these data with ELLs be helpful to them?

STRATEGY RESOURCES

1. Carol Hurst recommends titles for reading aloud to students from kindergarten through high school.

   http://www.carolhurst.com/profsubjects/reading/readingaloud.html

2. The National Center for Quality Afterschool provides an overview of the goals for read-alouds for young students. The site includes a video of a read-aloud and sample lesson plans.

   http://www.sedl.org/afterschool/toolkits/literacy/pr_read_aloud.html

3. Read-Alouds Move to the Middle Level—The authors provide an overview of the benefits of reading aloud to adolescents and share their findings from observations of middle school read-alouds and interviews with teachers. They provide excellent examples of read-alouds in middle schools.

   http://www.nysut.org/educatorsvoice_12345.htm

4. Scaffolding Language in a Language Rich Classroom Read-Alouds: open-ended questions, modeling, discussing word meanings (2 minutes)

   http://www.youtube.com/watch?v=lmJoOjLQM3U&feature=related

Strategy

30

Developing Community for Classroom Conversations

The first thing that teachers must do to promote academic conversations is to create a classroom community in which all students feel welcome and each student is encouraged to share his or her promising ideas. (Michaels et al., 2007). Members of this community must recognize that ELLs and FEP learners come to the classroom with different levels of experience and proficiency with both social and academic language. A central explicitly stated goal must be to support and scaffold the abilities of each student as he or she engages in academic discussion.

THEORY AND/OR RESEARCH UNDERLYING THE STRATEGY

For ELLs to develop academic oral language proficiency, they must engage in ongoing, meaningful classroom conversations. These conversations are likely to take place when the teacher explicitly and consistently models routines and norms for thoughtful conversation and conveys his or her expectations to students. In this supportive classroom setting, ELLs and FEP learners gradually "develop norms of discourse and students from widely varying backgrounds begin to listen to one another, build on one another's ideas, and participate productively in complex deliberative practices" (Michaels et al., 2007, p. 12). If ELLs are unaccustomed to participating in a student-focused classroom where students have time to discuss important issues, they will need to learn these routines (Michaels et al., 2007). Social conversations are a good way to ease into academic conversations.

IMPLEMENTING THE STRATEGY

1. Arrange the classroom so that students can easily engage in academic conversations: Clustering desks and creating an area for class meeting times provides a physical structure that facilitates classroom conversations. Strategy 1 in this textbook provides guidelines for arranging space to encourage academic conversation.

2. Provide time and routines for social conversation to build community; it is important that students know one another. Fisher et al. (2008) recommend easily implementable, grade-appropriate activities, such as *Getting to Know You Bingo, Find Someone Who,* and student-to-student interviewing. Each of these activities, which are shown in Table 30.1, builds on students' current knowledge and encourages students to get to know each other and converse socially. These activities range from questioning that requires one-word responses to interviewing that requires gradually more expansive responses. These activities scaffold increasingly academic conversations, which will be more challenging for ELLs. The time spent on these activities will ultimately result in more collaboration, cooperation, and active learning (Fisher et al., 2008). (While in-class social interaction frequently occurs in early elementary school, middle and secondary grade students whom I have interviewed often do not have this experience, and they may not even know their classmates' names.)

3. Explicitly model the conversation to ensure that students of all proficiency levels have language structures that enable them to participate in the conversations, including language forms that will extend conversation, such as "Could you say more . . . ?" and clarifying questions, such as "Could you explain what you mean by . . . ?" (These structures may not be immediately accessible to ELLs at lower levels of proficiency.)

4. Model wait time to show students how long 20 to 30 seconds is. Wait time in a classroom is extremely useful to ELLs at all levels.

5. Display conversation extension forms (What do you mean by . . . ? Can you say more about . . . ? Could you please explain . . . ?) in a prominent place in the room.

6. Gradually release responsibility to students.

Table 30.1	Three Activities to Build Community Through Social Conversations

1. ***Getting to Know You Bingo*** is an engaging game that requires students to learn more about each other by completing bingo cards. Cards are easily made using standard sheets of paper divided into boxes and a copy machine. Boxes may include descriptors such as "Has lived in a different city, state, or country; has a dog, cat, hamster, fish, younger or older brother, or sister; likes to eat apples, rice and beans, or fish for breakfast; speaks Mandarin, French, or Spanish." In order to fill their cards, students must find someone in the class that fits the description. Students write the matching student's name in the appropriate box. Using *Picture Card Getting to Know You* is a good variation for younger children and ELLs. Picture cards can be made using pictures on the Internet, clip art, or pictures found in magazines and newspapers.

2. As a variation to Getting to Know You Bingo, students can use teacher-made charts to *Find Someone Who* has two brothers or likes to play the violin, eat pizza, play baseball, and so on. Similar to Getting to Know You Bingo, students circulate throughout the room to find someone who _____. The person who plays the violin, eats pizza, and so on signs the card.

3. *Personal Interviews* also enable students to learn more about each other, are likely to generate conversation, and provide students with the opportunity to practice

(Continued)

(Continued)

language forms. Work with students to generate a list of probing questions that will help students get to know each other. Create handouts for the questions that students generate and using the whiteboard, document camera or overhead projector display questions for students. With the help of another student (or faculty member), model the interview process, asking questions, and then probing for more information using language forms such as, "Could you say more . . . ?" Students then use the questions to interview one another in pairs and introduce their partners to the class.

Interviews can be modified for *Starting* and *Emerging* ELLs in the following ways: If there is more than one ELL who speaks the same language, pair these students together and encourage them to conduct the interview in their first language as well as in English. Students report to the class together, or if the ELL with the lower level of proficiency is not comfortable speaking in front of the class, the student with the higher proficiency level may report out. When there is only one speaker of any language, assign a buddy to conduct the interview using visuals (similar to Picture Bingo). During the interview, the ELL can teach the buddy several new words in her or his language, which the buddy can then teach the class. (See strategy 4 in this book.)

Source: Getting to Know You Bingo, Find Someone Who, and Personal Interviews are adapted from *Content Area Conversations: How to Plan Discussion-Based Lessons for Diverse Language Learners* (Chapter 4), by D. Fisher, N. Frey, and C. Rothenberg, 2008, Alexandria, VA: Association for Supervision and Curriculum Development (ASCD).

Fisher et al. (2008, p. 80) also suggest the use of sentence frames to scaffold ELLs' language. Table 30.2 illustrates sentence frames for the interview assignment. Questions 5 and 6 lend themselves to elaboration.

Table 30.2	Sentence Frames
Interview Question	*Frame*
1. Where do you live?	I live _____.
2. What languages do you speak?	I speak _____.
3. How many brothers and sisters do you have?	I have _____ brother(s) and _____ sister(s).
4. How long have you lived in the house you live in now?	I have lived there for _____.
5. What is your favorite hobby (thing you like to do) and why?	My favorite hobby is _____ because _____.
6. If you could go anywhere, where would you go and why?	I would like to go to _____ because _____.

When Mr. Gordon introduces the interview protocol to his third grade students, he posts the interview questions on the Smart Board. He models the entire interview process at the front of the room with a student volunteer. As he models, he refers to each interview question. Mr. Gordon also provides sentence frames (Fisher et al., 2008) to facilitate the participation of ELLs with proficiency levels *Emerging* through *Expanding*. (ELLs with *Starting* proficiency levels will benefit from interviewing in their first language and being able to communicate with a combination of gestures, first language, and English.)

After Mr. Gordon models the interview process, he checks for student understanding, and then places students in pairs to practice. He creates these initial pairs with student comfort levels in mind—his goal is to keep affective filters low. Whenever possible, he places ELLs who speak the same primary language together. As students conduct their interviews, Mr. Gordon circulates and eavesdrops on interviews to ensure that students can use the protocol. He redirects students when appropriate, and he provides additional scaffolding as necessary. Once Mr. Gordon has informally assessed that students can use the protocol, he requires students to use the protocol independently to conduct another interview.

Student Language Objective

1. Use oral language to learn more about students and to share information about yourself.

Assessment

Observe ELLs (and others) as they mingle within the classroom. Are they on task? Can they complete the social conversation tasks with or without the support of the scaffolds, which include sentence frames or buddies who may or may not speak their primary language? Are they able to use language forms to extend conversation and to ask for clarification? Record observations so that you will be able to evaluate student progress and share this assessment with the ELL.

REFLECTIONS

1. How do the activities provided in this strategy help to establish a community that facilitates classroom conversations? Review the TESOL proficiency levels. How do scaffolds enable ELLs at each proficiency level to participate?

2. What other scaffolds might be useful?

STRATEGY RESOURCE

1. *Guided Construction of Knowledge in the Classroom: Teacher, Talk, Task, and Tools* provides a clear discussion of Accountable Talk with excellent examples that illustrate how students from culturally and linguistically diverse backgrounds learn together in the Classroom Community.

   http://www.parentseducationnetwork.org/resources/documents/HowEffectiveTalk.pdf

Strategy 31

Fostering Academic Discussions With Accountable Talk

THEORY AND/OR RESEARCH UNDERLYING THE STRATEGY

Accountable Talk has been shown to increase the quality of academic conversations of students from culturally and linguistically diverse backgrounds (Michaels et al., 2007) and to scaffold both academic content and academic language (Goldenberg, 1992/1993). ELLs and FEP learners who have not had substantial experience engaging in academic conversations within the classroom will need to learn the language and language structures to do so. It requires time to fully implement Accountable Talk, yet improvements in academic language and content-area understanding make this time well spent.

In the Accountable Talk classroom, the teacher begins by modeling the conversation process and forms of language. Following the teacher's model, ELLs and FEP learners are able to engage in focused academic talk in small groups while the teacher circulates and provides additional modeling as needed. To make academic talk more accessible to ELLs and FEP learners, the teacher may provide additional scaffolding, including sentence frames and charts with the academic words and expressions that ELLs and others will use (Fisher et al., 2008). As a result of these scaffolds, ELLs are able to understand and produce language structures.

The TESOL performance indicators provide an overview of what ELLs at each proficiency level will be able to produce when they are provided with effective instruction. These indicators are quite general. You also should use your knowledge of developmentally appropriate conversations in your content area and for the age of students in your classroom.

IMPLEMENTING THE STRATEGY

1. Model academic language as a normal part of classroom practice. When academic terms and expressions (e.g., *predict, investigate, form hypotheses*) are consistently modeled in the classroom, ELLs and other students are likely to learn and use these words in context (Beck et al., 2002; Fisher et al., 2008). The modeling of

academic conversations should also include attentive listening, providing wait time, and extending conversations with expressions such as "That is an important point, could you say more?" "Could you explain what you mean by . . . ," and "Why do you think . . . ?" ELLs and other students who consistently hear these phrases begin to use them to extend academic conversations within their small groups and with the larger class (Michaels et al., 2007).

2. Explain why you are teaching the strategy, including the usefulness or value of the strategy (e.g., "Having conversations about the text will help you to learn more from your reading") and the specific use of the strategy (i.e., to summarize, clarify parts of the text that are confusing, to question the text, and to predict what the remainder of the text will be about).

3. Model Accountable Talk by ensuring that students are (1) accountable to the community (e.g., they listen, request clarification, disagree respectfully), (2) accountable to knowledge (e.g., they are specific, get the facts straight, ask questions requiring evidence), and (3) accountable to standards of reasoning (e.g., they build arguments, link evidence with claims, and make clear statements). (Michaels et al., 2007)

4. Display language forms prominently within the classroom so that students can access these as scaffolds. Another effective technique is to print language forms on one side of manila folders and to place these folders on students' desks, so that ELLs and FEP learners have language forms as scaffolds when needed for conversation. See Table 31.1.

5. Make academic talk accessible to all students by placing key terms and academic language on word walls (or personal word walls using manila folders), referring to these during the talk, and paraphrasing in student-friendly language.

6. Pose questions that foster critical thinking about a topic. These questions generally encourage the discussion of multiple perspectives and viewpoints, rather than focusing solely on a right answer. They provide students with opportunities to make connections to their learning and to build academic language. These questions can frame components of instruction in one content area or branch across content areas. For example, "Who has rights to natural resources?" is a question that could be used in environmental science, social studies, or a multidisciplinary unit (Colombo & Furbush, 2009). The most important quality of an academic question is that it fosters meaningful academic conversation that requires students to use content-area knowledge and concepts to actively participate in a classroom discussion. This type of discussion increases knowledge and conceptual understanding as well as language proficiency.

7. Explain the expected outcome of the academic conversation so that students know what they are expected to do during the conversation. For example, "Using the academic vocabulary words from the math unit and the language forms we have practiced for extending and clarifying discussion points, discuss the best strategies for solving the math problem you have been given. Then collaboratively solve this problem."

8. Model academic language and classroom practices to extend student responses. Use the academic words and phrases that you would like students to develop: "What did the analysis show?" "How did you estimate the area?" "Could you explain how setting conveys theme in this story?" "Could you explain your thinking based on what you read?"

9. Scaffold students' language by encouraging them to use precise vocabulary, but do not turn the lesson into an IRE activity, rewarding students for using precise

vocabulary and correcting them when they are less precise. The goal is to extend academic talk in a meaningful way.

10. Provide wait time so that all students will have an opportunity to participate. ELLs need time to think about how they will express themselves in English. Provide 20 to 30 seconds or longer of wait time.

11. Provide sufficient time for students to respond, and ask questions that serve to scaffold and extend students' responses. For example, "Hmmm . . . good point. Could you say more about how you think these are different?"

12. Build group and individual accountability for academic discussions and content-area learning by ensuring that each student participates in his or her small group. Cooperative learning activities such as Numbered Heads Together (Kagan Publishing, 2008—described in the Strategy in Action section that follows) and the Jigsaw are useful in keeping students accountable.

Table 31.1	Make Accountable Talk Transparent Classroom Display
Principles	*Sample Language Forms*
We Are Accountable	
To Our Community	Take your time. We will wait.
	Could you say more about...?
	Does anyone want to add to that?
	I would like to add....
	I agree because ....
	I disagree because ...
To Knowledge	How do you know...?
	On what do you base...?
	Where did you find...?
To Standards of Reasoning	I think ... because [evidence]
	Why do you say...?
	What evidence supports...?

Source: Based on *Guided Construction of Knowledge in the Classroom: Teacher, Talk, Task, and Tools,* by S. Michaels, M. C. O'Connor, R. Sohmer, and L. Resnick, n.d., San Francisco: Parents Education Network.

Strategy in Action

Mrs. Rojas's students (ELLs and FEP learners) are learning about perimeter. As part of this class, she wants students to solve a problem involving perimeter, to be able to discuss how they solved the problem, and explain why they used that particular process. Students work in groups of three. Mrs. Rojas introduces a problem: She provides students with a map drawing of a very irregular plot of land and tells them the following: "Here is a map of your land with a scale. You want to know the perimeter and area of this land. How will you determine the most precise measurements for perimeter and area?" She writes the question on the whiteboard. She encourages students to use their math books, other diagrams, and the formulas on the classroom walls. They must collaborate together to decide the process that they will use and to solve the problem.

Mrs. Rojas explains the language objective of the lesson using the vocabulary words *process* and *precision*. She makes these words more comprehensible to ELLs by paraphrasing *process* and defining *precision*: "Today in your groups you will discuss the ways that the *process*—that is, the *way* you measured the perimeter—might affect the *precision* of the measurement—or how close it is to the real distance."

Mrs. Rojas also uses other academic words that she expects ELLs and other students will use in this discussion: *perimeter, approximation, area, estimate,* and *precision*. She has posted these target academic words on a word wall and points to each word as she reviews it.

Mrs. Rojas knows that Jonathan, an ELL with a *Developing* to *Expanding* level of English language proficiency, may need additional time to explain what he means in English. She provides wait time before she calls on students (20–30 seconds), which enables Jonathan to raise his hand to participate. When he volunteers to explain why he thinks his group's measurement of the perimeter of the classroom differed from another, Ms. Rojas provides time for him to gather his thoughts. After about 10 or 15 seconds, Jonathan is able to explain, "I think their measure stick is different." She scaffolds, "Why do you think that? Could you say more about what you are thinking?" This gives Jonathan the opportunity to explain his thoughts.

One way that Mrs. Rojas ensures the participation of each student is by using Numbered Heads Together (Kagan, 2008), a collaborative grouping strategy that promotes the active participation of each student in a group. In Numbered Heads Together, students work in small groups to solve a problem, and each member in the group is responsible for ensuring that other students in her or his group are able to respond.

Using Academic Sentence Frames

Strategy 30 provided an example of a sentence frame used to scaffold conversational language. Frames are even more useful to students when they engage in academic conversation. Here, frames provide a structure that enables ELLs to process content while they practice language. While the frames initially may sound artificial, they provide a way for ELLs to enter into academic conversation with FEP learners in the classroom and to practice linguistic structures (Fisher et al., 2008). Frames are gradually removed as students master the structures, thus releasing responsibility to students. Table 31.2 illustrates a frame used in one sixth grade science classroom. Students who are working with these frames also have access to a word wall.

Table 31.2	Sentence Frames Following a Science Experiment

1. Our team investigated _____

2. Our team explored _____

3. We found _____

4. Our findings showed_____ (Note: The impersonal or author-evacuated stance has been shown to be difficult for ELLs [Graham & Perrin, 2007].)

5. Our findings suggested _____ (Note: Hedging [e.g., *suggested* rather than *showed*] is difficult for ELLs [Hinkel, 2004]).

Generally, _____ (Note: This is another example of hedging.)

Passive voice is also difficult for ELLs. If a discussion will benefit from passive voice, sentence frames should be provided.

Assessment

The purpose of this assessment is to measure and chart the progress of ELLs and other students toward developing Accountable Talk when they are provided with rich and appropriately scaffolded instruction as well as ongoing opportunities to engage in academic discussions within the classroom. (For instruction to be appropriate, it must be comprehensible to ELLs at all proficiency levels. ELLs cannot participate if they do not understand the conversation.) For a description of oral language proficiency levels, please see Table VI.2. Table 31.3 illustrates an observation assessment for Lia, whose English proficiency level is *Developing*. Table 31.4 illustrates an observation assessment for Sophal, whose level of proficiency is *Starting*.

Table 31.3	Assessment: *Developing Proficiency*	
Student: Lia C.		
Date: 10/2 Proficiency Level: Developing Accommodations: Sentence frames and vocabulary words on manila folder tented on desk Visuals, including text and picture book illustrating the water cycle Repetition of key points Frequent think-pair-share to check for understanding		
Accountability to Community		
Actively Listens (1–5)	Requests Clarification (1–5)	Disagrees Respectfully—Adds to Group's Understanding (1–5)
5—Actively listens and looks to picture book and folder . . . gestures (nods) to indicate understanding. Uses facial expressions to indicate confusion.	3—Through gestures and expressions.	3—With scaffolding and time to practice statements with team member.
Accountability to Knowledge		
Specific and Accurate (1–5)	Gets the Facts Correct (1–5)	Ask Questions Requiring Evidence (1–5)
5—Lia demonstrates content-area understanding through gestures, nods, and by turning the books she is using to the appropriate section. She points to appropriate picture as she tries to explain her point.	5—Lia demonstrates content knowledge through gestures, nods, and by turning the books she is using to the appropriate section to show evidence.	5—For example, she asked Jeff, "Why do you say the water in the glass evaporates?"
Accountability to Standards of Reasoning		
Builds Arguments	Links Claims and Evidence	Makes Statements Clear
4—Lisa told her group, "I think tension because I can see this on p. 10. Here is the picture." This is illustrated by quote about tension.	4—Yes, see Builds Arguments.	4—For her level of English proficiency, Lia makes clear statements and supports these statements with visuals.

Table 31.4	Assessment: *Starting Proficiency*

Student: Sophal

Date: 10/2
Proficiency Level: Starting
Accommodations: Sentence frames and vocabulary words on manila folder tented on desk
Visuals, including text and picture book illustrating the water cycle
Repetition of key points
Frequent think-pair-share to check for understanding

Accountability to Community

Actively Listens (1–5)	Requests Clarification (1–5)	Disagrees Respectfully—Adds to Group's Understanding (1–5)
2—Actively listens for 5–10 minutes when students remember to use visuals. (More than this seems like overload.) Appropriate for proficiency level. His buddy helps by pointing to visuals.	2—With buddy, he points to visuals and tries short phrases— "This is tension?"	1—Without primary language support, Sophal is not yet able to do this.

Accountability to Knowledge

Specific and Accurate (1–5)	Specific and Accurate (1–5)	Specific and Accurate (1–5)
2—Sophal is able to point to pictures to illustrate points and match correct words to pictures.	2—Sophal uses pictures and gestures to illustrate concepts.	See above

Accountability to Standards of Reasoning

Builds Arguments	Links Claims and Evidence	Makes Statements Clear
See above	2—When I (teacher) position myself next to him, he points to illustrations and gestures to ask if he is correct.	See above

REFLECTIONS

1. How does Accountable Talk benefit ELLs and other FEP learners in the content-area classroom?

2. How are scaffolds useful in building academic language during Accountable Talk? Consider a unit that you teach that lends itself to Accountable Talk. How would you build sentence frames and other scaffolds to enable all ELLs to participate in academic conversation?

Strategy Resources

1. 🗐 *Accountable Talk in Reading Comprehension: A Technical Report* by Wolf, Crosson, and Resnick (2006), which studied the effect of Accountable Talk on Reading Comprehension.

   http://www.cse.ucla.edu/products/reports/r670.pdf

2. 🗎 Mathematically Accountable Talk: Teaching Students to be Mathematically Smart

   Adapted from the work of Daro and Resnick, this very short article provides an overview of how Accountable Talk works in the mathematics classroom, and it includes a link to an excerpt from Resnick.

   http://www.math.utep.edu/Faculty/duval/class/random/mathaccttalk.html

UNIT
VII

Strategies for Enhancing Reading and Writing

I teach English language arts, and I am working to ensure that all my students are prepared to pass the state tests, which include reading and writing. I am not sure how to help the English language learners who were placed in my classroom this year.

—Grade 4 Teacher

Novice and veteran teachers across grade levels and across content areas frequently express concerns about their ability to help ELLs to read and write at grade level and to support ELLs' use of these abilities to learn content and share their knowledge and understandings with others. In the United States, the gap in reading and writing between FEP learners and ELLs has been and remains substantial. In 2002, the National Literacy Panel was formed to address this gap (August & Shanahan, 2006). The Panel identified, assessed, and synthesized research in the area of literacy in English as a second language. As a result of this review of research, the Panel identified six components essential to second language English literacy. The first five of these components—phonemic awareness, phonics, comprehension, fluency, and vocabulary—are consistent with a previous study on first language literacy that was released in 2002 by the National Reading Panel. The sixth factor identified as critical to second language reading and writing by the National Literacy Panel is oral language. In fact, according to the National Literacy Panel research, "The reason for the disparity between word- and text-level skills among language-minority students is oral English proficiency" and "Well-developed oral proficiency in English is associated with English reading comprehension and writing skills for these students" (August & Shanahan, 2006). An overview of the development of vocabulary and oral language proficiency as well as selected strategies for teaching vocabulary and oral language were presented in Units V and VI of this book. Thus, this unit provides strategies for developing phonemic awareness, phonics, comprehension, and fluency in reading. It is important to keep in mind that these strategies must build on and foster oral proficiency to be effective for teaching ELLs.

WHAT YOU WILL LEARN

Unit VII includes an overview of theory, strategies, and vignettes to provide you with a general understanding of the following:

1. The process of reading.

2. The strengths and needs ELLs bring to the classroom with regard to reading and writing.

3. Several research-based strategies to support ELLs' development of reading and writing.

4. When and how to seek support from specialists (teachers of ESL, reading, or special education).

Unit VII differentiates for Grades K through 3, when students are learning to read, and Grades 4 through 8, when students are reading to learn and continually developing more sophisticated reading skills that will enable them to learn content from text. It also differentiates between ELLs who have had very different preparation with regard to reading: (1) ELLs who are preliterate in both their primary language and English, and (2) ELLs who are able to read or write near grade level in their primary language. Of course, many ELLs fall in the middle of this range—they are able to read in their primary language, but not yet able to read at grade level. For the purpose of this unit, these ELLs are grouped with ELLs who read at or near grade level in their primary language. Before discussing literacy instruction for ELLs, it is important to discuss the process of reading.

THE PROCESS OF READING

Reading is a highly complex, language-based process that integrates the reader's world and experiential knowledge, her knowledge of text structure and features, and her ability to make sense of written symbols. It involves making meaning from print in a variety of contexts, and it is thus intimately connected with language development. Reading involves an ongoing interaction between top-down processes, such as inferencing, predicting, problem solving and constructing meaning and bottom-up processes, including letter recognition, linking letters with sounds, word identification, accessing word meaning, and chunking words into phrases. Top-down processes are influenced by language development, culture, background knowledge, and general preparation. Bottom-up language processes are developed through exposure to print and direct instruction as needed (Birch, 2008, p. 10). Figure VII.1 illustrates the interaction of top-down and bottom-up processes.

| Figure VII.1 | Interaction of Top-Down and Bottom-Up Knowledge and Strategies |

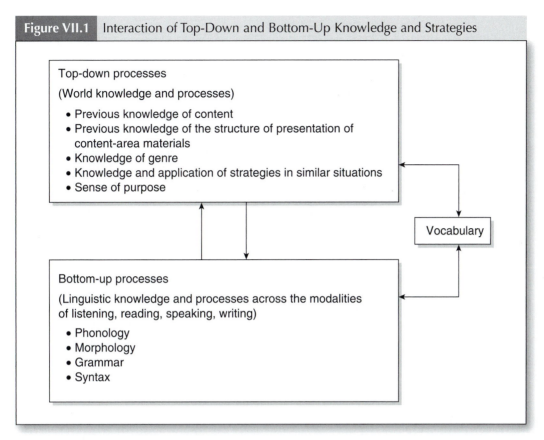

Source: From *Teaching English Language Learners: Content and Language in Middle and Secondary Mainstream Classrooms,* by M. Colombo and D. Furbush, 2009, Thousand Oaks, CA: Sage. Based on English L2 Reading: Getting to the Bottom, by B. Birch, 2008, New York: Routledge.

LEARNING TO READ—READING TO LEARN

Students in kindergarten through third grade spend a great deal of their instructional time learning how to read. This learning depends on oral language development (August & Shanahan, 2006; Nation, 2009), facility with language (i.e., vocabulary, rhyming, and alliteration) (Chall, 1983), and engagement with appropriate instruction (Nation, 2009). Reading development is likely to follow fairly predictable stages. The matrix in Table VII.2 illustrates the stages of reading, based on Chall's (1983) seminal work—which remains a commonly used model of reading development. The stages are based on the optimal reader, are approximate, and depend on educational opportunities. Children who are learning to read in a language other than English will show similar development (Birch, 2008).

According to Chall's model, Stage 1 readers are focused on the relationship between the sounds and symbols on the page, the lower-level processes of decoding and encoding Early in this stage, readers concentrate on sounding out and identifying words. Oral language plays an important role because readers must know the words they are sounding out. Ongoing opportunities to read with teachers and peers and to independently read books for pleasure provide necessary practice with bottom-level processing. Readers should have access to books that are matched to their reading level and interests. Again, the role of oral language is apparent: Readers must know at least 95% of the words they encounter to read for pleasure. With appropriate opportunities for practice,

Table VII.2	Chall's Stages of Reading		
Learning to Read			
Stage 0	Stage 1	Stage 2	Stage 3
Birth—Preschool	Grades K–2	Grades 2–3	Grades 4–8
Children acquire oral language and an awareness of sounds within words that words can be broken into parts, and that parts can be put together to form new words. They also acquire knowledge of print. Most children can identify letters, write their names, and hold a book right-side up and turn the pages.	Children learn the relationship between letters and the sounds they make. They learn to decode and recode, focusing on the bottom-up skills of processing letters and the corresponding sounds.	Children's ability to decode and recode becomes automatic. They become less conscious of the bottom-up processes, which enables them to attend to top-down processes. Comprehension improves. Students at this stage must read extensively at *their independent reading level* to practice these new skills.	Children begin to read to learn. Growth in background knowledge and vocabulary are important to this stage. Initially, reading materials provided to students in this stage should begin with topics about which students have background knowledge.

Source: Based on the seminal work *Stages of Reading,* by J. S. Chall, 1983, New York: Harcourt Brace.

bottom-level processing becomes so automatic that readers are no longer conscious of it. Readers are able to focus their attention on comprehension and fluency.

Early readers' ability to comprehend text is also facilitated by regular ongoing exposure to read-alouds, picture books, and storytelling. These top-down, language-rich experiences continue to provide readers with exposure to vocabulary; practice with predicting, confirming, and inferencing; and experience with the structure of narrative and expository text.

By the end of third grade, most FEP learners in U.S. schools who are not experiencing difficulties will be able to combine bottom-up processes with top-down processes to read English text. At this stage, readers are able to recognize many words automatically and read accessible materials with expression and fluency. Gradually, the focus in the third grade and beyond shifts from learning to read to reading to learn. Although readers continue to develop reading strategies necessary to access increasingly sophisticated texts, they will also be expected to read to acquire and learn new information in English language arts, social studies, science, and mathematics.

PRELITERATE ELLS

ELLs who, for whatever reason, have not learned to read in English or in another language will need to learn how to read. Research (i.e., Collier, 1992; Cummins, 1991; Hakuta, 1986) suggests clear benefits to teaching ELLs to read in their first language and then scaffolding the transfer of first language reading strategies to English. However, teaching reading in a student's first language is not always possible; some languages are low incidence, and it may be difficult to find reading materials in the languages and teachers who speak the language. In some states, politics and policy have mandated that ELLs must be taught to read in English.

Preliterate ELLs will experience the same stages of reading as FEP learners; however, they will be forced to learn to read in a language that is new to them. They will require effective reading instruction that builds oral language proficiency in English and that introduces sound-symbol relationships (phonics) using words in the ELL's mental **lexicon** (Nation, 2009).

> *Lexicon:* the vocabulary knowledge stored in one's mind.

ELLs Who Are Literate in Another Language

Regardless of grade level, English language proficiency, and first language, ELLs who have learned to read in one language do not need to learn to read again. They are able to transfer their first language reading strategies and skills to English reading. They will need to develop oral language proficiency in English to make sense of English text. They may also need learning opportunities that provide background knowledge prior to reading in order to effectively use their top-down reading strategies.

Bottom-up strategies and skills (phonemic awareness, alphabet scripts, alphabetic principles) transfer more readily when the first language is similar to English. For example, positive transfer is facilitated by languages that use the same directionality, left to right and top to bottom, and Roman alphabet script as English, such as Spanish or Italian. Readers of languages that feature different directionality (right to left and/or bottom to top) will need to learn English print conventions. Readers of languages with different alphabet systems, such as Arabic or Greek, will need to learn the English alphabet system and the sound-symbol relationships within the English alphabet system. Languages that use symbols (i.e., Mandarin) are thought to foster strategies to process the written letters as pictures; reading in English will require strategies that are effective with an alphabetic system (Birch, 2008).

Even ELLs who have learned to read using a Roman alphabet will need to learn the sounds of English and the sound-symbol relationships. For example, in Spanish or German, each letter makes the same unique sound. In contrast, English letters and combinations of letters can make different sounds (e.g., the consonant *c* in the words *receive* and *recount*; the vowel *a* in *can, cane,* and *farm*; and consonant blends, such as *sh, ch*). Whereas most vowel systems have five sounds, English has 12, and that does not include regional variations and dialects (Birch, 2008).

ELLs will also need to learn the English sounds that do not exist in their primary languages, develop new decoding strategies that are effective in reading English, learn the English sound-symbol relationships (phonics), and use English morphemes (the smallest elements of meaning, such as *s, es, ed, ing, er, est*).

The Role of the Regular Classroom Teacher

In kindergarten and Grade 1, it is likely that the instructional needs of ELLs (preliterate and readers in their primary language) will resemble the needs of FEP learners. Regular classroom teachers are likely to dedicate substantial classroom time to immersing students in experiences that build oral language and to using rich literature to teach young students the alphabet principle, phonics, and decoding and encoding skills. The structure of this instruction benefits ELLs in the classroom, and the classroom teacher who has the knowledge specified by the TESOL standards can provide much of the ELL's reading instruction—monitoring progress and requesting support from specialists if needed. During this time, ELLs should also receive ongoing support from an ESL teacher, and ELLs who appear to have difficulty hearing sounds in words that they know will likely benefit from additional instruction from a reading specialist.

As grade levels progress, preliterate ELLs will require a more formal, team approach, with services provided by a classroom teacher who has a depth of understanding of TESOL standards, a reading specialist with substantive expertise in second language literacy, and an ESL specialist who can support oral language development. The combined and well-coordinated efforts of this team will enable the ELL to learn content as he or she develops oral language and literacy in English.

STRATEGIES IN THIS UNIT

Because reading is a meaning-making process, any instruction should be provided using meaningful and purposeful learning activities and materials, beginning with assessment of what the ELL knows and continuing with building on the ELL's current abilities. This unit includes eight strategies that build on the literacy abilities and skills of ELLs.

First, Strategy 32 illustrates the Language Experience Approach; next, Strategy 33: Assessing and Supporting the Conventions of English Print is included for ELLs who are preliterate as well as for ELLs who read in another language. We know that good readers use a variety of strategies that help them make sense of the text. Explicitly teaching reading comprehension strategies in reading and content-area classrooms provides all students with what Adler (2001) referred to as a conscious plan for making sense of text. The strategies that students learn also help them to self-monitor their comprehension. Teaching ELLs comprehension strategies is the objective of Strategies 34, 35, and 36 (Summarizing Text—The GIST; Building Comprehension for ELLs With Reciprocal Teaching; and Using Text Structure). Readers Theatre (Strategy 37) is included to build fluency in English reading. Strategies 38 and 39 focus on writing in English: Interactive Writing is the focus of Strategy 38, and Revising and Editing: Teaching Writing Conventions is presented in Strategy 39. The strategies in this unit are consistent with the TESOL Standards for teachers (Table VII.3) and students. The TESOL performance indicators for students are separated into kindergarten through Grade 3, which are generally considered the grades in which learning to read occurs (Table VII.4), and Grades 4 through 8, when the focus switches to reading to learn (Table VII.5).

Table VII.3	TESOL Standards for Teachers

Domain 1: Language

1.a.2. Apply knowledge of phonology (the sound system), morphology (the structure of words), syntax (phrase and sentence structure), semantics (word/sentence meaning), and pragmatics (the effect of context on language) to help ELLs develop oral, reading, and writing skills (including mechanics) in English. (p. 29)

1.b.2 . . . [U]nderstand theories and research that explain how L1 literacy development differs from L2 literacy development. (p. 35)

1.b.5. Understand and apply knowledge of the role of individual learner variables in the process of learning English. (p. 37)

Domain 3: Planning, Implementing, and Managing Instruction

3.b.6. Provide standards-based instruction that builds on students' oral English to support learning to read and write. (p. 51)

3.b.7. Provide standards-based reading instruction adapted to ELLs. (p. 51)

3.b.8. Provide standards-based writing instruction adapted to ELLs. Develop students' writing through a range of activities, from sentence formation to expository writing. (p. 52)

Source: TESOL (2010). *TESOL/NCATE Standards for the Recognition of Initial TESOL Programs in P-12 ESL Teacher Education.* Alexandria, VA: TESOL.

Table VII.4	Reading and Writing

Based on TESOL Performance Indicators Grades K–3, Assuming Ongoing Appropriate Instruction, Instructional Materials and Depending On Grade Level

TESOL Standards 1–5: ELLs read and write to share social and cultural information and ideas.

Level 1—Starting

Reading: When ELLs are provided with visuals, they begin to make meaning from English text. With appropriate instruction, ELLs identify pictures that represent family members, common objects (e.g., books), and common areas within the school (e.g., cafeteria) or within the community (e.g., homes, stores, school). They match words with pictures, connect pictures to realia, and match symbols or icons with pictures (e.g., smiley faces to pictures that convey happiness).

Writing: When ELLs are provided with visuals, they are able to combine these with simple words or phrases to convey meaning in writing. ELLs draw, copy words/phrases/ sentences, and write words or phrases with invented spelling to describe events. When provided with cloze activities that are appropriate for Level 1 proficiency, ELLs complete these activities to express ideas.

Level 2—Emerging

Reading: Visuals continue to play an important role in reading English text. ELLs identify letters in words accompanied by illustrations that represent common objects. They match and sort pictures/drawings with words. ELLs use short sentences to convey the meaning of popular icons (e.g., Golden Arches = McDonalds has Happy Meals). They depict characters and sequence story elements using graphic organizers.

Writing: ELLs at this level continue to blend visuals with text to convey meaning. They label drawings of familiar people or objects in developmentally appropriate ways (e.g., scribbles, invented spelling, more conventional spelling), create lists of known people and items, write short sentences about favorite activities, and write about events and stories using writing models and graphic organizers.

(Continued)

Table VII.4 (Continued)

Based on TESOL Performance Indicators Grades K–3, Assuming Ongoing Appropriate Instruction, Instructional Materials, and Depending On Grade Level

Level 3—Developing

Reading: ELLs continue to use visuals and organizers to make meaning from written text. They match names of objects with pictures, match words with pictures, sort labeled pictures of known objects by initial letters, sequence story events using words and visuals and graphic organizers, and "draw or select written responses to visually or graphically supported descriptive paragraphs" (TESOL, 2006, p. 65).

Writing: ELLs copy words that match pictures, illustrate and label everyday events at developmentally appropriate levels (e.g., scribbles, invented spelling, more conventional spelling), copy or create lists, and draw and label familiar people, objects, places, and events. ELLs at this level write about familiar topics using graphic organizers and writing models; they are able to write compare and contrast statements and paragraphs using graphic organizers.

Level 4—Expanding

Reading: ELLs in kindergarten continue to rely on visuals within text to make meaning (as do many young English speakers), whereas ELLs in Grades 1 through 3 require fewer visuals to construct meaning but continue to use graphic organizers to access meaning from text. ELLs in kindergarten and early Grade 1 identify common words in their environment, sequence text with visuals, construct meaning from books with print, and use titles and illustrations to make predictions and inferences from written text. They identify frequently encountered words when they are accompanied by illustrations, sequence events using picture cards with text, and are able to arrange scrambled sentences accompanied by visuals.

Writing: Using scaffolds such as invented spelling, word banks, teacher modeling, and drawings, ELLs write personal stories about special events and share knowledge from books and classroom activities (beginning with copying text and using invented spelling to writing short phrases and sentences). ELLs in Grades 1 through 3 begin to write sentences and paragraphs to describe events or stories, begin to use transition words to sequence text (at first, then, last), and to develop grade-appropriate writing conventions when working with a partner, such as identifying capital letters.

Level 5—Bridging

Reading: At this level, ELLs require visuals to a similar degree as native English speakers. They continue to benefit from graphic organizers and modified grade-level texts and continue to require additional support with vocabulary and complex text structures.

Writing: ELLs complete writing tasks at levels similar to native English speakers. They continue to benefit from support with vocabulary (word walls, word banks, academic conversations) and support to appropriately use transitions and prepositions (word walls and academic conversations).

Source: Based on TESOL Performance Indicators: TESOL (2006). *PreK–12 English Language Proficiency Standards* (pp. 47–97), Alexandria, VA: TESOL.

Table VII.5	Reading and Writing

Based on TESOL Performance Indicators Grade 4–8, Assuming Ongoing Appropriate Instruction, Instructional Materials,and Depending On Grade Level

TESOL Standards 1–5: ELLs read and write to share social and cultural information and ideas.

Level 1—*Starting*

Reading: ELLs use illustrations, graphic organizers, and predictable patterns to construct meaning from text. With these supports, they are able to identify words and match labels (words/phrases) with visuals (e.g., models, diagrams, charts).

Writing: ELLs can make lists of people (family and historical) and events, label relatively simple content-area charts, graphs, and tables, and use bilingual or picture dictionaries to produce words and phrases.

Level 2—*Emerging*

Reading: ELLs continue to use visuals, graphic organizers, and peer support to make meaning of written text. They "use context and illustrations at the sentence level" (TESOL, 2006, p. 69), recognize sentence patterns in leveled texts, recognize sequence of events, begin to use elements of text structure (i.e., headings, diagrams, highlighted words) to make meaning from text, and classify and/or categorize statements, descriptions, or processes.

Writing: ELLs use visuals and writing models to write short paragraphs to describe people, events, stories, or experiences. ELLs in Grades 6 through 8 edit for language conventions using word processing programs, peer-editing teams, and writing models.

Level 3—*Developing*

Reading: ELLs continue to use visuals, graphic organizers, and peer support to construct meaning from written text. They read text at the paragraph level. They sort illustrated text according to genre using discourse structures such as "Once upon a time" (TESOL, 2006, p. 71) and use context clues to make meaning of text. ELLs follow illustrated directions in content-area text and sort information in expository text and narrative using graphic organizers. They can locate information in text and are able to order paragraphs about events.

Writing: ELLs create lists, organize and present information in graphs and charts, and write short stories with main ideas when presented with models of writing. ELLs revise and edit their writing with peers with the support of models and checklists. ELLs in Grades 6 through 8 write about events using multiple sources and compare and contrast people, places, and events.

Level 4—*Expanding*

Reading: ELLs continue to use visuals and graphic supports to access progressively challenging text. ELLs interpret and evaluate expository and narrative text and use multiple strategies to make inferences. They are able to draw figures, create charts, or plot information following steps in text. They synthesize, summarize, and draw conclusions from information from multiple written sources. ELLs at this level also self-monitor and self-correct when reading appropriate text with a partner or in small groups.

(Continued)

Table VII.5	(Continued)

Based on TESOL Performance Indicators Grade 4–8, Assuming Ongoing Appropriate Instruction, Instructional Materials, and Depending On Grade Level

Writing: ELLs are able to maintain journals and logs. They write personal narratives and thesis papers with clear details to support their positions. They are able to revise and edit their writing using feedback from teachers or peers as well as using reference books and word processing programs.

Level 5—*Bridging*

Reading: At this level, ELLs require visuals to a similar degree as native English speakers. They continue to benefit from modified grade level texts and graphic organizers. ELLs make and validate inferences from cues provided in decontextualized text. They use discourse features to identify and compare narrative and expository text.

Writing: *ELLs elaborate narrative and expository text they have written. They write to provide explanations and describe cause and effect relationships. They defend their arguments using logic and clear supporting details. They are able to self-evaluate their writing using rubrics and checklists and to revise and edit their writing for different audiences. They continue to benefit from word banks and word walls.*

Source: Based on TESOL Performance Indicators: TESOL (2006). *PreK–12 English Language Proficiency Standards* (pp. 47–97), Alexandria, VA: TESOL.

STRATEGY RESOURCES

1. August, D., & Shanahan, T. (2006). *Developing Literacy In Second Language Learners: Report Of The National Literacy Panel On Language-Minority Children And Youth.* Mahwah, NJ: Lawrence Erlbaum. (This is a 15-page summary of the purpose, methodology, and findings of the NLP.)

   http://www.cal.org/projects/archive/nlpreports/executive_summary.pdf

2. Dr. Jeanne Paratore, Boston University professor, introduces this Annenberg Production on the teaching of reading for diverse readers. The series features research, a description of ELLs in U.S. schools today, presentations, and an in-class video that includes literacy instruction for ELLs at different proficiency levels. It features the importance of support for primary languages and building on backgrounds and culture, and it differentiates instruction depending on language proficiency and literacy levels in the first language. It shows excellent examples of using first language in the classroom to support learning.

   http://www.learner.org/resources/series175.html?pop=yes&pid=1880# (Approximately 30 minutes)

3. Video—*Stages of Reading* by Dr. Luisa Moats, who discusses Dr. Chall's stages *http://www2.scholastic.com/browse/article.jsp?id=4449* (Approximately 2 minutes)

4. Strategies for Reading Comprehension. This resource is particularly useful for Strategies 38 through 40. ReadingQuest.org has compiled graphic organizers with strategies for building reading comprehension in the social studies. Most of these are adaptable to other content areas.

   http://www.readingquest.org/strat/

The Language Experience Approach

Strategy 32

The Language Experience Approach (LEA) is based on the principle that instruction should begin with the background experiences and knowledge of the learner. It uses the learner's background, vocabulary, and syntax to generate reading material that is relevant and therefore likely to be both accessible and pleasurable. The LEA can be used with learners of all ages. In one variation of the LEA, students experience a phenomenon together. This can be an outing or event such as a field trip, party, fire drill, and so on or an observation of an object, photo, painting, or other visual image. Based on the group's experiences or observations, learners describe the event, object, photo, or image. The teacher scribes their exact words on chart paper or on the whiteboard. The teacher may or may not guide the students in editing their writing. The final written work is displayed in the classroom and becomes reading for the group.

Alternatively, the LEA can be implemented with individual students (Ashton-Warner, 1963). In this version of the strategy, the learner draws a picture and discusses the picture with the teacher, who scribes the learner's exact words. (In cross-age tutoring, an older student may also act as the scribe.) Each student's picture and writing become her or his reading for the following day. Writings are collected and compiled into a book that the student can continue to read.

A third variation of the LEA incorporates comprehensible input (Krashen, 1981, 1982) and reinforcement to increase the accessibility of the LEA to ELLs at all proficiency levels (Moustafa & Penrose, 1985). In this version, rather than writing the student's words exactly as he or she says them, the teacher extends and builds the language that the ELL produces. For example, in response to a field trip to a petting zoo, the student draws a boy feeding a goat. The student identifies "goat." The teacher extends it by pointing to the boy and the action in the picture: "The boy is feeding the goat." The teacher reads the line and the student then reads along with the teacher.

Regardless of the variation of LEA used, the LEA text becomes the reading for those group members or individuals who helped to create it. Because the LEA text builds on the language the ELL has already developed, it can also be used for teaching and reinforcing decoding skills, phonics, conventions of print, and text structure. Using the text that ELLs have written increases the likelihood that the instruction will be relevant and appropriate for ELLs.

Theory and/or Research Underlying the Strategy

The LEA is consistent with the philosophy of John Dewey (1938), who maintained that learning should flow from the learner's experiences. It can be traced back at least to Ashton-Warner's (1963) use of it in successful reading instruction for Maori children in New Zealand. The LEA builds on students' background knowledge to develop reading, and it provides a scaffold from oral to written language. Because the LEA builds on student's knowledge and language, the text is meaningful to students and is likely to result in successful reading (Jones, 1986). The LEA can be very effective for ELLs and FEPs alike. When teaching ELLs with lower oral language proficiency levels it is advisable to use the version of the LEA that extends and scaffolds language.

Implementing the Strategy

Traditional—For Use With Large or Small Groups

1. Plan an event to engage students or select a photo or object with features that will interest students.

2. Prepare "Who, What, When" questions that will guide students to construct a narrative about the experience. For example, when discussing an outing or event, ask the following: "What did we do this morning?" "Who did that?" "Then what happened?" Also prepare questions that spawn rich description as well as critical and creative thinking, such as "Why do you think . . . ?" "How did it look to you?" and "What/Why did you feel . . . ?"

3. Explain to the class that they will create text about the experience, photo, and so on.

4. Call on individual volunteers to contribute information about the event. During this process, check regularly for understanding and provide wait time to encourage the participation of all students.

5. Using an overhead or chart paper, scribe the sentences just as the students dictate them. It is essential to capture the words of the students and to extend the language of ELLs with lower levels of English language proficiency.

6. When the text is complete, read the text with the correct intonation and prosody. (Option: You may engage students in revising and editing the text.)

7. Guide the students in a reading of the text as you point to the words.

8. Display the text prominently as part of the classroom reading.

9. Once the students have read the text several times and are familiar with its structure and language, the text may be used to teach phonics, text structure, or the conventions of written English.

Variations

1. Individual LEA

1. Ask each student to draw a picture or bring in a photo or object that represents an experience or symbolizes something that is important to her or him.

2. Conference with the student and ask him or her about the object.

3. Write the student's words exactly as he or she speaks them.

4. Place the text with the picture. This text becomes the student's reading for the following day.

5. Compile the student writings into a reading book for her or him.

6. Keep the book in the class library, readily available to the student and displayed as is appropriate. (Option: The text may be used to teach phonics, text structure, etc.)

Source: Adapted from *Teacher,* by S. Ashton-Warner, 1963, New York: Simon and Schuster.

Combining Comprehensible Input With LEA

1. Review the TESOL performance indicators for ELLs.

2. Begin the lesson for ELLs with lower levels of proficiency individually, in pairs, or in a small group. For comprehensible input, take a picture walk through a book or look at a visual together. (See LEA—Resource #1 in Strategy Resources.)

3. Prompt the ELLs with Who, What, Where questions (i.e., "Who is on the motorcycle?").

4. Scaffold and extend ELLs' responses using the pictures (i.e., ELL responds, "motorcycle," teacher acknowledges the response, and scaffolds, "The man is on a motorcycle.").

5. Write the extended response, saying the words as you write them.

6. Read the sentence to ELLs, and have the ELLs read the sentence with you.

7. Finally, go through the book with the student-written text, reading it page by page with the ELL.

Source: Adapted from "Comprehensible Input Plus the Language Experience Approach: Reading Instruction for Limited English Speaking Students," by M. Moustafa and J. Penrose, 1985, *The Reading Teacher,* 38(7), 640–647.

The student language objectives in each Strategy in Action example are the same.

1. Describe the experience (object or photo) in your own words.

2. Listen to the teacher and follow along as she reads the text.

3. Read the text with the teacher.

4. Read the text with a partner (or individually).

STRATEGY IN ACTION

Grade 1

Mrs. Garcia's first-grade class is comprised of 18 students who have varying degrees of English language proficiency. Students are seated on cushions arranged in a semi-circle, with Mrs. Garcia seated in the middle on a low chair so that she is close to the level of students and so that every child is able to see her. Next to Mrs. Garcia is an easel with lined chart paper. Mrs. Garcia explains that they are going to write a story about their field trip and that they will begin by talking about some pictures of the farm. (The previous day, Mrs. Garcia, the children, and several parent volunteers picked apples at a local farm.) Mrs. Garcia has large pictures of the farm, apple trees, and apples displayed on the wall at the eye level of the children. As she points to the first picture, students excitedly raise their hands to share what they remember. To ensure that ELLs with lower levels of English proficiency have the opportunity to speak, Mrs. Garcia tells students they will "stop, tell a neighbor." "Telling a neighbor" provides ELLs with time to practice their language before they speak in front of the larger group. After Mrs. Garcia and the students discuss each picture, they begin to write their story by generating a title together. Mrs. Garcia writes the title on the top of the chart paper, and while pointing to it, she reads the title aloud. Mrs. Garcia and students then read the title in chorus. Mrs. Garcia asks the children who, what, where, when, and why questions to guide their narrative of apple picking. Mrs. Garcia scribes the students' words, and then Mrs. Garcia and students read each line together. When they are finished, they read the narrative in its entirety. The narrative is kept on display in the room, is read regularly, and is used to teach and reinforce phonics as needed.

Grade 5

Mr. Collins is a regular education fifth grade teacher. This year's class consists of 22 students who speak English as a primary language, one ELL with a *Bridging* proficiency level, two ELLs with *Developing* to *Expanding* proficiency levels, and Pao, an ELL with *Emerging* English proficiency. When Pao arrived, a paraprofessional was assigned to Mr. Collins's classroom. On this day, while the paraprofessional works with one of Mr. Collins's guided reading groups, Mr. Collins works individually with Pao and implements an LEA to teach the vocabulary that Pao will need for science, to provide background knowledge for science class, and to construct reading materials that will be useful to Pao. Mr. Collins knows that Pao will be able to use illustrations to construct meaning from text, identify words, and match word labels with visuals. (See the TESOL Performance Indicators at the beginning of this unit.) Using a picture book, *The Moon Seems to Change* (Branley, 1987), Mr. Collins guides Pao through the different phases of the moon. First they look through the book together. Then, they return to the beginning of the book to label pictures of the moon's phases and other objects in the illustrations. Mr. Collins helps Pao construct simple sentences that he will be able to read, such as "The moon orbits the Earth." He explains the sentence using TPR to build comprehensibility. Using trimmed 4 × 6 sticky notes, Mr. Collins and Pao write text for selected pages of the book. Mr. Collins then reads through the pages while Pao follows along; then he and Pao read the text together.

Extensions to LEA

Once you and your students have read the text together several times, you can use text that was created using LEA to teach conventions of print, such as directionality, spaces to separate words, punctuation, and the use of upper- and lowercase letters. Once ELLs have demonstrated that they know the words in the writing (such as *man* in the previous example from the video found in the Language Experience in Action video in the Strategy Resources section of this strategy), you can use these known words to teach phonics.

REFLECTIONS

- How could you use the LEA with ELLs at your grade level and in your content area?

- Could you use the LEA with groups of students, or would you likely use it with individual students? Why?

STRATEGY RESOURCE

Language Experience In Action—Student and teachers take a picture walk through a book about a motorcycle, and then the teacher engages Starting ELLs in an LEA with comprehensible input.

http://www.youtube.com/watch?v=FmGdmqzPo60&feature=related (Approximately 10 minutes)

Strategy

33

Assessing and Supporting the Conventions of English Print

It is important to understand some of the difficulties that ELLs might encounter with English print so that you can adjust the type and amount of reading ELLs are required to complete, provide support to individual ELLs as they read, and work collaboratively with ESL and reading specialists. The purpose of Strategy 33 is to make you aware of some of the difficulties that ELLs might encounter and to enable you to prepare for discussions with the ESL or reading specialist. While reading through this strategy, it may be helpful to refer to the performance indicators for reading for your grade level (Table VII.4 and Table VII.5).

THEORY AND/OR RESEARCH UNDERLYING THE STRATEGY

ELLs enter U.S. schools with different levels of English proficiency and different preparation in the areas of reading and writing. Prior to beginning formal reading instruction in English, you will need to ensure that ELLs know grade-level concepts about English print. For example, they will need to know that pages of a book are turned from front to back (readers of Japanese turn pages from back to front) (Nation, 2009, p. 9). They will also need to know that print is read from top to bottom and from left to right, that words are signified by the spaces between them, and that words are put together in sentences that begin with capital letters and end with stops (periods, exclamation points, or question marks). The majority of ELLs who read in their first languages will be aware of at least some of these standard conventions.

Depending on grade level, ELLs will also have some level of phonemic awareness (words can be broken into sounds) and know the shapes of the letters and the symbol-sound relationship of letters. ELLs who can read in their first languages will most likely have phonemic awareness—they do not need to relearn this in English. If ELLs are readers of languages with other alphabet systems, they will need to learn the shapes of the letters and symbol-sound relationships. Nation (2009) and Birch (2008) suggested that learning letter shapes is too important to leave to chance. ELLs should receive explicit instruction for the letters that they do not know, and this instruction should begin with letters in words that are in ELLs' oral language (i.e., survival words such as *bus, book,* and *bathroom*). ELLs will need to learn to decode English letters with automaticity (see Chall's [1983] stages of reading 1–2) before they can fully comprehend grade-level text and read to learn.

As with any instruction, it is important to begin by determining what the ELL knows. Intake assessments for younger students will likely include an assessment of letter recognition. Intake assessments for ELLs who are preliterate or who read in non-alphabetic languages should include this assessment as well. If results from these assessments are not available, the regular classroom teacher, reading specialist, or ESL specialist can administer a quick assessment to determine an ELL's ability to identify letter shapes. Observation of the ELL as she or he reads will also reveal knowledge of the concept of print (front to back, top to bottom, and left to right).

IMPLEMENTING THE STRATEGY

In Kindergarten Through Grade 3

1. Assess ELLs' knowledge of print concepts by 1) observing students as they handle books, 2) reviewing students' writing (scribbles, whether in the first or second language) for directionality (top-bottom, left-right) and knowledge of words (spaces between words), and 3) assessing letter knowledge, knowledge of alphabet principle, and phonemic awareness using standard classroom assessments that are modified using words that are in the ELL's lexicon

2. While you continue to build an ELL's oral proficiency in English, teach the bottom-up skills that assessments indicate the ELL needs using words the ELL knows. (An LEA text generated by the ELL is useful for this purpose.)

3. Solicit the help and support of ESL and reading specialists.

4. Regularly assess the progress of ELLs.

5. If a paraprofessional is assigned to the classroom, provide him or her with strategies for supporting oral language development (see Unit VI of this book) and reading strategies (this unit). Stress to the paraprofessional that any instruction must build on the language the ELL already knows. Prepackaged phonics sheets are not useful. I once observed a second-grade ELL with *Developing* proficiency trying to make sense of the image of a candle (*vela* in Spanish), accompanied by the letter c. His facial expression conveyed his confusion as he asked the teacher, "Missy, *c* is for *vela*?"

6. Provide one-on-one skills support to the ELL while the paraprofessional supports the instruction of other students in the class.

In Grades 4 Through 8

1. Access the ELL's intake assessment and request information regarding previous schooling (report cards, parent's account, etc.). If the ELL has attended school in Grades 1 through 3, it is likely that she has learned to read.

2. If the ELL has not attended school, he may not be able to read in his first language. Regardless of the ELL's age, assess knowledge of the concept of print by observing him as he handles books and points to words. Record your observations

and share these with the ESL specialist; whenever possible, collaboratively plan instruction with ESL and reading specialists.

3. Review the intake assessment to determine the first language of the ELL. Readers of alphabetic languages will transfer knowledge of print concepts and the alphabetic principle to reading in English. (ELLs may need explicit instruction in sounds that differ between the first language and English.) If the language has a non-alphabetic writing system or if the alphabetic system differs from English, ELLs will benefit from direct instruction in the English writing system.

4. Provide ELLs with content-area reading materials that are consistent with their proficiency levels. As performance indicators suggest, ELLs at earlier stages will require illustrations, graphic organizers, and predictable patterns to make meaning from print. Reading must be comprehensible—that is, within the language-proficiency level of the ELL. (Unit IV provides suggestions for leveled readers and strategies for making reading comprehensible.)

5. Ensure that the preliterate ELL receives instruction in reading, preferably from a reading specialist who has substantive expertise in second-language reading.

6. Observe the ELL in the classroom as she participates in large group instruction, engages in small group discussions, and completes tasks individually. Record her progress in reading, language use, and content knowledge.

7. Meet regularly with the ESL specialist to share observations regarding the ELL's progress and to plan instruction.

8. Provide content in ways that do not involve reading (see Unit IV).

STRATEGY IN ACTION

Grade 5

When Mr. Collins and members of the fifth grade team are informed that Li, a new student from China with very limited English proficiency, will be placed with their team, they request that Ms. Joanna Rei, the school's ESL specialist, attend their regular team meeting to review the ELL's intake assessment results as well as any records from Li's previous school. Ms. Rei is able to tell them that Li received instruction in English as a foreign language while in China. She speaks very little English, but she is able to read and write in English at a basic level, which indicates that she understands the conventions of English print. Mr. Collins and Ms. Rei arrange an ESL schedule for Li for English language development. Ms. Rei will also determine Li's approximate reading level so that Mr. Collins can be sure that any content-area instructional materials he provides are comprehensible.

Grade 8

Ana, an ELL from Guatemala who has a *Starting* level of English proficiency, is newly enrolled in Ms. Juliana Pompei's seventh grade English language arts class. On Ana's first day, Ms. Pompei provides her with the literature anthology book, the picture book *Evangeline for Children* (Moore & Couvillon, 2002). (Ms. Pompei's students are approximately halfway through reading *Evangeline: A Tale of Acadie* (Longfellow,

1847). Ms. Pompei has requested Ana's records and the support of an ESL specialist in the classroom. Neither has yet arrived.

Ms. Pompei observes as Ana looks through the anthology, turning the pages until she finds pictures. She also watches as Ana looks through the picture book, looking like she is trying to make sense of the photos. While groups of students read, Ms. Pompei sits briefly with Ana to look through and talk about the picture book. She speaks to Ana using a combination of English and her very limited Spanish. Ana seems relaxed and begins to speak to Ms. Pompei slowly in Spanish. Ms. Pompei has taught ELLs with *Starting* and *Emerging* proficiency in previous years and feels confident that, with the right support, Ana will learn English quickly enough to participate in classroom discussions. Near the end of the class, Ms. Pompei distributes a notice about her homework policy. As she approaches Ana's desk to try to explain that she will get the policy in Spanish, she observes Ana trying to make sense of the notice. She also notices that Ana is holding the paper upside down.

That evening, Ms. Pompei translates the policy document using free online software. She knows the translation will be imperfect but that Ana should be able to recognize some of the words. On a hunch, she writes the alphabet letters on 3 × 5 index cards. The next day, as students are working in groups, Ms. Pompei provides Ana with the translated document—there are no images on the document to indicate directionality. Ana studies the paper right-side up and upside-down. This is Ms. Pompei's first indication that Ana does not yet know how to read. She then shows Ana the *A* card and says "A" in Spanish. Ana repeats "A." When she shows Ana the *B* card, Ana seems unable to respond. Ms. Pompei continues in the same manner with several more cards.

At the end of the day, Ms. Pompei contacts the building ESL specialist, the guidance counselor, and the reading specialist to request a meeting to plan for a complete assessment and an appropriate instructional plan for Ana. After assessing Ana, the team develops a plan that includes two hours of ESL and reading instruction each day and classroom support from regular classroom teachers to ensure that Ana makes rapid progress in learning to read in English.

REFLECTIONS

1. Why is a team approach necessary to build oral language proficiency and teach reading in English to preliterate ELLs? What role can the regular classroom teacher play in this process?

2. How might Ana's preliteracy have gone unnoticed in another classroom?

3. Ana's situation is extreme. What other behaviors might indicate that a student cannot yet read?

Strategy

34

Summarizing Text: The GIST

Strategy 34 presents two ways to support the development of text summarization skills for ELLs: the *Generating Interaction between Schemata and Text (GIST)* (Cunningham, 1982) and a variation of the GIST (Muth & Alvermann, 1999). GIST strategies are appropriate for ELLs with proficiency levels from *Developing* to *Bridging,* providing that the text is comprehensible. GIST strategies are most appropriate for ELLs in Grade 4 and above.

THEORY AND/OR RESEARCH UNDERLYING THE STRATEGY

Research suggests that one strategy used by effective readers to monitor their understanding is pausing periodically in their reading to summarize what they have read (Cunningham, 1982; Harvey & Goudvis, 2000; Wormeli, 2005). The evidence seems clear that teaching readers strategies such as summarization is likely to improve their reading (Pressley, 2001).The GIST is a focused strategy to support students in summarizing passages of text in order to get their gist.

IMPLEMENTING THE STRATEGY

Part 1. GIST (Cunningham, 1982)

In the paragraph version of the GIST, a paragraph of three to five sentences is used. The paragraph must have a gist, or central idea. Working with the teacher, students read one sentence at a time and summarize that sentence in 15 or fewer words. They then read the second sentence and summarize it, incorporating the summarization of the second sentence into the first and making adjustments to the original sentence, but using no more than 15 words. Students continue in this fashion, sentence by sentence, continually incorporating sentence summaries into the 15-word limit. Because the GIST requires students to talk about text, it supports English language development as it increases reading comprehension. The text must be comprehensible to the ELL.

Teaching Students the Strategy

1. Make a copy of the paragraph, leaving space at the bottom of the sheet for a GIST summary guide—15 lines, each large enough to write one word.

2. Explain why you are teaching the strategy, including the usefulness or value of the strategy (e.g., "The GIST is one strategy that will help you learn to summarize. Stopping to summarize as you read will help you to understand the text.").

3. Using an overhead projector or document camera, display the paragraph, covering all but the first sentence. Model the strategy to show students how it works. Explain to students that they will summarize the paragraph sentence by sentence and that their final summary will consist of no more than 15 words. They will be able to add, erase, or move words as they summarize each sentence.

4. Read the first sentence with students and ask them to summarize it.

5. Write each word of their summary on a line.

6. Revise the summary until students are satisfied with it.

7. Once the summary statement is complete, have students read it.

8. Allow them to make changes to the GIST summary sentence they have created.

9. Once you and students have completed the first GIST summary sentence, students read the first and second sentence of the paragraph together.

10. Students again dictate their summaries, but this time they incorporate the summary of the present sentence into the existing GIST summary, using no more than 15 words in total.

11. Continue with the remainder of the paragraph, following Steps 5 through 9

12. Once students seem comfortable using the GIST in the large group, assign another paragraph for them to summarize in small groups. Circulate throughout the room and monitor student progress as they create GISTs. Next, allow students time to create GISTs independently and monitor student individual progress.

13. When based on your observations and your review of students' GISTs, students are proficient in their use of this strategy, introduce longer sections of text, provide practice, and monitor student progress (Step 12).

> **Writing Connection:** Summarizing is particularly useful in writing to learn. Summarizing activities provide additional opportunities to support ELLs with word choice and grammar.

Part 2. GIST (Muth & Alvermann, 1999)

In this version of the GIST, students are provided with a paragraph from which they select 8 to 10 words they believe are important and then write a summary using these words.

1. Pair ELLs with FEP learners.

2. Provide students with a paragraph, as in the original version of the GIST, display it on the overhead or document camera, and provide students with individual copies.

3. Tell students that they will identify approximately 8 to 10 words that are important to the meaning of the paragraph.

4. Provide a few minutes for students to work in pairs to select words.

5. Write the words that students have selected on the overhead.

6. Have students work together to write a summary statement using as many of the words as possible.

7. Provide time for students to practice the strategy in pairs (ELLs with FEP learners) while you circulate and monitor understanding.

8. Next, allow students time to create GISTs independently while you circulate and monitor individual progress.

9. Once students have demonstrated their ability to use this form of the GIST, implement it with a longer text passage by doing the following:

   a. Write sentence summaries for each paragraph in the passage.
   b. Read through the sentence summaries and write a topic sentence for these.

10. Assess students' final summaries to check for understanding—A Ticket-to-Leave assessment (see Strategy 15 in Unit III) works well here.

Student Language Objectives:

1. Write a summary in 15 words or less for each paragraph.

2. Use paragraph summaries to summarize sections of text.

STRATEGY IN ACTION

During the first semester of each year, Mr. Collins uses both versions of the GIST to help ELLs and FEP learners build their reading comprehension and to prepare for the end of unit science tests. The textbook is dense, and Mr. Collins finds that when he uses the GIST to guide students through the text, their comprehension of science content increases. He begins by having students use the GIST to summarize paragraphs. Gradually, students learn to use GIST paragraph summary sentences to summarize larger sections of the text. Mr. Collins finds that spending time on reading strategies such as the GIST early in the school year is worthwhile because it prepares ELLs and FEP learners to learn content by reading the text.

REFLECTIONS

1. How might the GIST be a useful strategy in your content area and for your grade level?

2. Review the textbooks that you use and select a paragraph that would be appropriate for teaching the GIST. Try the using the GIST strategy with this paragraph. Then try the GIST strategy with a section of the text. Does it work as a summarization tool for your textbook?

OTHER USEFUL STRATEGIES TO SUPPORT SUMMARIZATION

1. Ask learners to cross out all information that is trivial using a red pencil and all information that is redundant with a blue pencil; or ask learners to underline topic sentences and provide a topic sentence when one seems missing from the paragraph.

2. Ask students to rate the importance of information in the text. Tell them to think about preparing mini books from the text that will contain only the most important information. Then, ask them to use their colored pencils to cross out information in the text that is not critically important. Once they have completed crossing out redundant and trivial text, ask students to read through the remaining text and to ascertain if this is the text they should include in their mini books.

3. Engage learners in conversations about what they kept and what they crossed out. Ask questions regarding the material that is most important.

Source: Adapted from "Reciprocal Teaching of Comprehension-Fostering and Comprehension Monitoring Activities," by A. S. Palinscar and A. L. Brown, 1984, *Cognition and Instruction, 1,* 117–175.

STRATEGY RESOURCE

Reading Comprehension Strategies for English Language Learners, by Ellen Douglas, provides an overview and strategies in use for three strategies that are effective with ELLs and other students in the classroom: Think-Pair-Share, Think Alouds, and GIST.

http://www.learnnc.org/lp/pages/724

Strategy 35

Building Comprehension for ELLs With Reciprocal Teaching

Reciprocal Teaching is a multifaceted strategy that fosters comprehension and the self-monitoring of comprehension (Palinscar & Brown, 1984). In reciprocal teaching, students work together in groups to summarize, question, and clarify text and to make text predictions. The group structure used in Reciprocal Teaching facilitates the meaningful participation of ELLs and FEP learners. By engaging students in structured dialogue about text, teachers are able to model and scaffold each component of Reciprocal Teaching. Students function as apprentices to the teacher, gradually taking on greater responsibility for their roles.

THEORY AND/OR RESEARCH UNDERLYING THE STRATEGY

Reciprocal Teaching, a strategy meant to be used while reading, was developed, piloted, and tested by Palinscar and Brown (1984). Reciprocal Teaching makes four invisible behaviors of expert readers, summarizing, generating questions, clarifying, and predicting, visible to all students. Through a combination of direct teaching and coaching, the teacher provides structured scaffolding to enable students to adopt the role of teacher in each of these four areas. Each area requires readers to check their understanding of content and monitor their understanding of the text. Instruction in these areas is recommended for second language readers by Nation (2009).

In Reciprocal Teaching, students begin by participating at the level at which they are able. Palinscar and Brown (1984) explained that the learner first participates as an observer, then as a novice, soon as an apprentice, and finally as an expert. As students use Reciprocal Teaching to discuss text with one another, they gradually become more proficient and more sophisticated in their ability to adopt each of the following roles: summarizer, questioner, clarifier, and predictor.

Each component of Reciprocal Teaching serves to activate students' background knowledge, enhance student comprehension, and build students' ability to monitor their comprehension. Thus, Reciprocal Teaching can be thought of as both a comprehension-fostering and a comprehension-monitoring activity (Palinscar & Brown, 1984, p. 121).

An additional benefit to Reciprocal Teaching is that it promotes academic discussion about the reading for ELLs and FEP learners.

Although Reciprocal Teaching requires substantial instructional time (Palinscar and Brown recommend 10 sessions), the effects on readers' comprehension and monitoring of comprehension appear to be lasting.

IMPLEMENTING THE STRATEGY

The goal of implementing this strategy is to enable all students to participate at the level at which they are capable, to enable them to experience success while using the strategy, and to situate the strategy in the actual reading of the text (Palinscar & Brown, 1984, p. 122).

1. Choose readings that are challenging but accessible to the group of students. Students must be able to read the text.

2. With new passages, introduce the reading by engaging ELLs and FEP learners in a discussion to activate and build background knowledge.

3. With passages in progress, ask learners to discuss the topic and main points of the passage that has already been read.

4. Assign a short passage to be read silently.

5. Once all students have completed reading the passage, think aloud to demonstrate how to summarize the passage, ask questions about the main ideas, clarify (when appropriate), and make predictions.

6. Assign readers to be teachers for a short passage (short segment or paragraph) that follows, and then assign the passage to be read silently.

7. Immediately after the reading, ask each learner-teacher to lead the group—beginning with the summary (Student 1) and followed by questions (Student 2), then clarifications (Student 3), and finally predictions (Student 4).

8. Scaffold each learner-teacher with prompts such as "What question do you think a teacher might ask?" and instructions such as "Remember that a summary is a shortened version. It doesn't include details." Support learner-teachers in modifying with prompts such as "If you are having a hard time thinking of a question, why don't you summarize first?" (p. 121).

9. Provide explicit praise and feedback: "That summary is very clear" or "You provided a lot of good detail, could you provide the main ideas in the summary?" "The question you asked is very clear," and so on.

10. Explain to learners that Reciprocal Teaching will help them to understand what they have read and to measure their understanding as they are reading. Tell students that they can use Reciprocal Teaching strategies to think through the text as they read silently. Explain that when they are able to talk about what they have read in their own words and can guess the questions that teachers will ask or questions they might encounter on a reading test, they have likely understood the passage.

11. Provide practice, circulating to assess each student's ability to use the strategy.

12. Once you have assessed students' strategy use and are confident that they can apply each of the four strategies at some level of proficiency, students can begin to work in groups of four.

13. Prepare students to read text by providing sticky notes in various colors (one color for summarizing, one for questioning, one for clarifying, and one for predicting). Read through a passage with students, modeling how you would use the sticky notes to summarize, question, clarify, and predict. (Students can use colored highlighters in place of sticky notes to mark text that has been photocopied for this purpose.)

14. Prepare and distribute note cards indicating students' roles within their groups—summarizer, questioner, clarifier, and predictor.

15. Allow students to use their marked text (marked with sticky notes or highlighters) to work within their groups. Students then discuss the text from the perspective of each role: The summarizer provides the key summary points; the questioner poses questions as a teacher might, such as making connections to previously learned concepts or reading; the clarifier addresses the confusing parts, attempting to respond to questions about clarity; and the predictor makes predictions about the text.

16. Students in each group then pass cards to the left or right so that eventually each student plays each of the roles in reciprocal teaching. Table 35.1 provides a graphic organizer that students in groups can use to take notes as they engage in Reciprocal Teaching.

Source: Adapted from "Reciprocal Teaching of Comprehension-Fostering and Comprehension Monitoring Activities," by A. S. Palinscar and A. L. Brown, 1984, *Cognition and Instruction, 1,* 117–175.

Table 35.1 Reciprocal Teaching			
Summarizing	*Questioning*	*Clarifying*	*Predicting*

Strategy in Action

Mrs. Linda Clark regularly uses Reciprocal Teaching to build content-area reading comprehension skills in her fifth grade social studies class. She began by modeling summarizing, questioning, clarifying, and predicting with a large group; she then worked with small groups of students in a coaching role, helping them to expand their use of each strategy. Students in Mrs. Clark's classroom are now accustomed to participating in Reciprocal Teaching and know the process.

Mrs. Clark has 24 students in her classroom: 21 FEP learners and three ELLs with English proficiency levels of *Emerging, Developing,* and *Expanding.* Students are learning about the U.S. Constitution. Maya, the ELL with *Emerging* proficiency, and Hector, the ELL with *Developing* proficiency, are reading the same texts as other students in the classroom, but glossing and simplified sentences in the margins have increased the comprehensibility of their texts. The glossing and simplification has made the text accessible to Hector, but it continues to be challenging for Maya. To support Maya's reading, Mrs. Clark has found similar text materials in Spanish. Dan, the ELL with *Expanding* proficiency, has access to the simplified text if and when he needs it, but he is encouraged to read the regular text, which is at his instructional level..

In preparation for Reciprocal Teaching, Mrs. Clark has placed students in heterogeneous groups with four students in each group. She placed Maya in a group with Denise, an FEP English-Spanish bilingual learner. This placement will enable Maya to participate using a combination of Spanish and English. This day, she placed Hector in a group with FEP learners. (At times, she places Hector and Maya together for extra support, but her informal assessment of Hector suggests that he will be able to participate in an all English discussion of this section of text.) Dan is also participating in a group of FEP learners.

For homework, students have been assigned to read two pages of the text and to use sticky notes and highlighters to practice the four components of Reciprocal Teaching (summarizing, questioning, clarifying, and predicting) and to generate notes for discussion. When Mrs. Clark assigned homework, she also assigned the role that each student would play in her or his group. Thus, each student engaged with the reading in preparation for their discussion by either summarizing, questioning, clarifying, or predicting.

During the following day's discussion, students worked with each section of the text, first summarizing, then questioning, then clarifying, and finally predicting. Students jotted down notes using Table 35.1. At the end of each section, students who had questions or were confused about the text had the opportunity to check their understanding. Mrs. Clark circulated and took notes about the quality of individual students' interrogation of the text. (One example of a Reciprocal Teaching assessment checklist is included in the Strategy Resources section at the end of this strategy.) Mrs. Clark also joined groups and coached students to scaffold the level of their summarizations, questions, clarifications, and predictions. For example, she listened in on one group as Danny asked (in relation to women's roles), "What would it be like if our mothers couldn't work or couldn't vote?" A few minutes later, Liza predicted, "My prediction is that we will learn more about how women got jobs and were able to be mayors and stuff later."

REFLECTIONS

1. Review your content-area texts and other reading materials to ensure that materials are at the appropriate reading level of students. Which sections would benefit from Reciprocal Teaching? How would students benefit from working through these sections using Reciprocal Teaching?

2. How are the sticky notes and highlighters useful to students when they read independently? How might knowing that they will participate in a Reciprocal Teaching group the following day motivate them to read and serve to improve their comprehension?

Strategy Resources

1. 🗐 An overview of Reciprocal Teaching and the research that underlies this strategy. Smith, J. A., & Reutzel, D. D. (2006). *Reciprocal teaching*. USU Emma Eccles Jones Center for Early Childhood Education online.

   http://www.liberty.k12.ga.us/jwalts/RecipTeaching/reciprocal_teaching.pdf

2. 📄 Reciprocal Teaching Checklist

   http://www.liberty.k12.ga.us/jwalts/RecipTeaching/CHECKLIST.pdf

3. 📄 Reciprocal Math

   http://www.liberty.k12.ga.us/jwalts/RecipTeaching/Reciprocal%20math.pdf

4. 🎬 *Using Reciprocal Teaching Strategies to Boost Reading Comprehension* illustrates Reciprocal Teaching with older students, including using a variety of questions, both literal and inferential.

   http://www.youtube.com/watch?v=vbzuycoHwts

Strategy

Using Text Structure

36

As ELLs and FEP learners read in the content areas, they encounter various genres and text structures within these genres (e.g., compare and contrast, sequence of events, cause and effect). This strategy for teaching text structure, which is based on the work of Rhoder (2002), is appropriate for ELLs with English proficiency levels from *Developing* to *Transitioning*.

THEORY AND/OR RESEARCH UNDERLYING THE STRATEGY

Teaching students about text structure provides them with advance organizers that facilitate their ability to comprehend text (Ausubel, 1978). Instruction in text structure is particularly useful for ELLs, who must learn the syntax and the structure of English writing (Nation, 2009). Once students know the structure of text, they are more able to organize it and reorganize it using graphic organizers (Rhoder, 2002). Direct instruction in text structures (including the most common ones, such as cause and effect, compare and contrast, and sequence of events) and in the cue words that signal text structure is useful to readers (Rhoder, 2002)—and especially to ELLs who are working to make sense of English text as they develop English proficiency. The implementation of this strategy is based on content-area texts.

IMPLEMENTING THE STRATEGY

1. Begin by providing curriculum-free examples. For example, use the following to illustrate cause and effect: Tamara spends every vacation at the beach. Maria does not like the beach. Therefore, Maria refused to go on vacation with Tamara.

2. Elicit examples from students.

3. Explain the ways that ideas are related. For example, something happened: Maria refused to go on vacation with Tamara. Someone or something made it happen: Tamara spends every vacation at the beach and Maria does not like the beach.

4. Use questions to show students how they can identify text structure.
    a. What has happened? (Maria refused to go on vacation with Tamara.)
    b. Why did it happen? (Maria doesn't like the beach.)
    c. Who made it happen? (Tamara—she always goes to the beach.)
    d. What cue words tell you who, what, or why? (*therefore*) (Rhoder, 2002, p. 502)

5. Use a cause and effect graphic organizer, as follows, to illustrate the events.

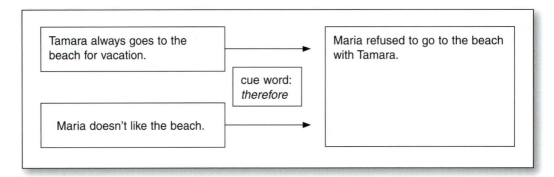

1. Use the student-generated examples to provide practice and to enable students to discover cue words that identify cause and effect structure, such as *so, because, therefore, thus, as a result, so that,* and so on.

2. Call students' attention to the graphic organizer, and explain that they can use blank graphic organizers to help them map text information and see relationships.

3. Practice in groups using brief sections of simple text. The focus is on using the strategy, not on unpacking complex content. During this time, students ask questions, map text, and identify cue words. (Several forms of cause and effect organizers are available online at no cost.)

4. Once students are comfortable using the strategy with simple texts, guide students through a passage in their text using large group instruction. Repeat previous steps.

5. Provide students with time to discuss their maps or organizers. Many texts are "inconsiderate," in that they combine topics in sections. They also may include more than one type of text structure. In these cases, there is no one correct answer. Providing students with time to discuss their graphic organizers will help them to think more deeply about the structure of the text.

Source: Based on "Mindful Reading: Strategy Training That Facilitates Transfer," by C. Rhoder, 2002, *Journal of Adolescent & Adult Literacy, 45*(6), 498–512.

Other Structures

Compare/Contrast

- Simple example: Facts and ideas are presented that are the same (ice cream and soup are both food) and/or different (ice cream is cold and soup is hot). A Venn diagram works well for compare and contrast. Cue words include the following: *the same, both, alike,* or *more, but, less, instead of, in contrast* (Rhoder, 2002, p. 504).

Sequence of Events

- Simple example: Topics are presented in a way to show what has, will, or should happen. When you build a model car, first you read the directions, then you lay out the parts, next you build the car, and finally you display the car. A sequence map (Figure 36.1) is effective for mapping a sequence. Cue words include the following: *first, second, third, at the beginning, next, then,* and *finally*.

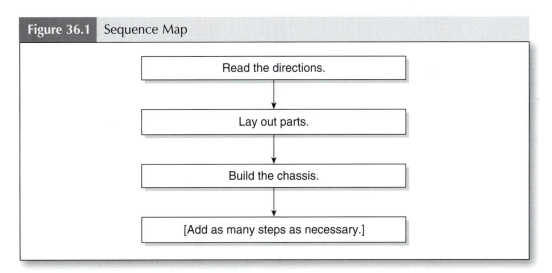

Figure 36.1   Sequence Map

> Read the directions.
>
> Lay out parts.
>
> Build the chassis.
>
> [Add as many steps as necessary.]

STRATEGY IN ACTION

Student Language Objectives:

1. Use compare and contrast maps to map the text.

2. Identify cause and effect cue words (or compare and contrast or sequence of events cue words, depending on text to be read).

Mrs. Allen guides the students in her fourth grade social studies class in the use of a cause and effect graphic organizer. She begins by using simple examples: "Billy took the candy from his little sister, so she started to cry," and "It snowed really hard last night. The roads were closed; therefore, we didn't have school." After providing students with practice using graphic organizers and several non-curricular examples, she guides students through a section in their social studies books about the beginning of the Revolutionary War.

Ms. Dina Sands' students are reading about the process of conducting experiments in science. She prepares them for this by introducing them to sequence structure. She begins with the simple example of making a sandwich. Students then complete the sequence graphic organizer together. After providing practice using the graphic organizer, Ms. Sands takes students through the strategy using the textbook.

REFLECTION

- Teaching strategies (such as identifying text structure and cue words) and providing adequate practice take substantial instructional time, yet research indicates that when students have a repertoire of strategies they are more competent content-area readers. How can you work with your schedule to provide adequate instructional time for strategy instruction?

Strategy

37

Readers Theatre

Readers Theatre is one way to help students develop fluency in reading. It is an enjoyable reading experience for ELLs and FEP learners in that they read with expression and participate in repeated readings of a text. It is also a highly motivational reading strategy because students use their voices, "facial expressions, and bodies" to interpret the "emotions, beliefs, attitudes, and motives of characters" (Carrick, 2001, para 2). Readers Theatre also serves to develop pronunciation skills for ELLs. Similar to choral reading, there is little risk involved in Readers Theatre. Students who feel they are ready for solo parts may be given solo parts of different lengths, and students who do not yet feel confident with their reading can read their parts in pairs or in small groups.

THEORY AND/OR RESEARCH UNDERLYING THE STRATEGY

Readers Theatre promotes confidence and fluency in readers, including readers who have been insecure and have read haltingly in the past (Martinez, Roser, & Strecker, 1998/1999). One way this occurs is by providing readers the opportunity to listen to good reading models, and thus enabling them to understand how the reader's voice can be used to make sense of the text. They begin to understand understand that reading aloud can make text come alive (Martinez et al., 1998/1999).

IMPLEMENTING THE STRATEGY

Implementing the Strategy is presented in three parts: Preparing for Readers Theatre, Day 1, and Days 2 through 5.

Preparing for Readers Theatre

1. Create a script from a book, which is easy to do. Use the text as it is, simply adding brief narration to describe story action that is only depicted by an illustration and dividing long narration into more than one speaking part (Martinez et al., 1988/1999, p. 329). It is advisable to use a shorter script until students know the routine.

2. Readers Theatre scripts can also be purchased or found at no cost online. Resources can be found at the end of this strategy.

Day 1

3. Provide each student with a copy of a script, which can vary in length. You might provide two copies (one to be kept at school, the second to be taken home so that students can practice).

4. Read the title with students, encouraging them to make predictions about the text. (Walker [1996] suggests that older students might benefit from reading the script silently in order to get its gist.)

5. Read the text aloud with expression.

6. Ask for feedback. Did students like the story? Did it remind them of another story?

7. Assign parts that students will practice and read. Initially assign shorter parts and parts that can be read in pairs or small groups to ELLs and FEP learners who are not strong readers. As students' confidence grows, be sure to assign longer and solo parts.

8. Students highlight the parts of the script they will practice and read.

9. Students read through their parts and identify words they do not know.

10. Review the meaning of the vocabulary words with ELLs and FEP learners, and ensure that they recognize words when they are pronounced correctly. (They will need to be able to pronounce words for Readers Theatre, and it is easier for students to learn words that they can pronounce. This does *not* mean that ELLs need to pronounce words without accents.)

Days 2 Through 5

11. Students read through the scripts in small groups and practice reading their lines with expression.

12. Circulate and provide coaching (Martinez et al., 1998/1999) to support and scaffold, such as "I really like the way that you read that part. Your expression, stress on that word, and intonation really help listeners understand how your character is feeling," and "Remember the way you felt when . . . ? I wonder how this character is feeling now. Can you read the part to convey this?" or "How could you

read this to show this question mark?" "Could you read it again, pausing at the comma," . . . "stopping at the period?" and so on.

13. On Day 5, students perform the reading in the large group, with each student reading his and her part.

Source: Based on "Internet Resources for Conducting Readers Theatre," by L. Carrick, 2001, *Reading Online, 5*(1).

Strategy in Action

At the beginning of each school year, Mrs. Patricia Tabor engages her third grade learners in a unit about themselves and their families, which helps students to get to know one another and to make connections between home and school. As a culminating project, each student will make a square about herself or himself, and the squares will be sewn together into a quilt, which is displayed throughout the year. This year, Mrs. Tabor has 26 students in her class, including five ELLs (one with *Emerging*, two with *Developing*, one with *Bridging,* and one with *Expanding* proficiency levels). In addition, she has four students who are having difficulties with reading.

Mrs. Tabor begins by having students interview one another (Strategy 30) and then interview members of their families to learn more about their families' histories and interests. (Unit VIII focuses on involving parents and discusses guidelines and parameters for interviewing families and the need for sensitivity to families' circumstances.) During the early stages of this instructional unit, Mrs. Tabor engages students in Readers Theatre using *The Name Quilt* (Root, 2003). (Mrs. Tabor will use Readers Theatre throughout the school year. She has found that it builds fluency and engages even the most reluctant readers in reading.) She begins by making a copy of the book and dividing the reading into parts, which she has labeled. The book has 18 pages that include text and illustrations. The remaining pages are illustrations only. There are only two character parts in the book: that of Sadie and that of Grandma. In preparation, she divides the narration into 12 parts and labels them Narrator(s) 1 through 12.

In planning for Readers Theatre, Mrs. Tabor reviews her roster and places ELLs with *Emerging* and *Developing* proficiency with FEP learners. She assigns longer parts to students who have demonstrated confidence in their ability to read. For example, Yessica, the ELL with *Bridging* proficiency, will read Sadie; Alison, an FEP learner, will read Grandma. There are several substantial narrator parts, including one for the introduction to the book, that Mrs. Tabor decides to assign to pairs and trios—ELLs working with FEP learners. She creates a casting handout so that each student knows his or her part. On Day 1, Mrs. Tabor reads the book aloud to students, involving them in using illustrations as well as the text to make predictions and discuss the story. She explains Readers Theatre to them, and once she has checked for understanding, she distributes copies of the labeled text along with the casting handout. She provides students with time to read through their parts in pairs and trios. (The students with individual parts work together.) Mrs. Tabor circulates and explains words and language about which students have questions.

Student Language Objectives: Day 1

1. Follow along as Mrs. Tabor reads the story to ensure you understand the story.

2. Highlight your part on the script.

3. Review your part to ensure you understand it.

4. Rehearse your part with a partner.

Student Language Objectives: Days 2 and 3

1. Read your part with expression and fluency.

2. Perform *The Name Quilt,* written by Phyllis Root and illustrated by Margot Apple.

The parts for each student are relatively short, so Mrs. Tabor has scheduled three days for the lesson. (With longer scripts, she plans for five days.) On Day 2, students work in the teams that were formed on Day 1 and rehearse their parts. Mrs. Tabor circulates, scaffolds, and encourages. She ensures that students can read their parts with expression and fluency. Near the end of Day 2, students come together and read through their parts together so that the story flows. On Day 3, Mrs. Tabor invites the assistant principal, the second grade teacher, and her class to hear the production.

REFLECTIONS

1. How does Mrs. Tabor ensure that all students (ELLs and FEP learners) are included in meaningful ways?

2. What are some reading selections at your grade level that might lend themselves to Readers Theatre?

Writing in the Classroom

Writing must be a meaningful process for students—one in which communication, content, and audience precede attention to writing conventions. Students (ELLs and FEP learners) are more likely to write, revise, and edit their work when they write about topics that are relevant and meaningful to them. Writing instruction should build student enthusiasm for engaging in writing and for sharing her or his ideas. Conventions must be taught as a way to help the writer convey his or her ideas more clearly to the reader. Teachers of writers (and emergent writers) can help students uncover their interests by listening to and conversing with them, expressing genuine interest in their ideas. These conversations extend to discussions of students' writing, including their accomplishments, what worked well, how they understood how to convey an idea, and what they were thinking about as they wrote (Graves, 1994).

Quality writing instruction requires time: Classrooms should provide time for students to engage in writing at least four days each week. During this time students should have opportunities to plan, write, discuss their writing with teachers and peers, and publish selected writing for a larger audience. Writing instruction should also include mini-lessons led by teachers (and later by student writers) that focus on the different aspects of writing, including writing conventions. Instruction should help student writers to become increasingly responsible for their own writing—and for being readers of their writing (Graves, 1994).

As ELLs write for meaning, they will need additional support with English vocabulary and English syntax, grammar, and spelling to help them to convey their ideas with precision and make these ideas clear to their audience.

Two writing strategies are presented in Unit VII: Strategy 38, Interactive Writing, and Strategy 39, Revising and Editing: Teaching Writing Conventions. These strategies should be embedded in a quality writing program. Readers are encouraged to read Graves (1994) and Calkins (1994). While Graves and Calkins do not focus on writing instruction for ELLs, their philosophies and instructional recommendations are consistent with quality instruction for ELLs.

Strategy
38

Interactive Writing

Interactive writing provides a model of the writing process for students, scaffolding their abilities to write for a variety of purposes and audiences. Interactive writing within a meaning-focused writing program provides a useful scaffold for ELLs as they begin to write in English and has been shown to improve writing as well as reading abilities (Craig, 2003). Initially a strategy for primary-grade students, interactive writing has been used successfully to scaffold the writing of students in upper grades (Wall, 2008). An interactive writing session can be led by the teacher or by a more competent peer, as in cross-grade tutoring, or it can be conducted collaboratively with small groups of students. As a teacher-led activity, the writing group may consist of either the entire class or of small groups of students. When working with the entire class, whiteboards can be distributed to students so they can actively participate throughout the process (Wall, 2008).

Teacher-led interactive writing can be effective when introducing a new genre or when attempting to strengthen students' abilities to write in a relatively new genre, such as when introducing writing sequence of events or cause and effect in science or social studies. It can also be effective following a writing mini-lesson such as varying the length of sentences. During the teacher-led activity, one student scribes and acts as the teacher while students compose and negotiate text. The teacher serves as the "more knowledge-able other" (Vygotsky, 1978, as cited in Wall, 2008). As the group of students contributes ideas and sentences, the teacher scaffolds responses through questioning, such as "Let's check to see if we are describing the order of events?" "Is that the word you want there?" "Is there a way to combine these sentences?" In interactive writing with a more capable peer, the peer, rather than the teacher, provides the scaffolding and support to students as they try out new structures and language.

Collaborative interactive writing can be accomplished with pairs or small groups of students. Students share the pen, write together, and make revisions and edits as they work through a piece of writing. An additional benefit of interactive writing is that it has the potential to increase vocabulary and language structures for ELLs.

THEORY AND/OR RESEARCH UNDERLYING THE STRATEGY

Interactive writing is based on the sociocultural theory of learning, in which students work together with a more knowledgeable other to write at a level that is beyond which

223

they are capable of writing independently (Vygotsky, 1978). Research has shown that when interactive writing is part of a quality writing program, it is instrumental in improving students' writing (Wall, 2008).

IMPLEMENTING THE STRATEGY

1. Decide on a writing skill you will teach to improve the writing of students in your classroom (e.g., summarization, blending sentences, using transition cue words, etc.). This can be a skill that is needed by the entire class or one that is needed by a group of students.

2. Prepare a mini-lesson to teach this skill and to model and scaffold students' application of this skill.

3. Teach the mini-lesson.

4. Engage students in an interactive writing lesson in which they will apply the skill from the mini-lesson.

5. Ask for a student volunteer (or appoint a student) to scribe.

6. Collaborate with students as they suggest ways to write a narrative or expository text or to revise or edit an existing piece of writing.

7. Function as the more knowledgeable other by questioning, scaffolding, and making suggestions for extending students' writing.

STRATEGY IN ACTION

Grade 4

Ms. Allen is teaching her fourth grade students how to write a description of the process they used to solve a mathematics word problem. She believes it is important for students to think about the processes they use rather than to memorize the steps for solving a problem. Writing, helps students to develop the habit of thinking through, expressing their thinking, and identifying where they may become stuck in the process. Once students understand how to write these descriptions, Ms. Allen will require students to explain their thinking in their math journals as they work to solve problems that are particularly challenging for them.

Ms. Allen explains that there is more than one way to solve each problem but that, for the purpose of this interactive writing lesson, they will solve a problem together and then write about the process. As they work through this process, students suggest ideas and Ms. Allen scaffolds their responses; one of the students scribes the text on the whiteboard. Ms. Allen and the students create the text together, read it through for accuracy, revise it, and edit it until they are satisfied with the product. Students then work together in pairs to solve a mathematics word problem and to write about the process they use. Ms. Allen groups students heterogeneously (according to mathematic ability and English proficiency level) to engage in this interactive writing process. She circulates to ensure that students are able to solve their problems and write about the process they used. Once students have demonstrated their ability to write about solving the problem, she regroups students homogeneously according to mathematical ability and heterogeneously for English language proficiency, and she differentiates the mathematics word problems according to each group's mathematics level.

Grade 8

Ms. Janice Norton has been working with students on making revisions to their research papers. Today, she presents a mini-lesson on paragraph structure in which she guides students through a review of several paragraphs to decide if each sentence in the paragraph supports the paragraph's main idea and to look for the ways in which the sentences are connected to one another. Following Ms. Norton's mini-lesson, students engage in interactive writing in pairs (heterogeneously grouped by English language proficiency levels) to make revisions and edits to one paragraph in each student's text.

REFLECTIONS

1. How could you use interactive writing in your content area? How might it improve students' writing skills?

2. What mini-lesson on writing would benefit the students in your classroom, and how would you follow up on this lesson using an interactive writing activity?

STRATEGY RESOURCES

1. Interactive Writing

    In this video, the teacher presents a mini-lesson on summarizing leading to interactive writing between pairs of students. Dedicating more time to student talk and less to teacher talk would make this lesson more effective. (9:34)

    http://www.youtube.com/watch?v=0C10VDEoChg&feature=related

2. ReadWriteThink provides interactive writing lessons for grades kindergarten through 8. Teaching Audience Through Interactive Writing (Grades K–2)

    http://www.readwritethink.org/classroom-resources/lesson-plans/teaching-audience-through-interactive-242.html

Nature Reflections: Language Practice for English-Language Learners (Grades 3–5)

http://www.readwritethink.org/classroom-resources/lesson-plans/nature-reflections-interactive-language-882.html

Describe That Face: An Interactive Writing Game (Grades 6–8)

http://www.readwritethink.org/classroom-resources/lesson-plans/describe-that-face-interactive-1125.html

Creative Writing Through Wordless Picture Books (Grades 6–8)

http://www.readwritethink.org/classroom-resources/lesson-plans/creative-writing-through-wordless-130.html

Revising and Editing: Teaching Writing Conventions

Strategy 39

All students need to learn standard English writing conventions. As with other elements of writing, writing convention strategies should be taught in a meaningful context. ELLs and FEP learners should have a purpose for learning and applying the conventions of English print (Celce-Murcia, 2007; Larsen-Freeman, 2003). Graves (1994) recommended teaching students that they must learn the conventions of writing so that their writing is clear to them (they are saying what they intended to say) and clear to others (others understand the writer's message).

The expectations for writing conventions will differ depending on the grade level of the student—in early grades, students write primarily to share personal information and familiar stories. As students progress through the grades, they must develop the ability to write about content and concepts using more abstract and more impersonal forms.

Throughout the grades ELLs have varying levels of proficiency in English and differ in the quantity and quality of education they have received in their first languages. ELLs who are preliterate will need to learn to write to share meaning with others as well as the conventions of standard English. While all preliterate ELLs will need substantial classroom support and additional support provided by ELL specialists, the level of support will increase for older ELLs, who will need to learn to write across the content areas.

Instruction should begin with what ELLs know, teaching letters that form known words, and writing about topics about which the ELL has first hand knowledge. ELLs who are literate in their own languages will need to learn the form and conventions of writing in English. Teaching writing conventions in an authentic and meaningful context requires beginning with the knowledge and abilities that individual ELLs bring to the writing experience and providing scaffolding that enables each ELL to improve her or his writing.

Revising offers an authentic opportunity for teaching writing conventions. Not every piece of writing will benefit from revision. Instruction should guide students in their selection of pieces of writing they will revise. Graves (1994) suggested the following guidelines for choosing work for revision:

1. The student knows the subject well.

2. The work will be displayed without the author, such as on bulletin boards or in class books.

3. The student understands that writing conveys meaning to the reader.

4. The student is aware of the audience for the piece of writing. (p. 279)

227

THEORY AND/OR RESEARCH UNDERLYING THE STRATEGY

Providing opportunities for ELLs to write for authentic purposes and for authentic audiences is important to teaching all aspects of writing, including planning, writing, revising, and editing. Scaffolding the writing skills of ELLs by building on what they know and can do, and providing focused instruction on writing conventions they need is consistent with sociocultural theories of second language development (Graham & Perin, 2007) and the Zone of Proximal Development (Vygotsky, 1978).

IMPLEMENTING THE STRATEGY

1. Review the English language proficiency performance indicators that correspond to the grade level of the ELLs in your classroom (Tables VII.4 and VII.5), as well as samples of the writing that ELLs have produced in your classroom.

2. Introduce and teach conventions as a means to understand writing.

3. Find out what students already know about print conventions and how they know what they know. (For example, they report using a period to show a stop or a long pause or a comma to show a string of ideas.)

4. Develop mini-lessons on writing conventions based on the needs of ELLs and FEP learners. These mini-lessons might include conventions at the sentence level, such as punctuation (comma, period, colon, semicolon), capitalization, grammar, and word choice; at the paragraph level, such as main ideas (sentences support the main idea of the paragraph), sentence order, and transitions between sentences; or at the essay level (coherence). The focus of each 10-minute mini-lesson is using one convention to convey precise meaning to the reader.

5. Maintain a loose leaf binder in which you keep each mini-lesson for future use (Graves, 1994), and organize these for easy retrieval.

6. Teach the mini-lesson using authentic writing. Books that students read provide exemplars, as do some sections of students' writing. Share your own writing with students and engage in a think-aloud regarding the convention that is being taught.

7. Provide students with opportunities to practice interactive writing in small groups or in pairs during peer review.

8. Guide students to read text to uncover how good writers effectively use writing conventions (how does the writer show, tell, etc.?).

9. Once students can read the writing of others to understand how conventions are used to convey meaning, have them read their own writing as readers.

10. Hold conferences with the students to discuss specific pieces of writing they have revised and how they engaged in the revision process.

Source: Based on principles of second language acquisition and on *A Fresh Look at Writing* (pp. 191–240), by D. H. Graves, 1994, Portsmouth, NH: Heinemann.

When Mrs. Joanne Allen began teaching fourth grade, she taught writing in very traditional ways. She planned a lesson, assigned a topic about which students would write, marked their work for revisions, and graded final papers. Mrs. Allen found that she spent most of her instructional and grading time focusing on the mechanics of writing. Although each year there were several students who appeared to enjoy her writing lessons and several more who dutifully engaged in the process, the announcement that they would write was usually met with sighs and groans. Six years ago, in response to the lack of student motivation and the generally lackluster student compositions, Mrs. Allen began to implement Writers Workshop. Students now choose their own topics, and Mrs. Allen provides 10- to 15-minute mini-lessons on a variety of writing topics that are based on the needs she has observed in her students' writing. (Initially, a lot of the mini-lessons were based on where writers find ideas for writing.)

This year, Mrs. Allen's classroom consists of 24 students, six of whom are ELLs. Mrs. Allen has found that Writers Workshop works very well for ELLs as well as FEP learners. ELLs are learning to write as they learn English, so Mrs. Allen encourages them to write in their primary languages if they want to do so. This enables ELLs to organize their thoughts and get their words on paper. She encourages ELLs and other students to illustrate their stories prior to writing and provides additional time for ELLs to discuss their ideas with an FEP learner or with her prior to beginning to write. Using the illustrations during these discussions helps Mrs. Allen to scaffold the writing of ELLs and FEP learners.

Mrs. Allen uses her own writing and samples of students' published work to teach students to revise and edit. Over the past five years, students have published their writing in class books, and several copies are kept in the classroom library.

Today, Mrs. Allen has planned a lesson on word choice and especially on choosing action words that make writing come alive. She explains that she has just drafted a letter to her aunt in Arizona to tell her about a birthday party she attended for her niece and nephew, Christine and Jules, and that she would like to share one paragraph with them. "It's just a draft," she reminds students, "I may want to make several types of revisions, but right now I think I would like to just look at some of the action words."

Mrs. Allen uses the document camera to display her paragraph. She also displays some pictures of the party to make the event more comprehensible to the ELLs in the classroom.

On Sunday, I *went* to a birthday party for Christine and Jules. Paul *rented* a waterslide for the party. When we *arrived* about 10 children *played* on the waterslide. They *took* turns *going down* the slide. Some children *went* really fast, and the older children *did* tricks when they came down. Everyone *landed* in a pool at the bottom of the slide. When they *landed,* water *splashed* from the pool and *landed* on everyone. It was so hot out that the water *cooled* us.

Paul *cooked* hamburgers and hotdogs on the grill for everyone. After *playing* in the water all day, the children *were hungry.* They *ate* all the food, and then *ate* cake and ice cream. We *sang* happy birthday, and then Christine and Jules *opened* their presents.

Mrs. Allen reads through the writing once and explains any words that students do not know. She reads through it again, thinking aloud about the parts that she thought conveyed images of the party well and the words she was less sure about. She asks for student input: "What do you notice about the action words that you might you change?"

Callie volunteers, "The first thing I notice is that you say *landed* three times. I think I would change that."

Mrs. Allen points to the sentence, reading through it again. "You are right," she tells Callie. "Maybe we could brainstorm some other words that might fit here." The students suggest alternatives to *landed*, which Mrs. Allen jots down on the whiteboard. Collectively, they rewrite the sentence:

Everyone *flew* into the pool at the bottom of the slide. When they *landed*, water *splashed* from the pool and *rained down* on everyone.

They then return to the beginning of the paragraph to decide if they will keep the underlined words or make changes. Following this mini-lesson, Mrs. Allen asks students to select a piece of writing from their folders that they think will benefit from a revision of the action words. Some students consult one another about word choice using quiet voices, whereas other children work independently on their writing.

REFLECTIONS

1. How do you think it benefits ELLs and FEP learners to use authentic writing when learning to make revisions?

2. How will lessons such as Mrs. Allen's serve to develop English language proficiency as well as skill in writing?

STRATEGY RESOURCE

1. 📄 📑 ReadWriteThink provides several ideas for lessons and mini-lessons in revision.

   http://www.readwritethink.net/search/?resource_type=6&sort_order=relevance& q=revising+writing&old_q=&srchwhere=full-site

UNIT VIII

Strategies for Involving Families and Communities

How am I supposed to communicate with families when we don't speak the same language and I don't know their culture?

—Preservice Teacher

we had parent-teacher's night and none of the families of our ELLs came. How am I supposed to involve parents who won't come to school?

—Grade 4 Teacher

As educators, we know that relationships between children's schools and their families are important. In fact, home–school relationships have been associated with higher student grades, lower incidences of discipline problems, higher rates of high school graduation, and increased enrollment in institutes of higher education (August & Hakuta, 1997).

> **Majority Culture:**
> middle class and English speaking

While home–school relationships are important to the educational well-being of all students, these relationships are even more important for students whose culture, language, and economic status differ from that of the **majority culture.**

ELLs are certainly among this group of students; ELL parents are generally not fully English proficient, the culture of the home differs from the culture of the school, and because of language barriers, ELL parents are disproportionally represented among the monetarily poor. Because of these differences, ELLs often transition from one world to another as they go from home to school each day. Home–school partnerships are powerful tools for providing education that is relevant to ELLs in learning environments and they demonstrate value for ELLs' home culture and language.

When ELLs' family members participate in events and activities within their children's schools, ELLs are more likely to see school as a welcoming place that values their presence and are more likely to see learning as relevant. Learning becomes understood as something that occurs within schools and within their families (National Family, School, and Community Engagement Working Group, 2010, p. 5).

Family involvement also extends beyond the walls of the schools and the formal educational setting. As children transition from elementary to middle school, the role of parental involvement includes helping students understand the value and possibility of continuing education and having regular and ongoing conversations that make clear the link between studying, schoolwork, future employment, education, and community involvement and improvement.

Although home–school partnerships have the potential to improve educational opportunities for ELLs and FEP learners, these partnerships are often the exception rather than the norm. Many schools and school systems have been less than successful in involving ELL families, and families who are not accustomed to the culture and structure of American schools may not know how to become involved. This is particularly true for families who come from countries and cultures where the teacher is held in the highest regard and it is considered disrespectful to question him or her.

For ELL parents who are recent arrivals in the United States, U.S. schools are foreign places. The culture of the school—the language, the norms for behavior, dressing, and eating, and even the types of food that are served—is very different from the culture within many families, causing parents to feel a sense of disequilibrium before they reach the school door.

ELL parents who are the second generation in the United States may have had negative experiences with schools as they themselves struggled to learn content and academic English. For these parents, schools are likely to feel like unwelcoming places.

It is also often difficult for families from different cultures to understand the structure of the U.S. school system with regard to preparing students for educational opportunities beyond K–12. Parents who have not attended college or have not attended college in the United States often do not have any notion of how K–12 education begins to prepare students in middle school for college opportunities. As a result, students in the middle years may not see connections between school and their lives.

Negotiating the front door of the school is a less than welcoming experience for many parents. Due to necessary security structures, visitors must ring a bell, identify themselves in response to a voice in English, and then wait to hear the loud click that unlocks the door. Once inside the building, many parents are greeted by signs in English that they do not fully comprehend and a secretary or front office administrator who may not speak their language. Even when parents are explicitly invited to school events, barriers exist. Invitations, often written only in English, may arrive at homes in a sea of school announcements and papers. Invitations are also often extended to parents only, which creates an additional burden for parents who do not have childcare for younger children as well as for those parents who are more comfortable attending events with their extended families. While many barriers to home–school partnerships exist, it is possible to actively involve families in school and to tap into the knowledge that exists within each family (Colombo, 2004, 2007; González et al., 2005).

The Parent Partnership for Achieving Literacy (PAL) project (Colombo, 2004, 2007) provided outreach and educational services to ELL families in Grades PK through 8. Services, designed in response to the needs identified by ELL parents, were provided at the school district's central administration building, which was located in the ELL families' neighborhood. The ongoing opportunities for meaningful involvement provided by PAL helped to build trust and reciprocity between parents and teachers. ELL parents actively participated in family literacy nights and family ESL classes. Teachers were also invited to participate in family literacy nights and ESL classes, which provided a welcoming venue for parents and teachers to get to know one another and a comfortable environment to talk about their children. PAL evenings also included speakers who explained the expectations of the school and ways in which teachers expected parents to participate. They explained ways that families could support the learning of their children, such as reading with younger children, storytelling in their own language, discussing the school day and homework, and so on.

In the Funds of Knowledge project (González et al., 2005), teachers engaged in professional development and action research to prepare for visits to the homes of their students who were Mexican American and whose families spoke Spanish as a first language. During these visits, teachers learned about the strengths and knowledge that exists within families, discussed this knowledge with other participating teachers and researchers, and applied their learnings to the curriculum. In this way, the Funds of Knowledge project parents were active participants in shaping the curriculum and the way that teachers approached instruction.

Both the PAL program and the Funds of Knowledge project are examples of meaningful ways that schools can actively involve parents. This unit builds on the understandings gained from PAL and Funds of Knowledge to provide you with strategies that will help you to build relationships with the families of your ELL students.

WHAT YOU WILL LEARN

Unit VIII provides theory, research, vignettes, and strategies to help you do the following:

1. Understand the importance of building partnerships with the families and communities of ELLs.

2. Begin to recognize your own perspectives and biases and to think about how the perspectives of ELLs and their families may differ from your own.

3. Extend an invitation to the families of the ELLs in your classroom.

4. Communicate with the families of ELLs in your classroom.

5. Learn about programs in which home visits have been conducted successfully.

6. Build on the strengths and body of knowledge that exists within the families of ELLs.

STRATEGIES IN THIS UNIT

Actively involving families requires sustained effort. Teachers, administrators, and school personnel will need to build, cultivate, and maintain trusting relationships with parents who are, for whatever reason, unfamiliar with the structure of the school or not comfortable coming to the school. This unit provides four strategies: Strategy 40: Extending the Invitation, which focuses on outreach and providing a welcoming environment for ELL families; Strategy 41: Communicating With the ELL Parent includes ways to inform and have discussions with the ELL parent; Strategy 42: Visiting Homes and Communities; and Strategy 43: Building Funds of Knowledge Into Classroom Instruction, which helps you learn what to do with the knowledge you have gained during the home visits. The strategies in this unit are consistent with the TESOL Standards for Teachers as illustrated in Table VIII.1.

Table VIII.1	TESOL Standards for Teachers

Domain 2: Culture

2.a. *Understand and apply knowledge about cultural values and beliefs in the context of teaching and learning. (p. 41)*

2.b. *Understand and apply knowledge about the effects of racism, stereotyping, and discrimination to teaching and learning. (p. 41)*

2.c. *Understand and apply knowledge about cultural conflicts and home events that can have an impact on ELLs' learning. (p. 41)*

2.d. *Understand and apply knowledge about communication between home and school to enhance ESL teaching and build partnerships with ELL families. (p. 42)*

2.g. *Understand and apply concepts of cultural competency, particularly knowledge about how an individual's cultural identity affects their learning and academic progress and how levels of cultural identity will vary widely among students. (p. 43)*

Domain 5: Professionalism

5.b.6. *Support ELL families.(p. 75)*

Source: TESOL Teacher Standards Tables: TESOL (2010). *TESOL/NCATE Standards for the Recognition of Initial TESOL Programs in P–12 ESL Teacher Education*, Alexandria, VA: TESOL.

STRATEGY RESOURCE

The document *Building Collaboration Between Schools and Parents of English Language Learners: Transcending Barriers, Creating Opportunities* by Robin Waterman and Beth Harry (2008), provides an overview of the benefits of increased participation for ELL parents as well as suggestions for involving parents.

http://www.nccrest.org/Briefs/PractitionerBrief_BuildingCollaboration.pdf

Strategy

Extending the Invitation

40

As much as they value education and want the best for their children, for many reasons, some ELL families do not feel comfortable in the school setting. All of us have biases, and it is possible that if we feel comfortable in schools, we may view families who do not participate in school events through a deficit lens. Yet it is when we can see differences, rather than deficits, that we are able to begin to understand the perspectives of others.

Strategy 40 provides resources and ideas for understanding one's own biases as well as steps for assessing the current climate of the school environment and ways to create an environment that welcomes all parents.

THEORY AND/OR RESEARCH UNDERLYING THE STRATEGY

Home–school partnerships enhance educational opportunities for ELLs and FEP learners. We are all influenced by our cultures in ways in which we are not even fully aware. We are like fish swimming in water—we may not notice the water (our cultural medium), yet it influences everything we do and know (Kluckholn, 1949). By becoming aware of our own perspectives and biases, we can better understand the perspectives of others (Howard, 2006).

IMPLEMENTING THE STRATEGY

This is a three-part strategy. Extending an invitation to families begins by creating a welcoming environment and connecting with the community. Neither the invitation nor the connection is likely to happen if you see families through a deficit lens—that is, if you believe that your way of doing things is the only way to do them. Extending an invitation begins by thinking about your own perspectives, and therefore, the first step of this strategy involves a reflection and two brief online quizzes to help you begin this process. The goal of Part 1 of this strategy is to become aware of what you know and how you know it. Part 2 of the strategy then guides you on a walk-through of your building and classroom to look for evidence of a welcoming environment, and Part 3 focuses on making initial contact with ELL families.

Part I. Reflection

1. Consider this reflection:

   "We all have an internal list of those we still don't understand, let alone appreci-ate. We all have biases, even prejudices, toward specific groups. In our workshops, we ask people to gather in pairs and think about their hopes and fears in relating to people of a group different from their own. Fears usually include being judged, miscommunication, and patronizing or hurting others unintentionally; hopes are usually the possibility of dialogue, learning something new, developing friend-ships, and understanding different points of view. After doing this activity hun-dreds of times, I'm always amazed how similar the lists are. At any moment that we're dealing with people different from ourselves, the likelihood is that they carry a similar list of hopes and fears in their back pocket."

   Source: From *Waging Peace in Our Schools,* by L. Lantieri and J. Patti, 1996, Boston: Beacon Press (as quoted in DuPraw & Axner, 1997).

1. Take the brief quizzes that are found in the Strategy Resources section. Review the answer keys. Reflect on your results and reaction to the results.

2. Discuss the quizzes and the Cross-Cultural Communication Challenge with colleagues.

3. With a colleague, discuss your hopes and your fears with regard to relating to ELL parents.

Part II. School and Self-Inventory

1. Take a walk through your school, beginning at the front door, proceeding to the main office (or other area to which visitors are directed), and finally heading through the main corridors on the way to classrooms. Is the setting welcoming to families? If so, how? Is it welcoming for ELL families who speak the languages represented in your school? If so, how?

2. Stand outside the door to your room and look at it as though you were a visitor. Is your classroom welcoming? How so? Would it be welcoming if you spoke the language of each student in your class? How can you make it more welcoming?

3. Find the streets where each of your students live. Are you familiar with these neighborhoods? What do you know about them?

4. Are you familiar with the stores, community service buildings, and so on in each area? What might you learn from your ELL student's neighborhood?

Part III. Initial Outreach

1. Determine whether there is an interpreter for the languages of students in your classroom.

2. Find out from the home language survey and from your ELL student if his or her parents speaks some English. If they do, you can make a phone call home to introduce yourself and invite the parent to come to the school at his or her convenience. If not, you will need the services of an interpreter to accomplish this.

3. Invite the family, not just the parents, to visit the school. This may include younger siblings, grandmother, another member of the extended family, and perhaps a cousin who can speak more English—the concept of family must be extended. Offer at least some time options that complement the parents' schedules (e.g., early morning or evening).

4. Invite the family to come to the classroom with the purpose of getting to know one another a bit and so that they will know the classroom in which their child spends her or his days and receives instruction. Do not wait until there is a problem or an issue to contact parents.

5. Learn to say a few words, including a brief greeting, in the language of the parent. This gesture will show parents that you value their participation and their language.

6. While it is preferable to be able to fluently speak the language of the parent and to reach out in a bilingual format, this is not always possible. For a friendly visit, if the ELL student speaks some English, he or she can assist in interpreting and can show the family his or her desk, work in the classroom, and so on.

7. Arrange a tour of your school for parents in your grade (Colorín Colorado, 2007).

8. Visit the grocery stores, offices, and areas in the ELLs' communities. Be visible.

9. Encourage your principal and others to create a welcoming atmosphere for parents.

STRATEGY IN ACTION

Ms. Jeanine Carter is a fifth grade regular classroom teacher. She has 10 ELLs in her class of 26 students. At the beginning of the year, Ms. Carter begins a schedule for contacting homes and introducing herself. She contacts the families of seven students each week. Several of the ELLs in her classroom speak Spanish at home. While Ms. Carter's Spanish is not nearly proficient, she can communicate well enough to greet parents, introduce herself, and tell the parents that she is happy to have their child in her class. She also extends an open invitation for them to call or to visit the classroom. Ms. Carter has identified a paraprofessional in the building who can assist her in making phone calls to the two families for whom Portuguese is a first language. She is trying to locate someone who speaks Shona, the language spoken by Chipo, an ELL from Zimbabwe, and she feels confident that she will be able to do so during the first quarter of the school year. With Chipo's help, she has invited Chipo's family to the school to see the classroom and to meet her.

Ms. Carter continues to make follow-up phone calls according to the schedule she has developed. This enables her to speak with families very briefly, approximately once a month. She limits these calls to a few minutes each, just long enough to tell parents something that their child has learned or something positive that they have done in the classroom. She dedicates one half hour a week to this.

Ms. Carter has been reaching out to parents for several years. She finds that when she contacts parents in this way, parents are willing to respond to her if there is a problem to discuss. Parent participation at regular school events has increased slightly for Ms. Carter's parents, and several parents regularly stop by the classroom to say hello when they arrive at school to pick up their children at the end of the day.

Mr. Dan Clark is a physical education teacher in a suburban school adjacent to a large urban area. Most of the ELLs in Mr. Clark's classes live in this urban area. Mr. Clark has mapped out a jogging route that takes him through the urban neighborhoods of many of the students he has in his physical education classes. Mr. Clark is greeted by students and their parents and neighbors when he jogs through the neighborhood. Mr. Clark's students often mention seeing him when they are in school. He has found a way to connect home and school.

REFLECTIONS

1. Review your responses to the quizzes. Were you surprised by any answer? If so, which and why?

2. Why do you think it is useful to extend the invitation to the family rather than to limit it to the parents?

3. Have you tried to involve the families of the students in your classroom? Have you been successful? What might be the reasons for your success? Based on this strategy, what might you do to increase your opportunities for success with families?

STRATEGY RESOURCES

1. 📄 Quizzes at the Multicultural Pavilion
   http://www.edchange.org/multicultural/quizzes.html

2. 📄 Review Working on Common Cross-Cultural Communication Challenges, published online by PBS
   http://www.pbs.org/ampu/crosscult.html

Strategy

Communicating With the ELL Parent

41

Connections between ELL families and their children's schools help to build bridges between the two worlds in which the ELL lives. The previous strategy provided ideas for reaching out to families. This strategy focuses on communicating with family members once they have arrived at school or during a home visit scheduled to discuss an issue about student behavior or school work. (This communication is different from the social nature of the outreach calls discussed in Strategy 40 and also the more extensive visits discussed in Strategy 42.)

THEORY AND/OR RESEARCH UNDERLYING THE STRATEGY

The positive influence of home–school relationships on the educational well-being of ELLs is clear (August & Hakuta, 1997). Language is often a formidable barrier in forging and sustaining positive relationships between schools and ELL families. Translations that are sent home can be poorly done, especially if they are machine translations or if the parent does not know the school system (Waterman & Harry, 2008); therefore, personal conversations that occur face to face or by phone are often better ways to communicate with family members who do not speak English (Waterman, 2006). Personal communication is likely to be more effective with family members who are not educated in their first language. It is always best to communicate in the language that the parent understands best, and this is especially true when there are serious issues, important school policies, and so on. The following strategy is adapted from Colorín Colorado (a full link to Colorín Colorado is provided in the Strategy Resources section at the end of this strategy). Also included is a video in which Pat Mora, a literacy expert and author of children's books, speaks about involving parents.

IMPLEMENTING THE STRATEGY

1. As often as is possible, communicate with families in their preferred language. This is critical if the issue is serious and family members must fully understand all aspects of the message.

2. Request a bilingual interpreter who speaks the language of the parents and English to attend meetings and discuss school issues, grades, report cards, discipline, and other sensitive issues. (For each language spoken within the school, the school district should provide an interpreter.)

3. Be sure to introduce non-English-speaking families to bilingual staff within the building or school system.

4. Encourage ELL and bilingual families who are even marginally involved in the school to reach out to other ELL families to build a network of support.

5. Through an interpreter, explain the U.S. school system so that parents understand its procedures and expectations. Be sure to include the following:

   a. A description of the policies and practices within your school, including the school calendar, trajectories from PK through Grade 12, and the administrative structure within the school.

   b. The curriculum and instructional materials used in your school. (Some parents may be accustomed to a national curriculum.)

   c. The expectations of teachers. As indicated by Colorín Colorado (2007), "Explain that teachers hope and expect that parents will help with homework, find tutors, read books, tell stories, take their children to the library, visit the classroom, and [otherwise] become involved in school" (para. 10).

   d. Information for parents on their rights. A link to an explanation of the rights of parents is available in the Strategy Resources section.

   e. Arrangement for home and community visits (the topic of Strategy 42).

6. When conducting a meeting with an ELL family member and an interpreter, build rapport with the family member by speaking to the parent directly and pausing to allow the interpreter to translate.

Source: Adapted from "How to Create a Welcoming Classroom Environment," Colorín Colorado, 2007.

Strategy in Action

When 11-year-old Farrah was placed in Mrs. Mia Carter's fifth grade classroom, Mrs. Carter reviewed her intake records and assessments. From these, she learned that Farrah had recently arrived from Iraq, where she had been a very good student. Because the school guidance counselor and Mrs. Carter scheduled a meeting with Farrah's parents and scheduled an English-Arabic interpreter to participate in the meeting, they learned that Farrah's Iraqi neighborhood had experienced ongoing bombings and gunfire. As a result, Farrah was easily startled by sudden and loud noises and she sometimes experienced difficulty sleeping. Without a meeting with parents and an interpreter, this serious situation would have remained largely unknown to the school. Because Mrs. Carter and the guidance counselor now have this information, they have been able to sensitize students to the fact that sounds and movements might frighten Farrah. Mrs. Carter is also sensitive to Farrah's tendency to become very tired in her classroom, a typical tendency for ELLs who must process language and content that is exacerbated when Farrah has not had sufficient sleep.

During this initial meeting, Mrs. Carter explained her curriculum, the type of daily assignments that students completed, and some of the long-range major assignments. With the help of the interpreter, she was able to explain that she would make adjustments to Farrah's assignments so that Farrah could learn content as she developed English language proficiency. Mrs. Carter also explained the developmental nature of English language acquisition and Farrah's schedule with ESL services. She told Farrah's family that the school was conducting a search for an Arabic tutor who could explain content to Farrah while Farah was learning English.

To keep Farah's parents informed about her progress, Mrs. Carter, the guidance counselor, the interpreter, and Farrah's parents set a schedule for biweekly phone conversations. The interpreter also provided contact information in case Farrah's parents had questions or concerns.

Following the meeting, Farrah's parents accompanied the guidance counselor on a tour of the school, which ended in Mrs. Carter's classroom. Mrs. Carter showed them her daily schedule, Farrah's desk, content-area instructional materials, and the instructional centers in the room.

REFLECTIONS

1. Find out what languages are spoken by parents of students in your school. Do the parents speak English as well? Find out if there is an interpreter for each language spoken. If there is not an interpreter, how is the school conducting meetings and discussions with ELL parents?

2. What are some of the problems that might arise when children interpret for their parents? Why do you think this is usually discouraged unless the conversation is very casual and upbeat?

3. Watch the video of Pat Mora and reflect on what you have learned.

STRATEGY RESOURCES

1. Pat Mora discusses how to reach out to parents and involve them in the classroom. (Running time: 4 minutes)

   http://www.colorincolorado.org/educators/reachingout/outreach#video

2. "Your Rights as the Parent of a Public School Student," from Colorín Colorado.

   http://www.colorincolorado.org/families/school/parentalrights

Strategy

42

Visiting Homes and Communities

Teachers have been making home visits for many years. The focus of these visits is often to discuss the progress of a child, what the parent needs to do to support the child and the work of the school, and the ways in which parents and teachers can work together to collaboratively solve any problem the child is experiencing. The type of home visit that is presented in this strategy is different. This strategy focuses on home visits with the goal of learning more about the family and the community—learning about the *funds of knowledge* within each home and family. *Funds of knowledge* refers to the ways of knowing and doing that exist in each home, which, for example, include the interests and talents of the family members, the ways in which members of the family interact, and the various roles that children may play within the household, such as caretaker for younger siblings, assistant with household chores, and interpreter and translator for parents and other family members. Knowing about parents' strengths and talents provides segue to including family members in classroom activities, and knowing about children's roles helps teachers to understand how children learn within the home. The role that children play within their families also provides insight into the match or mismatch of instructional processes and materials and the student's learning. Knowing the knowledge that exists within the home can also help teachers to make instruction more relevant to students. The Funds of Knowledge project (González et al. (2005) forms the basis for Strategy 42.

THEORY AND/OR RESEARCH UNDERLYING THE STRATEGY

The Funds of Knowledge project, which was implemented in Arizona (González et al., 2005), helped teachers transition from viewing families who did not speak English as deficient to seeing the strengths that exist within every family. In this project, teachers visited families to learn more about the whole child, the interaction between the child and others in her or his family, and the interests of parents and extended family members. Funds of Knowledge involves socially mediated learning that is steeped in the research of Vygotsky.

In addition to helping teachers see parents and other family members as valuable and often untapped resources for the classroom, teachers' visits to homes increased the families' trust of teachers. The resulting family-teacher relationships were built on reciprocity which resulted in a greater family presence within the classroom.

Another such project is the Parent Teacher Home Visit Project (PTHVP), which promotes home visits that enable families and teachers to work collaboratively as equal partners in a child's education. In this model, teachers make at least two home visits: The focus of the first is relationship building and learning about families, the goal of the second visit is to share information about the school system with families. It is important to note that participation in the Funds of Knowledge project was voluntary, as is participation in the PTHVP project. Teachers are provided with training and ongoing support. In addition, all teachers and school staff who participate in the PTHVP project are compensated for their work. A link to the PTHVP project is included in the Strategy Resources section for this strategy.

IMPLEMENTING THE STRATEGY

1. Find out if your school and school district provide support in terms of training and compensation for home visits. Plan visits to homes or venues within families' neighborhoods with the goal of learning more about the strengths and talents within each family. As with any home visit, visit only homes and neighborhoods in which you feel safe, and visit with another teacher, a guidance counselor, or another member of the school's personnel, preferably someone who speaks the language of the family. Another version of the home visit is to contact a church or community organization within the community and arrange to meet with family members at that venue.

2. Contact families, explaining your interest in visiting their homes and communities: You are interested in ensuring that children see the extension between the school and home learning environment. The goals of meeting with families away from school are to build trust and collaboration, to find ways to tap into the different strengths that exist within every family, to learn about how the student learns at home, and to learn about strengths that family members may be able to share within the classroom.

3. Prepare to leave your perspectives of the way things should be done at the door. Your goal is not to judge how families measure up to your notion of family (González et al., 2005).

4. If you visit within the home, observe the ways in which things are done, the roles that individuals play, and the interactions between individuals in the family.

5. Notice artifacts that will help you learn about the strengths within families—instruments, artwork, language use, plants, and so on.

6. Talk with family members about knowledge that they share that might be included within the classroom curriculum—story telling, art, different languages, knowledge about the geography of different places, history, and so on.

7. Talk with family members about the activities that children engage in within the family, including caring for siblings, performing household chores, translating, and so on.

8. Keep a journal of your visits, noting what you have learned, what might be incorporated into your curriculum and instruction, and how you can make connections between knowledge within the home and the curriculum to increase the relevance of your teaching.

Strategy in Action

Mrs. Carter has always believed that parents want what is best for their children. When she first began teaching at her present school, which is approximately 10% ELL and 60% low income based on free and reduced lunch statistics, Mrs. Carter was disappointed that she had little participation from ELL families. From general conversations with her students, she knew that several families attended the same neighborhood church. She contacted the bilingual minister of the church, explained that she would like to meet with families to get to know them better, and asked if there were days and times that a room in the church could be available for this purpose. The minister offered to attend the first meeting.

Only one parent attended the first session. Although Mrs. Carter was disappointed, she had heard that it would take time to build trust and develop a core group of parents who might attend meetings. She talked with the parent and explained that her goals were to get to know family members, to share with them what their children were learning in school, and to learn about their ideas for working together. She asked the parent to talk with other family members in the community to encourage them to attend the next meeting.

Mrs. Carter now meets with families at the church venue four times a year. She knows several of her students' parents as well as their extended families, including grandparents and siblings. Mrs. Carter keeps a journal in which she documents meetings; this has enabled her to see growth in the number of family members who attend the meetings as well as the deepening sense of trust that has evolved. It also allows her to keep notes about the strengths and talents of family members, which she taps into to enhance her classroom instruction. For example, during one visit, Mrs. Carter learned that one of the parents played the guitar during church services. She invited the parent to come to the classroom to play and to teach students a traditional song. Since that time, several family members have visited her classroom to read and tell bilingual stories. One Hmong family member brought traditional textile art to tell about Hmong history, geography, and art. Building on funds of knowledge within the classroom is the topic of Strategy 43.

Reflections

1. How might knowing about families help you to build on students' knowledge?

2. What have you done to increase classroom connections with families who appear to be hard to reach?

3. How do you feel about conducting visits within homes or community centers? What are your hopes and fears?

STRATEGY RESOURCES

1. 🗐 Carrie Rose, the executive director of the Parent Teacher Home Visit Project (PTHVP), describes the PTHVP project in this issue of The Family Involvement Network of Educators (FINE) newsletter.

   http://www.hfrp.org/publications-resources/browse-our-publications/the-parent-teacher-home-visit-project

2. 🎬 The Parent Teacher Home Visit Project (PTHVP) video illustrates the benefits of home visits for building positive and caring relationships with families. (Running Time: 15 minutes)

   http://www.pthvp.org/video.html

Strategy

43

Building Funds of Knowledge Into Classroom Instruction

As educators, we know that students have greater opportunities for learning when instruction is relevant. Infusing the *funds of knowledge* (González et al., 2005) from families and communities into classroom instruction helps to connect home and school learning and increases the likelihood that students will view instruction as relevant. Also, bringing the knowledge from diverse homes including language, customs, and artifacts, into the classroom, shows that these differences are valued and, thus, that students themselves are valued. Strategy 42 focused on the importance of communicating with families within their homes and communities and mentioned two resulting cases of parents coming to the classroom to share their talents and funds of knowledge. Bringing the knowledge of families and community members to the classroom is the focus of Strategy 43.

THEORY AND/OR RESEARCH UNDERLYING THE STRATEGY

Valuing differences in language and culture and acknowledging and recognizing these differences as strengths are hallmarks of a culturally responsive classroom (Au, 2006; Gay, 2000; Villegas & Lucas, 2002). When ELLs and FEP learners believe that the strengths they bring to the classroom are valued, their opportunities for educational success improve (Au, 2006). In addition, when teachers value differences in language and culture, they are less likely to view ELLs from a deficit lens, resulting in higher expectations for student achievement.

IMPLEMENTING THE STRATEGY

1. Find out about the funds of knowledge that exist in the families and communities of the students in your classroom (using home visits—Strategy 42—and student generated interviews—this strategy). Family members are more likely to participate in the classroom if they are invited by the teacher or if they are invited by

their own children.

2. Have students prepare interviews to conduct with family members as an assignment option. This can be done as part of a project on reading and writing biographies. Work with students to generate developmentally appropriate questions. Some families do not want to discuss their backgrounds for a variety of reasons, so the home biography <u>should be one choice</u> for an assignment.

3. Ask students to bring in artifacts and photos from home. For example, the Hmong textile art mentioned in Strategy 42 could serve as a springboard into oral storytelling. (Hmong weavings depict history, beliefs, everyday life, geography, world history, or art.) Photos from other countries, states, or regions can be used to discuss climate, customs, or ecosystems. Photos of machines (cars, household appliances, etc.) can be used to introduce a unit on technological change. As you might imagine, the uses for photos are nearly endless.

4. Ask students about their responsibilities at home. Knowing that a student cares for younger siblings during the summer months or prepares dinner most evenings illustrates his or her level of responsibility, and it may provide examples for instruction across the content areas.

5. Celebrate languages. All students will benefit from hearing languages other than English and from learning a few words in a different language. Invite and have children invite family members into the classroom to read a book from their culture in their primary language. With professional development funds, invest in an inexpensive video camera (approximately $129). Allow students whose family members work during the day to record their parents' story telling or storybook reading. Show these to the class and discuss them.

6. Encourage family members to visit the classroom to show slides of their native countries or trips to other countries or states that lend themselves to content-area study.

STRATEGY IN ACTION

Grade 7

Ms. Tamara Tabor's seventh grade class is preparing to read biographies for a combined English language arts and social studies unit. Mrs. Tabor has discussed the ways in which biographies often provide much historical information about the time in which the subject lived. She presents a student–home biography as one assignment option. She tells students the biography of her great-grandmother, who immigrated to the United States from Ireland in the early 1900s. She uses photos of her great grandmother in various settings, maps, and information about Ellis Island that she found on the Internet. She tells the story of her great-grandmother and about a period in Irish history and U.S. history.

Mrs. Tabor is sensitive to the needs of her students. She does not know if the families of her students are all living in the United States legally. Also, in the past, she has had students from families who have experienced war, conflict, persecution, and genocide. She understands that neither of these groups of parents is likely to want to share their past with the school. Mrs. Tabor ensures that this assignment is flexible. Again, using herself as an example, she explains that she would not have been able to interview her great-grandfather, who was sent to the United States alone as a young boy and who refused to talk about his experiences. Mrs. Tabor explains that Option 2 of the assignment is to identify a person who was influential in either the United States or their families' country of origin. She provides students with a clear example of this assignment, using Arthur Griffin, one of the founding fathers of the Irish Free State, who lived in Ireland at the time her great-grandmother immigrated to the United States. This year several members of her students' families, including two ELL parents, have agreed to come to the classroom to tell a story from their cultures.

Grade 4

Following Sr. Lopez's visit to Mrs. Carter's class to play the guitar, Lindsey Kielty told Mrs. Carter that her mother also played the guitar. Every few weeks, Sr. Lopez and Mrs. Kielty visit the classroom to teach students a song bilingually, Sr. Lopez singing in Spanish and Mrs. Kielty singing in English. Mrs. Carter has also had several mothers agree to come to her classroom to read a story from their culture in their first language using bilingual books: The parent reads in her first language, and either Mrs. Carter or a capable student reads the story in English. If no bilingual version is available, parents provide Mrs. Carter with an oral translation in advance so that she can explain the story to the students. In preparation for their visits, Mrs. Carter tells the students about the parent and the parent's place of birth. Students find the birthplace on the map and learn about the climate, geography, population, capital city, and industry. Mrs. Carter displays posters for each place they have studied in preparation for their guest performer.

Reflections

1. How might you build instruction into your classroom that includes the funds of knowledge of your ELL students?

2. What do you see as challenges as well as potential benefits?

3. What are your hopes, and what are your fears?

Strategy Resources

1. 📄📑 *Tapping Into Community Funds of Knowledge*, by Michael Genzuk, provides theories and techniques to help teachers understand and use the funds of knowledge that exist within their students' homes and communities. Funds of Knowledge Professional Development Document can be accessed online.

   http://www-bcf.usc.edu/~genzuk/Genzuk_ARCO_Funds_of_Knowledge.pdf

2. 🎞 *The Classroom Mosaic: Culture and Learning*, an Annenberg production, provides a discussion of culturally responsive teaching and the ways in which teachers can tap into household funds of knowledge and create culturally responsive classrooms. Gloria Ladson-Billings and Luis Moll provide theory and commentary. In-classroom videos demonstrate the effectiveness of using students' funds of knowledge.

   http://www.learner.org/resources/series172.html (You will need to log in and establish an account. There is no charge for this.)

References

Abdallah, J. (2009a). Benefits of co-teaching for ESL classrooms. *Academic Leadership Live, 7*(1). Retrieved July 5, 2010, from http://www.academicleadership.org/emprical_research/532.shtml

Abdallah, J. (2009b). Lowering teacher attrition rates through collegiality. *Academic Leadership. 7*(1). Retrieved July 4, 2010, from http://www.academicleadership.org/emprical_research/531.shtml

Adler, C. R. (Ed.). (2001). *Put reading first: The research building blocks for teaching children to read.* Jessup, MD: National Institute for Literacy. Retrieved December 1, 2009, from http://lincs.ed.gov/publications/pdf/PRFbooklet.pdf

Albright, L. K. (2002). Bringing the Ice Maiden to life: Engaging adolescents in learning through picture book read-alouds in content areas. *Journal of Adolescent & Adult Literacy, 45,* 418–428.

Alliance for Education. (2008). *What keeps good teachers in the classroom? Understanding and reducing teacher turnover.* Washington, DC: Author. Retrieved October 5, 2010, from http://www.all4ed.org/publication_material/TeachersLeaders

American Federation of Teachers. (n.d.). *Creating a classroom team: How teachers and para-professionals can make working together work.* Washington, DC: Author. Retrieved July 5, 2010, from http://www.aft.org/pdfs/psrp/psrpclassroomteam0804.pdf

Anderson, R. C. (1977). The notion of schemata and the educational enterprise: General discussion of the conference. In R. C. Anderson, R. J. Spiro, & W. E. Montague (Eds.), *Schooling and acquisition of knowledge* (pp. 413–431). Hillsdale, NJ: Lawrence Erlbaum.

Aronson, E., Blaney, N., Stephin, C., Sikes, J., & Snapp, M. (1978). *The jigsaw classroom.* Beverly Hills, CA: Sage.

Asher, J. (1965).The strategy of total physical response: An application to learning Russian. *International Review of Applied Linguistics, 3,* 291–300.

Asher, J. M. (2009). *The total physical response (TPR): Review of the evidence.* Los Gatos, CA: Sky Oaks Productions. Retrieved June 14, 2010, from http://www.tpr-world.com/review_evidence.pdf

Ashton-Warner, S. (1963). *Teacher.* New York: Simon and Schuster.

Au, K. (2006). *Multicultural issues and literacy achievement.* Mahwah, NJ: Lawrence Erlbaum.

August, D., & Hakuta, K. (Eds.). (1997). *Improving schooling for language-minority children: A research agenda.* Washington, DC: National Academy Press.

August, D., & Shanahan, T. (Eds.). (2006). *Developing literacy in second-language learners: A report of the National Literacy Panel on language-minority children and youth.* Mahwah, NJ: Lawrence Erlbaum.

Ausubel, D. (1978). In defense of advance organizers: A reply to the critics. *Review of Educational Research, 48,* 251–257.

Baker, C. (2006). *Foundations of bilingual education and bilingualism.* Clevedon, UK: Multilingual Matters.

Bandura, A. (1977). *Social learning theory.* Englewood Cliffs, NJ: Prentice Hall.

Bandura, A. (1986). *Social foundations of thought and action: A social cognitive theory.* Englewood Cliffs, NJ: Prentice Hall.

Barrett, J. & Barrett, R. (1978). *Cloudy with a Chance of Meatballs.* New York: Anteneum.

Beck, I. L., & McKeown, M. G. (2007). Increasing young children's oral vocabulary repertoires through rich and focused instruction. *Elementary School Journal, 107,* 251–271.

Beck, I. S., McKeown, M. G., & Kucan, L. (2002). *Bringing words to life: Robust vocabulary instruction.* New York: Guilford Press.

Berko, J. (1958). The child's learning of English morphology. *Word, 14,* 150–177. Retrieved October 5, 2010, from http://childes.psy.cmu.edu/topics/wugs/wugs.pdf

Bhatia, V. K. (1983). Simplification v. easification: The case of legal texts. *Applied Linguistics, 4,* 42–54.

Biemiller, A. (2000, Fall). Teaching vocabulary: Early, direct, and sequential. Perspectives, 26(4). Retrieved June 30, 2010, from http://www.wordsmartedu.com/Biemiller_Teaching_Vocab.pdf

Birch, B. (2008). *English L2 reading: Getting to the bottom* (2nd ed.). New York: Routledge.

Branley, F. M. (1987). *The moon seems to change: Let's read-and-find-out science 2*. New York: Harper Collins Children's Books.

Brown, C. L. (2005, Winter). Ways to help ELLs: ESL teachers as consultants. *Academic Exchange Quarterly*. Retrieved June 26, 2010, from http://www.thefreelibrary.com/ays+to+help+ELLs%3A+ESL+teachers+as+consultants-a0142636428

Calkins, L. (1994). *The art of teaching writing*. Portsmouth, NH: Heinemann.

Campbell, R. (2001). *Read-alouds with young children*. Newark, DE: International Reading Association.

Canale, M. (1983). From communicative competence to communicative language pedagogy. In J. Richards & R. Schmidt (Eds.), *Language and communication* (pp. 2–27). New York: Longman.

Canale, M., & Swain, M. (1980). Theoretical bases of communicative approaches to second language teaching and testing. *Applied Linguistics, 1*, 1–47.

Carlo, M. S., August, D., & Snow, C. (2005). Sustained vocabulary-learning strategy instruction for English-language learners. In E. H. Hiebert & M. L. Kamil (Eds.), *Teaching and learning vocabulary: Bringing research to practice* (pp. 137–154). Mahwah, NJ: Lawrence Erlbaum.

Carle, E. (1987). *The very hungry caterpillar*. New York: Penguin Putnam Books for Young Readers.

Carrick, L. (2001, July/August). Internet resources for conducting readers theatre. *Reading Online, 5*(1). Retrieved June 25, 2010, from http://www.readingonline.org/electronic/elec_index.asp?HREF=carrick/index.html

Carrier, K. A. (2005). Key issues for teaching English language learners in academic classrooms. *Middle School Journal, 37*(2), 4–9.

Cartledge, G., & Lefki, K. (2008). Culturally responsive classrooms for culturally diverse students with and at risk for disabilities. *Exceptional Children, 74*(3), 351–371.

Causton-Theoharis, J. N., Giangreco, M. F., Doyle, M. B., & Vadasy, P. F. (2007). The "sous-chefs" of literacy instruction. *Teaching Exceptional Children, 40*(2), 56–62.

Celce-Murcia, M. (2007). Towards more context and discourse in grammar instruction. *TESL-EJ, 11*(2), 1–6.

Chall, J. S. (1983). *Stages of reading development*. New York: Harcourt Brace.

Chomsky, N. (1965). *Aspects of the theory of syntax*. Cambridge, MA: MIT Press.

Christensen, L., & Karp, S. (2003). *Rethinking school reform: Views from the classroom*. Milwaukee, WI: Rethinking Schools.

Church, E. B. (2007, September). Off to a great start: Creating an effective classroom. *Scholastic Early Childhood Today*. Retrieved August 9, 2010, from http://www2.scholastic.com/browse/article.jsp?id=3747330

Clayton, M. K., & Forton, M. B. (2001). *Classroom spaces that work*. Turners Falls, MA: Northeast Foundation for Children.

Collier, V. P. (1992). A synthesis of studies examining long-term language minority student data on academic achievement. *Bilingual Research Journal, 16*(1–2), 187–212.

Colombo, M. (2004). Family literacy nights and other home-school connections. *Educational Leadership, 61*(8), 48–51.

Colombo, M. (2007). Developing cultural competence: Mainstream teachers and professional development. *Multicultural Perspectives, 9*(2), 10–17.

Colombo, M., & Fontaine, P. (2009). Building vocabulary and fostering comprehension strategies for English language learners: The power of academic conversations in social studies. *New England Reading Association Journal, 45*(1), 46–54.

Colombo, M., & Furbush, D. (2009). *Teaching English language learners: Content and language in middle and secondary mainstream classrooms*. Thousand Oaks, CA: Sage.

Colorín Colorado. (2007). *How to create a welcoming classroom environment*. Retrieved June 29, 2010, from http://www.colorincolorado.org/educators/reachingout/welcoming

Coxhead, A. (2000). A new academic word list. *TESOL Quarterly, 34*(2), 213–238.

Craig, S. A. (2003). The effects of an adapted interactive writing intervention on kindergarten children's phonological awareness, spelling, and early reading development. *Reading Research Quarterly, 38*(4), 438–440.

Crawford, J. (2004). *Foundations of bilingual education and bilingualism* (5th ed.). Los Angeles: Bilingual Educational Services.

Cummins, J. (1979). Cognitive/academic language proficiency, linguistic interdependence, the optimum age question. *Working Papers on Bilingualism, 9*, 1–43.

Cummins, J. (1981). *Bilingualism and minority-language children*. Toronto, Ontario, Canada: Ontario Institute for Studies in Education.

Cummins, J. (1991). Interdependence of first- and second-language proficiency in bilingual children. In E. Bialystok (Ed.), *Language processing in bilingual children* (pp. 165–176). Cambridge, UK: Cambridge University Press.

Cummins, J. (2000). *Language, power, and pedagogy: Bilingual children in the crossfire*. Buffalo, NY: Multilingual Matters.

Cunningham, J. W. (1982). Generating interactions between schemata and text. In J. A. Niles & L. A.

Harris (Eds.), *New inquiries in reading research and instruction, Thirty-first Yearbook of the National Reading Conference* (pp. 42–47). Washington, DC: National Reading Conference.

Cunningham, P. M., & Hall, D. P. (1998). *Month-by-month phonics for upper grades: A second chance for struggling readers and students learning English.* Greensboro, NC: Carson-Dellosa.

Dewey, J. (1938/1997). *Experience and education.* New York: Simon and Schuster.

DuPraw, M. E., & Axner, M. (1997). Working on common cross-cultural communication challenges. *Public Broadcasting System.* Retrieved June 30, 2010, from http://www.pbs.org/ampu/crosscult.html

Echevarria, J., Vogt, M., & Short, D. (2003). *Making content comprehensible for English language learners: The SIOP model.* Boston: Allyn and Bacon.

Echevarria, J., Vogt, M., & Short, D. (2007). *Making content comprehensible for English language learners: The SIOP model* (3rd ed.). Boston: Allyn and Bacon.

Feldman, K., Kinsella, K. (2003). *Narrowing the language gap: Strategies for vocabulary development.* New York: Scholastic. Retrieved June 17, 2010, from http://www.fcoe.net/ela/pdf/Vocabulary/Narrowing%20Vocab%20Gap%20KK%20KF%201.pdf

Fisher, D., Frey, N., & Rothenberg, C. (2008). *Content-area conversations: How to plan discussion-based lessons for diverse language learners.* Alexandria, VA: Association for Supervision and Curriculum Development.

Francis, D., Rivera, M. Lesaux, N., Kieffer, M., & Rivera, H. (2006). Practical guidelines for the education of English language learners: Research-based recommendations for instruction and academic interventions. (Under cooperative agreement grant S283B050034 for U.S. Department of Education). Portsmouth, NH: RMC Research Corporation, Center on Instruction.

Frayer, D., Frederick, W. C., & Klausmeier, H. J. (1969). *A schema for testing the level of cognitive mastery.* Madison, WI: Wisconsin Center for Education Research.

Freeman, D., & Freeman, Y. (1990). Welcome: By drawing on ELL students' first languages, you can help make learning English easier—and a little less scary (best practice). (English language learners). *HighBeam Research.* Retrieved June 30, 2009, from http://business.highbeam.com/523/article-1G1-168316479/welcome-drawing-ell-students-first-languages-you-can

Freeman, D. E., Freeman, Y. S., & Mercuri, S. P. (2002). *Closing the achievement gap: How to reach limited-formal-schooling and long-term English language learners.* Portsmouth, NH: Heinemann.

Freeman, D., & Freeman, Y. (2007, August). Welcome ELLs: How to make ELL students feel at home. *Scholastic.* Retrieved on June 25, 2010, from http://www2.scholastic.com/browse/articlejsp?id=3747021

Garrison, C., & Ehringhaus, M. (2007). Formative and summative assessments in the classroom. Retrieved June 18, 2001, from http://www.nmsa.org/Publications/WebExclusive/Assessment/tabid/1120/Default.aspx

Gay, G. (2000). *Culturally responsive teaching: Theory, research, and practice.* New York: Teachers College Press.

Giangreco, M. F. (2003). Working with paraprofessionals. *Educational Leadership, 61*(2), 50–53. Retrieved June 2, 2010, from http://www.uvm.edu/cdci/evolve/working.pdf

Giangreco, M. F. (2010). One-to-one paraprofessionals for students with disabilities in inclusive classrooms: Is conventional wisdom wrong? *Intellectual & Developmental Disabilities, 48*(1), 1–13. doi: 10.1352/1934-9556-48.1.1

Giangreco, M. F., Smith, C. S., Pinckney, E. (2006). Addressing the paraprofessional dilemma in an inclusive school: A program description. *Research & Practice for Persons With Severe Disabilities, 31*(3), 215–229.

Giangreco, M. F., Yuan, S., McKenzie, B., Cameron, P., & Fialka, J. (2005). "Be careful what you wish for . . ." Five reasons to be concerned about the assignment of individual paraprofessionals. *Teaching Exceptional Children, 37*(5), 28–34.

Goldenberg, C. (1992/1993). Instructional conversations: Promoting comprehension through discussion. *The Reading Teacher, 46*(4), 316–326.

Goldenberg, C. (2008). Teaching English language learners: What the research does—and does not—say. *American Educator, 32*(2), 8–23, 42–44.

González, N., Moll, L., & Amanti, C. (Eds.). (2005). *Funds of knowledge: Theorizing practices in households, communities, and classrooms.* Mahwah, NJ: Lawrence Erlbaum.

Gottlieb, M. (2006). *Assessing English language learners: Bridges from language proficiency to academic achievement.* Thousand Oaks, CA: Corwin Press.

Graham, S., & Perin, D. (2007). *Writing next: Effective strategies to improve writing of adolescents in middle and high schools—a report to Carnegie Corporation of New York.* Washington, DC: Alliance for Excellent Education.

Graves, D. H. (1994). *A fresh look at writing.* Portsmouth, NH: Heinemann.

Graves, M. F. (2010). *Teaching content-area vocabulary.* Presenters' handouts for the 55th annual convention of the International Reading Association, Chicago, IL. Retrieved May 30, 2010, from http://www.reading .org/General/Conferences/AnnualConvention/ PresenterHandouts.aspx

Hakuta, K. (1986). *Mirror of language: The debate on bilingualism*. New York: Basic Books.

Harmon, J. M., Wood, K. D., Hedrick, W. B., Vintinner, J., & Willeford, T. (2009). Interactive word walls: More than just reading the writing on the walls. *Journal of Adolescent & Adult Literacy, 52*(5), 398–408. doi:10.1598/JAAL.52.5.4.

Harvey, S., & Goodvis, A. (2000). *Strategies that work*. York, MA: Stenhouse.

Haynes, J. (2007, September). Collaborative teaching: Are two teachers better than one? *Essential Teacher, 4*(3). Retrieved June 24, 2010, from http://www .everythingesl.net/inservices/cooperative_teaching_ two_teach_83908.php

Heritage, M. (2007). Formative assessment: What do teachers need to know and do? *Phi Delta Kappan, 89*(2), 140–145.

Heritage, M. (2009). Using self-assessment to chart students' paths. *Middle School Journal, 40*(5), 27–30.

Heritage, M., Kim, J., Vendlinkski, T., & Herman, J. (2009). From evidence to action: A seamless process in formative assessment? *Educational Measurement: Issues and Practice, 28*(3), 24–31.

Hinkel, E. (2004). *Teaching academic ESL writing: Practical techniques in vocabulary and grammar*. New York: Lawrence Erlbaum.

Hinton, S. E. (1967). *The outsiders*. New York: Viking Press.

Howard, G. (2006). *We can't teach what we don't know: White teachers, multiracial schools*. New York: Teachers College Press.

Hymes, D. (1972). On communicative competence. In J. B. Pride & J. Holmes (Eds.). *Sociolinguistics* (pp. 269–293). Harmondsworth, UK: Penguin Books.

Jones, E. V. (1986). Teaching reading through experience. *Life Learning, 9*(7), 29–31.

Kagan Publishing. (2008). *Numbered heads together*. San Clemente, CA: Author.

Kinsella, K. (2005, November). Teaching academic vocabulary. *Aiming High Resource*. Retrieved June 27, 2008, from http://www.scoe.org/docs/ah/AH_kinsella2 .pdf

Kluckhohn, C. (1949). *Mirror for man*. New York: McGraw-Hill.

Krashen, S. D. (1981). *Second language acquisition and second language learning*. London: Pergamon Press.

Krashen, S. D. (1982). *Principles and practice in second language acquisition*. New York: Oxford.

Krashen, S. D. (1985). *The input hypothesis: Issues and implications*. New York: Longman.

Krashen, S., & Terrell, T. D. (1983). *The natural approach*. London: Pergamon Press.

Larsen-Freeman, D. (2003). *Teaching language: From grammar to grammaring*. Boston: Thompson-Heinle.

Lieberman, A. (1986). Collaborative work. *Educational Leadership, 44*(1), 4–8.

Lieberman, A. (1990). *Schools as collaborative cultures: Creating the future now*. Bristol, PA: The Falmer Press.

Longfellow, H. W. (1847). *Evangeline: A tale of Acadie*. Boston: William D. Ticknor.

Lowry, L. (1981). *Anastasia Krupnik*. New York: Bantam Doubleday.

Martinez, M., Roser, N. L., & Strecker, S. (1998/1999). "I never thought I could be a star": A reader's theatre ticket to fluency. *The Reading Teacher, 52*(4), 326–334.

Marzano, R. J. (2004). *Building background knowledge for academic achievement: Research on what works in schools*. Alexandria, VA: Association for Supervision and Curriculum Development.

Marzano, R. J., Pickering, D. J., & Pollock, J. E. (2001). *Classroom instruction that works: Research-based strategies for increasing student achievement*. Alexandria, VA: Association for Supervision and Curriculum Development.

McCauley, J. K., & McCauley, D. S. (1992). Using choral reading to promote language learning for ESL students. *The Reading Teacher, 45*(7), 526–533.

McDermott, G. (1987). *Anansi the spider: A tale from the Ashanti*. New York: Henry Holt.

McKeown, M. G., Beck, I. L, Omanson, R. C., & Pople, M. T. (1985). Some effects of the nature and frequency of vocabulary instruction on the knowledge and use of words. *Reading Research Quarterly, 20*(5), 522–535.

McLaughlin, M. W., & Talbert, J. E. (2010). Professional learning communities: Building blocks for school culture and student learning. *Collective Practice Quality Teaching, 27*, 1–3. Retrieved June 27, 2010, from http://www.annenberginstitute.org/ VUE/vue27-talbert

McLaughlin, C. W., Thompson, M., & Zike, D. (2008). *Physical science*. New York: McGraw Hill.

Michaels, S., O'Connor, M. C., Sohmer, R., & Resnick, L. (n.d.). *Guided construction of knowledge in the classroom: Teacher, talk, task, and tools*. San Francisco: Parents Education Network.

Michaels, S., O'Connor, C., & Resnick, L. B. (2007). Deliberative discourse idealized and realized: Accountable talk in the classroom and in civic life.

Studies in the Philosophy of Education, 27(4), 283–297. doi: 10.1007/s11217-007-9071-1

Moore, E., & Couvillon, A. (2002). *Evangeline for children.* New York: Pelican.

Moore Johnson, S. (2010). Once a teacher, always a teacher? *Harvard Education Letter, 26*(3), 6–8. Retrieved July 28, 2010, from http://www.hepg.org/hel/article/467

Moustafa, M., & Penrose, J. (1985, March). Comprehensible input plus the language experience approach: Reading instruction for limited English speaking students. *The Reading Teacher, 38*(7), 640–647.

Muth, K. D., & Alvermann, D. (1999). *Teaching and learning in the middle grades.* Boston: Allyn and Bacon.

Nagy, W. E. (2010). Teaching vocabulary to improve reading comprehension. Newark, DE: International Reading Association.

Nation, I. S. P. (2001). *Learning vocabulary in another language.* Cambridge, UK: Cambridge University Press.

Nation, I. S. P. (2008). *Teaching vocabulary: Strategies and techniques.* Boston: Heinle.

Nation, I. S. P. (2009). *Teaching ESL/EFL reading and writing.* New York: Routledge.

Nation, P., & Waring, R. (1998). Vocabulary size, text coverage, and word lists. In N. Schmitt & M. McCarthy (Eds.), *Vocabulary: Description, acquisition, and pedagogy* (pp. 6–19). New York: Cambridge University Press.

National Family, School, and Community Engagement Working Group. (2010). *Taking leadership, innovating change: Profiles in family, school, and community engagement.* Cambridge, MA: Harvard Family Research Project. Retrieved July 18, 2010, from http://www.hfrp.org/publications-resources/browse-our-publications/taking-leadership-innovating-change-profiles-in-family-school-and-community-engagement

National Middle School Association. (Producer). (2009, September 21). The culture of formative assessment [audio podcast]. Retrieved July 18, 2010, from http://www.nmsa.org/Publications/TodaysMiddleLevelEducator/tabid/1409/Default.aspx?name=formative%20assessment

Nias, J. (1998). *International handbook of educational change.* Portland, OR: Book News.

Office for Civil Rights. (1990). Policy regarding the treatment of national minority students who are limited English proficient. Retrieved April 8, 2010, from http://www2.ed.gov/about/offices/list/ocr/docs/lau1990_and_1985.html

Office for Civil Rights. (2000). Developing programs for English language learners. Washington, DC: U.S. Department of Education. Retrieved May 3, 2010, from http://www2.ed.gov/about/offices/list/ocr/ell/planoutline.html

Office for Civil Rights. (2005). Questions and answers on the rights of limited-English proficient students. Retrieved October 8, 2010, from http://www2.ed.gov/about/offices/list/ocr/qa-ell.html

O'Shea, D. J., McQuiston, K., & McCollin, M. (n.d.). Improving fluency skills of secondary-level students from diverse backgrounds. *Tips for Teaching, 54*(1), 77–80.

Palinscar, A. S., & Brown, A. L. (1984). Reciprocal teaching of comprehension-fostering and comprehension monitoring activities. *Cognition and Instruction, 1,* 117–175.

Paterson, K. (1991). *Lyddie.* New York: Dutton Children's Books.

Pickett, A. L., Likins, M., & Wallace, T. (2003). *The employment and preparation of paraeducators, the state of the art, 2003.* Logan, UT: National Resource Center for Paraprofessionals. Retrieved on June 25, 2010, from http://www.nrcpara.org/

Polacco, P. (2000). *The butterfly.* New York: Philomel Books.

Prelutsky, J. (1984). *The new kid on the block.* New York: Greenwillow Books.

Pressley, M. (2001, September). Comprehension instruction: What makes sense now, what might make sense soon. *Reading Online, 5*(2). Retrieved from http://www.readingonline.org/articles/art_index.asp?HREF=/articles/handbook/pressley/index.html

Reinhard, J. (1998). *Discovering the Inca Ice Maiden: My adventures on Ampato.* Washington, DC: National Geographic.

Rhoder, C. (2002). Mindful reading: Strategy training that facilitates transfer. *Journal of Adolescent & Adult Literacy, 45*(6), 498–512.

Richek, M. A. (2005). Words are wonderful: Interactive, time-efficient strategies to teach meaning vocabulary. *The Reading Teacher, 58*(5), 414–423. doi:10.1598/RT.58.5.1

Ritchie, D. A. (2001). *American history: The modern era since 1865.* New York: Glencoe McGraw-Hill.

Root, P. (2003). *The name quilt.* New York: Farrar, Straus and Giroux.

Sadler, D. R. (1989). Formative assessment and the design of instructional systems. *Instructional Science, 18,* 119–144.

Saphier, J., & Gower, R. (1997). *The skillful teacher.* Acton, MA: Research for Better Teaching.

Schmitt, N. (2008). Review article: Instructed second language vocabulary learning. *Language Teaching Research, 12*(3), 329–363.

Shore, K. (2005, March). Success for ESL students: 12 practical tips to help second-language learners. *Scholastic.* Retrieved June 26, 2010, from http://www2.scholastic.com/browse/article.jsp?id=4336

Simonsen, B., Fairbanks, S., Briesch, A., Myers, D., & Sugai, G. (2008, August 1). Evidence-based practices in classroom management: Considerations for research to practice. *Education & Treatment of Children.* Retrieved June 30, 2009, from http://www.highbeam.com/doc/1G1-183874069.html

Smith, J. A., & Reutzel, D. R. (2006, Spring). *Reciprocal teaching.* PowerPoint. Retrieved June 10, 2010, from http://www.liberty.k12.ga.us/jwalts/RecipTeaching/reciprocal_teaching.pdf

Stahl, S. (1999). *Vocabulary development.* Brookline, MA: Brookline Books.

Stahl, S. A., & Nagy, W. E. (2006). *Teaching word meanings.* Mahwah, NJ: Lawrence Erlbaum.

Stahl, S. A., Richeck, M. A., & Vandivier, R. J. (1991). Learning meaning vocabulary through listening: A sixth-grade replication. In J. Zutell & S. McCormack (Eds.), *Learner factors/teacher factors: Issues in literacy research and instruction* (pp. 185–192). Chicago: National Reading Conference.

Stahl, S., & Vancil, S. J. (1986). Discussion is what makes semantic maps work in vocabulary instruction. *The Reading Teacher, 40*(1), 62–67.

Stiggins, R. (2005). From formative assessment to assessment for learning: A path to success in standards-based schools. *Phi Delta Kappan, 87*(4), 324–328.

Stiggins, R. J., Arter, J. A., Chappuis, J., & Chappuis, S. (2004). *Classroom assessment for student learning: Doing it right—using it well.* Portland, OR: Assessment Training Institute.

Swain, M. (1985). Communicative competence: Some roles of comprehensible input and comprehensible output in its development. In S. Gass & C. Madden (Eds.), *Input in second language acquisition* (pp. 235–256). New York: Newbury House.

Swain, M. (2000). The output hypothesis and beyond: Mediating acquisition through collaborative dialogue. In J. P. Lantolf (Ed.), *Sociocultural theory and second language learning* (pp. 97–114). Oxford: Oxford University Press.

Swain, M. (2005). The output hypothesis: Theory and research. In E. Hinkel (Ed.), *Handbook on research in second language teaching and learning* (pp. 471–484). Mahwah, NJ: Lawrence Erlbaum.

TESOL. (2006). *PreK–12 English language proficiency standards.* Alexandria, VA: Author.

TESOL. (2010). *TESOL/NCATE Standards for the recognition of initial ESOL programs in P-12 ESL teacher education.* Alexandria, VA: TESOL.

Thomas, W. P., & Collier, V. (1997). *School effectiveness for language minority students.* (NCBE Resource Collection Series, No. 9). Washington, DC: National Clearinghouse for Bilingual Education.

Tomlinson, C. (2001). *How to differentiate instruction in mixed-ability classrooms* (2nd ed.). Alexandria, VA: Association for Supervision and Curriculum Development.

Tomlinson, C., & Edison, C. (2003). *Differentiation in practice: A resource guide for differentiated curriculum.* Alexandria, VA: Association for Supervision and Curriculum Development.

Tomlinson, C., & McTighe, J. (2006). *Integrating differentiated instruction and understanding by design: Connecting content and kids.* Alexandria, VA: Association for Supervision and Curriculum Development.

Trelease, J. (1995). *The read-aloud handbook* (4th ed.). New York: Penguin.

U.S. Census. (2008). *American community survey, 2008. Languages spoken at home by language.* Washington, DC: Author. Retrieved May 28, 2010, from https://www.census.gov/compendia/statab/cats/population/ancestry_language_spoken_at_home

VanDeWeghe, R. (2006). Deep modeling and authentic teaching: Challenging *students* or *challenging* students. *English Journal, 95*(4), 83–88.

Villegas, A. M., & Lucas, T. (2002). Educating culturally responsive teachers: A coherent approach. Albany: State University of New York.

Viorst, J. (1981). *If I were in charge of the world.* New York: Aladdin Paperbacks.

Vygotsky, L. (1978). *Mind in society.* Cambridge, MA: Harvard University Press.

Walker, L. (1996). *Readers theatre in middle school and junior high school.* Colorado Springs, CO: Meriwether.

Wall, H. (2008). Interactive writing beyond the primary grades. *The Reading Teacher, 62*(2), 149–152.

Wang, D. (2010). Team teaching and the application in the course English teaching methodology by CET and NSET in China. *English Language Teaching, 3*(1), 87–91.

Waterman, R. (2006). *Breaking down barriers, creating space: A guidebook for increasing collaboration between schools and the parents of English language learners.* Denver, CO: Colorado Department of Education.

Waterman, R., & Harry, B. (2008). *Building collaboration between schools and parents of English language learners: Transcending barriers, creating opportunities.* Retrieved May 5, 2010, from http://nccrest.org/Briefs/PractitionerBrief_BuildingCollaboration.pdf

Watson, S. M. R., & Houtz, L. E. (2002). Teaching science: Meeting the academic needs of culturally and linguistically diverse students. *Intervention in School and Clinic 37*(5), 267–278.

Wick, W. (1997). *A drop of water.* New York: Scholastic.

WIDA. (2009, March). What do we know about the formative assessment for English language learners and how do we develop a system accordingly? *FLARE, 1*(1). Retrieved October 5, 2010, from http://flareassessment.org/News/newsletter_Mar09.pdf

Wiggins, G., & McTighe, J. (1998). *Understanding by design.* Alexandria, VA: Association for Supervision and Curriculum Development.

Wiggins, G., & McTighe, J. (2005). *Understanding by design* (2nd ed.). Alexandria, VA: Association for Supervision and Curriculum Development.

Wolf, M. K., Crosson, A. C., & Resnick, L. (2006). *Accountable talk in reading comprehension instruction.* Los Angeles: Center for Research on Evaluation, Standards, and Student Testing. Available online at http://eric.ed.gov/ERICWebPortal/contentdelivery/servlet/ERICServlet?accno=ED492865

Wormeli, R. (2005). *Summarization in any subject: 50 techniques to improve student learning.* Alexandria, VA: Association for Supervision and Curriculum Development.

Zimmerman, B. J., & Ringle, J. (1981). Effects of model persistence and statements of confidence on children's self-efficacy and problem solving. *Journal of Educational Psychology, 73,* 485–493.

About the Author

Michaela Colombo is an associate professor in the Graduate School of Education at the University of Massachusetts Lowell. She teaches graduate courses to prepare preservice and practicing teachers to teach English language learners and provides professional development to inservice teachers in Massachusetts schools. Prior to joining the UMass faculty full time in 2004, she was the district-wide supervisor of the Bilingual/English Language Acquisition Department for the Methuen Public Schools in Massachusetts, where she worked extensively with English language learners, their families, and their teachers. During her time as the department supervisor, she implemented the Parent Partnership for Achieving Literacy (PAL) program, the central goal of which was to improve educational opportunities for English language learners by building two-way bridges between parents and mainstream teachers. She authored several articles about the PAL program that were published by *Educational Leadership*, *Multicultural Perspectives*, and *Phi Delta Kappan*. Colombo holds professional certification in bilingual education, elementary education (K–8), and ESL (PK–12). She has taught content-area subjects to English language learners in Grades 5 through 12, and she has taught English as a second language to young children and their parents in family literacy situations and to adults in workplace literacy settings. She is the lead author of *Teaching English Language Learners: Content and Language in Middle and Secondary Mainstream Classrooms*.

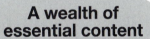